The military–humanitarian complex in Afghanistan

Manchester University Press

HUMANITARIANISM
Key debates and new approaches

This series offers a new interdisciplinary reflection on one of the most important and yet under-studied areas in history, politics and cultural practices: humanitarian aid and its responses to crises and conflicts. The series seeks to define afresh the boundaries and methodologies applied to the study of humanitarian relief and so-called 'humanitarian events'. The series includes monographs and carefully selected thematic edited collections which will cross disciplinary boundaries and bring fresh perspectives to the historical, political and cultural understanding of the rationale and impact of humanitarian relief work.

The military–humanitarian complex in Afghanistan

Eric James and Tim Jacoby

Manchester University Press

Copyright © Eric James and Tim Jacoby 2016

The right of Eric James and Tim Jacoby to be identified as the authors of this work has been asserted by them in accordance with the Copyright, Designs and Patents Act 1988.

Published by Manchester University Press
Altrincham Street, Manchester M1 7JA

www.manchesteruniversitypress.co.uk

British Library Cataloguing-in-Publication Data
A catalogue record for this book is available from the British Library

Library of Congress Cataloging-in-Publication Data applied for

ISBN 978 0 7190 9723 2 hardback

First published 2016

The publisher has no responsibility for the persistence or accuracy of URLs for any external or third-party internet websites referred to in this book, and does not guarantee that any content on such websites is, or will remain, accurate or appropriate.

Typeset by
Servis Filmsetting, Stockport, Cheshire
Printed in Great Britain by
CPI Group (UK) Ltd, Croydon, CR0 4YY

Contents

Figures, tables and boxes

Acknowledgements

We have many people to thank. At the University of Manchester, particular thanks goes to Sam Hickey, Admos Chimhowu, Christopher Rees, Kirsten Howarth and Carole Douguedroit and several other support staff. We also give hearty thanks to Tony Bebbington, George Holmes, Jenny Peterson, Ellie Sandercock and Siobhan McGrath. In Afghanistan, we would like to extend our most gracious thanks to the Center for Conflict and Peace Studies (CAPS), their director Hekmat Karzai and all the staff based in Kabul and the nearly 70 people interviewed for this research. In particular, we would like to thank Del-Agha Shakeeb for being a wealth of information and long-time friend. Finally, we thank our families for their continual love and support. This book is dedicated to everyone, both Afghan and expatriate, who has worked so hard and in some cases lost their lives to make Afghanistan a better and more secure place.

Preface

The origins of this book began nearly 15 years ago. About six weeks after the attacks of 11 September 2001, I boarded a plane for Dushanbe, Tajikistan, where I joined a couple of other aid workers. We made our way to the Afghan frontier a few hours' drive to the south. Once there, we came to the Amu-Darya River crossing and found it teeming with people – fighters, war correspondents and aid workers – waiting to transit. Standing on the shore, I took out our map and guessed we were at least 15 kilometers east of the frontline.

We watched more trucks go by and then, all of a sudden, explosive shockwaves rocked everything. On a ridge where Taliban forces held firm, a line of smoke several hundred yards across rose into the sky. I looked directly overhead and saw what appeared to be a B-52 about 40,000 feet up leaving a white contrail as it turned back to the south. Those around me watched for a few moments and then went back to waiting and taking care of mundane tasks. Once the bulk of weapons and ammo were shipped on the precarious barge, we made it across and onward to the village of Dashti-Qala as the sun set. That was my first day in Afghanistan.

The war came at a convenient time for me. With a freshly minted master's degree and an emergency medical technician's certificate, I was looking for my next relief job when 11 September 2001 happened. I might have used my degree for writing funding proposals (often wasted on slow-moving donor representatives), but it was the medical skills that helped save two local boys. They were playing with a disused mortar shell, which exploded, seriously wounding one and nearly killing the other. I had the smallest role in a response that was a collective effort of aid workers and Special Forces.

In the weeks that followed, the Taliban regime faded away and we expanded our relief efforts, including health, water, education and efforts to stimulate the local economy. This also included going to Kabul to establish a new office and programs there. In January 2002, the bombed-out road route to the south had just reopened and so I set out with a local driver named Ahmed in an old Russian UAZ jeep. After fording a river (Ahmed shut off the vehicle and we were then towed by a horse), we crossed tracks of desert and narrow fertile valleys before starting up the Hindu Kush mountains.

There is one passage open "year round" through the Salang tunnel. During the summer months, the route can be a pleasant drive with stunning views, but in the winter it can be deadly. We climbed the foothills to the tree line as a blizzard set in. As Ahmed continued with quiet confidence, he gained my trust and respect. We had only about three mutually intelligible words between us, and I reminded myself that Afghans have a love for poetry and proverbs, a few of which I had copied into my notebook before leaving. One saying goes, "There is a path to the top of even the highest mountain" (*ko ar qadar ke beland basha baz am sare khud ra dara*) – where there's a will, there's a way.

The snow fell heavily as we made our way up the mountain road. We passed massive military transports as well as 4x4 jeeps that lay stuck, spinning their wheels; ordinary cars were forced to stop or turn around long before this point. Along the upper reaches, landmine markers lined the way forward. At one point we started spinning toward one and then fishtailed across the road toward another. By luck and by pluck, Ahmed managed to negotiate each turn, climbing higher and higher toward the tunnel. Often shrouded in mist, the entrance is little more than an archway protruding from the side of the mountain. The opening was jammed with traffic, people yelled (those with Kalashnikovs seemed to be the loudest) as vehicles jockeyed for position to enter the tunnel. Without proper management of the traffic, at least an hour passed before it was finally our turn. Finally inside, we crept forward in first gear. There were deep, icy puddles, few lights and no ventilation; noxious fumes filled our jeep.

After about two and a half kilometers we made it through, covered in soot and the smell of exhaust. Several weeks later, during my second trip, an avalanche trapped traffic inside the tunnel, and because drivers left their motors running several people succumbed to the fumes. Making it down the southern route was no less of an adventure, with several close calls. I did not know what to expect as it grew dark. Still in the mountains, we had not yet reached the long Shomali plain, a long way off toward Kabul, when we pulled over to rest for the night.

I was feeling very vulnerable, the only foreigner at the Afghan truck stop, and Ahmed once again took me under his wing, finding a plate of pulao, hot chai and a warm mattress. As we prepared for the night, I read through my notes: "The first day you meet, you are friends. The next day you meet, you are brothers" (*yak roz didi dost, dega roz didi bradar*); friendship grows into brotherhood. It was proven to me that night, and many times since, that the hospitality of the Afghan is unrivaled. Even when language failed, I will forever recall the knowing glance so many Afghans have shared with me, as if to say, "I know this place is difficult, but we're here to help each other through it now."

I stayed on in Afghanistan for about another year and half, and have made it back most years since then. Looking back, that time was filled with more than a few close shaves. Even with high levels of insecurity, the truth is of course that I was relatively safe, in that statistics were on my side. The overwhelming suffering is borne by the local populace – Afghans in this case, but the same is true anywhere aid workers operate.

It was from these experiences that I found that people's conceptions of security, aid and peace are often incomplete and sometimes just wrong. Tim and I have put together our best effort in offering a better analysis and understanding of these issues. Far more than simply an academic concern, these issues have real consequences and we hope this contribution will help those engaged in making these situations better.

Eric James

Abbreviations

3-D	defense, diplomacy and development
ACBAR	Agency Coordinating Body for Afghan Relief
ADF	Afghan Development Framework
ADZ	Afghan Development Zones
AMI	Aide Médicale International
ANA	Afghan National Army
ANDS	Afghan National Development Strategy
ANSO	Afghan NGO Safety Office
AOG	armed opposition group
AREU	Afghanistan Research and Evaluation Unit
ARTF	Afghan Reconstruction Trust Fund
BAAG	British Agencies Afghanistan Group
CARE	Cooperative for American Relief Everywhere (US)
CBOs	community based organizations
CENTCOM	Central Command (US)
CIA	Central Intelligence Agency
CIDA	Canadian International Development Agency
CIMIC	Civil–Military Cooperation
CJCMOTF	Coalition Joint Civil–Military Operations Task Force
COIN	counter-insurgency
CPAN	Child Protection Action Network
CORDS	Civil Operations and Rural Development Support
DACAAR	Danish Committee for Afghanistan (consortium of three NGOs)
DDR	disarmament, demobilization and reintegration
DFID	Department for International Development (UK)
DOD	Department of Defense
GOA	Government of Afghanistan
HRW	Human Rights Watch
ICG	International Crisis Group
ICRC	International Committee of the Red Cross

IHL	international humanitarian law
INGO	international non-governmental organization
IOM	International Organization of Migration
ISAF	International Security Assistance Force
MSF	Médecins Sans Frontières
NATO	North Atlantic Treaty Organization
NDS	National Development Strategy
NGO	non-governmental organization
NSP	National Solidarity Program
OEF	Operation Enduring Freedom
OECD	Organisation for Economic Cooperation and Development
PCD	policy coherence for development
PRT	Provincial Reconstruction Team
SCA	Swedish Committee for Afghanistan
SIDA	Swedish International Development Agency
UN	United Nations
UNAMA	United Nations Assistance Mission to Afghanistan
UNDP	United Nations Development Programme
UNHCR	United Nations High Commission for Refugees
USAID	US Agency for International Development
VOLAG	Voluntary Agency (an older name for NGOs)

A note about spelling

In 1842, Mountstuart Elphinstone wrote that "it is always difficult to represent Asiatic words in our own characters, and this is increased in the present instance by want of a uniform system" (p. x). For example, he spelled place names this way: Caubul, Hindoo Coosh and Afghaunistaun. Today there is increasingly common spelling practice, which this book follows, except in direct quotes, where the original has been used.

Part I

Background to the military–humanitarian complex

1

Introduction

Humanitarianism and war in Afghanistan

On 4 June 2004, five staff members of the international NGO, Médecins Sans Frontières (MSF), were murdered in northwest Afghanistan. Within a month, the organization had withdrawn after more than two decades of providing assistance to the country. According to a senior MSF staff member, their departure was prompted by the Afghan authority's perfunctory investigation into the killings and because:

> The Taliban, whilst claiming responsibility for the assassinations, falsely accused us [MSF] several times of working for American interests. Ironic given that MSF has worked extremely hard to maintain its independence and distance from the coalition forces and has been repeatedly critical of their attempts to link military objectives with the provision of "humanitarian" assistance. Through these accusations, we are vulnerable to further attack ... On the way to the airport we pass unmarked white landcruisers, the trademark of aid agencies [sic]. For the last 24 years in Afghanistan MSF has been using these vehicles: they enable the population to identify us. Looking closely at these unmarked landcruisers, though, you see Western soldiers inside. I rest my case. (MSF 2004, p. 1)

As shocking as the killings were, the situation was not as clear cut as this relief worker describes it. One year later, MSF itself was not so certain about the blurring of the lines with the foreign military forces in Afghanistan: "The killings had no discernible motive and crossfire was discounted ... The reality is we do not know why these dreadful events took place; we only have suspicions and hypotheses" (MSF 2004, p. 1). While MSF returned to the country in 2009, and there were more deadly attacks later on such as the murder of 10 staff members of International Assistance Mission in 2010, this case remains important. It raises a fundamental question: how close or distant a relationship should humanitarian relief workers have with the military? In other words, should aid organizations integrate or separate their activities from the military?

In considering these questions, several issues spring to mind, including the proximity and visibility of partnerships, the blurring of the line between soldiers and relief workers, the notion of humanitarian space and the security of NGO staff. These underlying issues are embedded in a list of contradictory and unresolved debates based on commonly held assumptions that do not necessarily stand up to close inspection.

As a means to reach a better understanding of these questions, a distinction will be drawn between two approaches. The first is an integrated approach which is in support of or "for" close relations between humanitarians and the military, while the second is a segregated approach which is fundamentally "against" close relations between humanitarians and the military. This builds on the work of other researchers (see, for example, Pugh 1998, Ankersen, 2004, Jackson and Haysom 2013). Wider issues of management and decision making, humanitarian principles and the link between security and development are also involved in this relationship between humanitarians and the military. From among these concerns, an underlying policy question emerges: why should NGOs have a close or distant relationship with the military? This book seeks to lay bare this fundamental practical and policy-oriented question in relations between humanitarians and the military.

The purpose of this introduction is to present the key issues related to this book, all of which will be developed further in the subsequent chapters. First, five basic assumptions are offered relating to the military–humanitarian relationship, which will later be an important base line for the research presented in the book. Second, the case of Afghanistan is discussed with a view to its importance and its wider relevance. Third, several important definitions are offered. Finally, an outline of the structure of this book is presented, followed by a brief conclusion.

Assumptions

Despite a growing body of research and literature devoted to it, there is considerable ambiguity in the relationship between humanitarians and the military. It is therefore helpful to undertake an assessment of commonly held assumptions. This will serve as a starting point on which the underlying policy question rests (why should aid organizations have a close or distant relationship with the military?). Five sequential statements based on these assumptions are introduced here and explored later in the book. It is important to note that these assumptions are based on a set of propositions in the literature, policy making and commonly held opinions in the field. The assumptions help to inform whether humanitarians have an integrated or segregated policy toward relations with the military: in other words, whether organizational policies are for or against such relations. These assumptions are introduced here and later form five sequential sub-questions explored throughout this book.

The relationship between humanitarians and the military is "new"

Without a clear understanding of what took place before, without a commonly accepted history, phenomena appear to be new and their causes are poorly understood. While there has been prior research on a number of topics in this book (see, for example, Parmelee 1915, Hutchinson 1996, Moorehead 1998, Boli and Thomas 1999, Walker and Maxwell 2008), there is a surprising lack of reference to the historical roots of NGOs, humanitarianism and its connection to security. In discussing the development of NGOs, for example, widely read historical works by Hobsbawm (1994), Grenville (1994) and Keylor (1992) leave out mention of NGOs. Iriye argues that "to ignore them [NGOs] is to misread the history of the twentieth-century world" (1999, p. 424).

With this understanding, it is commonly assumed that the relationship between humanitarians and the military is relatively new. For example, some of the literature – and indeed some of those interviewed as part of this research – argues that the relationship began roughly with assistance provided to Iraqi Kurds in 1991. As Rana concludes: "the phenomenon of armed forces engaging in humanitarian action in the 1990s was a new and evolving concept" (2004, p. 568). If the assumed history of the relationship between humanitarians and the military extends only as far back as 1991, it is reasonable to conclude that humanitarians were always separate from the military prior to the end of the Cold War. Further, if separate, humanitarians must have been neutral when working in conflict-affected countries and they should remain that way regardless of the context or situation. This assumption is perhaps based on the fact that civil–military relations are now a norm in international relations and the aid sector, yet a cursory view of history reveals few historical examples because civil society and its actors were not typically part of the commonly accepted history. Further analysis reveals a different picture. The presence of aid organizations and the blurring of the lines between humanitarians and the military extend throughout the historical record and the ethical position has depended on political context.

Finding historical patterns in a time span of hundreds of years is difficult, but they are nonetheless still evident. To address fully the question of the origins of the military–humanitarian relationship, the development of specific technology, strategy and normative issues will be considered along with their contribution toward humanitarianism in war today. Technology has affected practices including health and medicine, media attention and the way wars are fought. Changes in strategy have made the military more disposed to interact with civilians. Humanitarian principles developed significantly with the policies and the codification of international humanitarian law (IHL). Thus, the origin of how humanitarians and the military have become involved in similar work is revealed. This book will therefore begin by showing how these three interrelated issues have influenced relations between humanitarians and the military.

Differences between humanitarians and the military cause inter-organizational friction

Humanitarians and members of the military are inherently and obviously different. Their appearance, resources, ways of operating and, most significantly, their mandates and aims appear to be poles apart. It is assumed that their culture and politics are dissimilar, to the point that they cannot communicate or function cooperatively to achieve a common end (Beauregard 1998, Tomlin 2000). It is commonly held that these differences lead to friction, causing dissonance between humanitarians and the military. This friction can be thought of as the "awkward, unequal, unstable, and creative qualities of interconnection across difference" (Tsing 2004, p. 4). Cultural differences are often immediately apparent between humanitarians and the military (Archer 2003, George 2005, Wheeler and Harmer 2006). Mutual disdain is shown through the "us and them" language revealed in labels such as "tree hugger" and "war monger" which have been heard in exchanges between relief worker and soldier.

For those who respond to them, disasters and post-conflict situations are typified by their lack of resources, acute time pressures and uncertainty, all of which contribute to high stress. In these situations, friction can lead to policy dysfunction (Janis 1989, Walkup 1997) and other problems such as poor decisions about programming and partnerships. This can then affect the external relations of an organization. Partnerships in particular can have unintended outcomes, such as potentially dangerous situations and compromised principles. When the agendas of the security and development sectors are mixed, as is the case for Afghanistan and Iraq, humanitarians are placed in a particularly difficult situation when it comes to their relationship with the military. In Afghanistan, this was seen in the design of the aid architecture, where aid organizations were meant to be part of a system and in partnership with government and security elements. In this way, the notion of coherence has been institutionalized and has become standard practice, on the basis that organizations would be less likely to experience inter-agency friction, to be "uncoordinated," to waste resources or to work at cross-purposes.

A close relationship with the military is dangerous for humanitarians

In humanitarian practice, the quest for security is the most contentious issue relating to the military–humanitarian relationship. Providing humanitarian relief is inherently dangerous and it is not surprising that threats increase with the amount of violent conflict (Stoddard et al. 2006, Fast 2007). The threat of violence, such as gunfire and kidnapping, can be targeted directly at humanitarians or, more frequently, occur independently as part of a wider insecure environment. Because of their apparently opposing mandates, it is a natural and intuitive assumption that any relationship humanitarians have with the military will compromise their security.

The situation is further complicated by the rationale that is often given for military relations with humanitarians (and in some cases for an intervention itself) – that they are to provide a secure environment. In various contexts since the end of the Cold War, the military has sought to expand safe access for humanitarians, and in some places it was relatively successful. This creates a contradiction. Given this complexity, the situation is not as simple as is commonly assumed. For instance, if military personnel took part in peacekeeping activities and the next day engaged in open conflict, it is unclear where the line between the two roles would be. In Afghanistan, the military presented multiple images as counter-terrorist, peace-keeper and promoter of reconstruction, which made the situation complex and common assumptions unreliable.

Principled positions are well established

There is a great deal of discussion, both in the literature and in the policy arena, regarding humanitarian principles (Leader 1998, Amos 2013). These principles serve as a framework for policy decisions, including the sort of relationships humanitar-ians have with the military, especially in light of the perceived failures of aid in the wake of the many humanitarian crises of the 1990s. In different historical cases, as will be discussed at length, beginning in Chapter 2, "classic" humanitarianism, which stressed certain key principles such as neutrality, was challenged by other humanitarian positions. In some circumstances, including Afghanistan during the 1980s, humanitarians even assumed solidarity with the people they sought to help. Thus, over recent decades principles have undergone not just a "broadening" by reformists but also a "deepening," by including human rights protection (Leader 1998, p. 296; De Waal 1995; Roberts 1996). When adopting what is called a neo-humanitarian position, relief workers may show preference for certain principles over others and, in the process, adopt a close or integrated policy toward the mili-tary. This suggests that while there is debate about the exact nature and applicability of humanitarian principles to particular contexts, it is assumed that organizations have established positions often solidified by written policies. In other words, it is thought that aid organizations have developed positions with regard to the military and that they typically seek neutrality and impartiality (Lilly 2002, Klingebiel and Roehder 2004, InterAction 2005, Frerks et al. 2006).

Official aid leads to co-option and politicization

As independent entities, aid organizations need to maintain some degree of autonomy in decision making and action. The reasons for this rest on the ability of aid organizations to fill perceived gaps by addressing needs at the community level and at the same time, depending an organization's mandate, to raise aware-ness of particular issues of social concern. This includes, controversially, holding governments accountable. An important part of this discussion centers on the type of partnerships in which aid organizations involve themselves. Co-option can be seen as a type of partnership (Brinkerhoff 2002), where one partner has little self-identity and there is a lack of mutuality and equality in decision making and of influence on action. In these relationships, an organization may abandon its original goals and fundamental core.

Many organizations espouse a virtual laundry list of humanitarian principles that emphasize their apolitical and independent positions. The implicit, and sometimes explicit (Chandler 2001, Donini et al. 2004,), assumption is that official aid and, by extension, relations with the military, lead to an unintended co-option and a politicized position. This notion of co-option stems from an assumption that humanitarians are unwilling partners (although American-based NGOs often appear less unwilling than others). In other words, humanitarianism became subsumed into a wider political and military agenda, despite the efforts of aid workers to remain neutral. Following this assumption, aid organizations "increasingly accept the necessity" (Lilly 2002, p. 1) of cooperating and working closely with the military. This co-option stems in part from an expanded understanding of what security means, which is examined more closely in Chapter 3. Particularly since the events of 11 September 2001, security has taken on a broader definition (Dannreuther 2014) and the military is now viewed as just one player in the security realm (Ignatieff 2004). There is even greater dissonance when some label NGOs "military security actors" (Herring 2007, p. 130). As the politicization and co-option of aid organizations are a regular occurrence, it is fair to say that an old-fashioned belief in apolitical humanitarianism can be laid to rest.

Afghanistan and its wider relevance

Afghanistan is chosen as the case study here because it provides an opportunity to analyze the assumptions and the underlying key question. Afghanistan as a case study contains several elements that are developed in later chapters, but the broad reasons are worth mentioning here. In any case study selection, Stake (2003) suggests that there are both intrinsic (important in and of themselves) and instrumental (providing insight into other cases) reasons that need to be considered.

In this case, there are several *intrinsic* reasons. The military–humanitarian relationship is rife with policy, practical and intellectual contestation. The presence of a large number of humanitarian and military actors with conflicting agendas only adds to the debate's significance. The situation in Afghanistan incorporates both peacekeeping and active war fighting. This has led to the creation of combined civil–military teams by governments who are at one and the same time donors to humanitarian action, supporters of the Afghan government and belligerents in the conflict on the ground. Their efforts are seen as a blurring of the line between civilian and military, at times a duplication of effort and a dilution of the military's "core function in providing security" (Linborg 2003, p. 1). Perhaps most importantly, Afghanistan has a policy environment that has generated a fractured response to the array of challenges there. This situation has led many to argue that humanitarians were "ill-prepared for a new reality in which *humanitarian space* became an oxymoron, and *aid politicization* a tautology" (O'Brien 2004, pp. 187–8, emphasis original; see also Stockton 2004a). Such a situation has a high intrinsic value in further study.

While there have been other studies of Afghanistan (Strand 2002, Vogelsang 2002, Saikal 2004, Marsden 2000) and the military–humanitarian relationship (Flavin 2004, Jackson and Haysom 2013), it is widely acknowledged that the link between the security and NGO sectors needs further research. Kraft is probably most blunt in stating that the link between security and development "has been largely unexplained" (2003, p. 115). For Duffield, this area "remains underresearched and its study has yet to establish its own conceptual language" (2001, p. 10). This is supported by Picciotto, who acknowledges that security is a "prerequisite of development but the role that development can play in promoting security has not been systematically researched" (2006, p. 2). The research undertaken for this book will help fill this gap in the literature. Nonetheless, it is perhaps more disconcerting that there are those who, while acknowledging the need for further research, do not see problems. For example, a director of civil–military affairs in the United States Department of Defense (DOD) has stated that "I haven't seen any real studies that show that behavior A causes this level of risk whereas behavior B causes this level of risk ... [humanitarians are] increasingly at risk almost no matter what we [the military] do" (Bristol 2006, p. 386). In other words, there is no scientific evidence to show that if a humanitarian group decrease their proximity to, or cooperation with, foreign military forces in a country like Afghanistan they are more prone to attack. One work that has sought to quantify the relationship between humanitarians and the military in Afghanistan is Watts (2004). Using statistical analysis and key informant interviews, Watts shows that certain factors (such as physical proximity to Pakistan) more than others (presence of military forces) account for greater insecurity among humanitarians, while others (including poppy cultivation, which reached a new high in 2014) do not. Only from about 2007 onwards has more definitive data been captured by international analysts.

As the issues associated with the military–humanitarian relationship extend far beyond Afghanistan, there are several *instrumental* reasons why that country has been chosen as a case study. In nearly every emergency response and reconstruction effort where foreign military forces have been present, debate has arisen as organizations try to adopt the most appropriate policies. Four cases in particular serve to illustrate this wider relevance and will be returned to in the final chapter of this book. In Iraq, following the United States-led invasion in 2003, some aid workers protested against the international political and military strategy and only some decided to acquiesce to the pressures to implement government-funded projects. In Liberia, the UN's effort integrated the civil and military aspects of peacekeeping and state building after years of civil war. Alongside military peacekeepers, aid organizations helped to demobilize tens of thousands of soldiers. Following the Kashmiri earthquake in 2005, aid groups cooperated with military forces in the relief effort. Finally, following the 2004 Indian Ocean tsunami, relief workers openly collaborated with the military that had rushed in to help. For example, those NGOs often critical of the military were known to have unloaded and used supplies from military helicopters. If these high-profile events are anything to go by, the widely held belief in the humanitarian principles of neutrality and independence are no longer rigid or sacrosanct and the opportunity for aid to be used in place of political action remains ever present. From these examples, it is obvious that the context and the responses, indeed how the military–humanitarian relationship has been carried out, vary considerably. The case of humanitarians working with the military in Afghanistan and other contexts has unclear implications. This has led humanitarians to develop and then alter their policies, shifting them according to the scenario or context in which they operate. As a former Civil Military officer and UN civil–military coordinator in Afghanistan, Taylor (2004, p. 1) observed: "The civil–military relationship in Afghanistan is setting a precedent that will fundamentally change the relationship of the military and the assistance community for the future." This continues to have implications in crises from Syria to Somalia and from Haiti to Ukraine.

Key concepts

In this book, a number of common terms are used to label specific concepts. These labels are sometimes used as a synecdoche to denote specific cases even while the word may have wider meaning. The "Afghans," for instance, may be used to mean either the people or their government. In particular, four key concepts are discussed here – NGO, partnership, humanitarianism and the military – with the aim of introducing a common understanding for the research.

Non-governmental organization (NGO): The definition of NGO varies widely but there are several common elements. These include the fact that an organization was formed to benefit targeted populations in some way, that it has membership in civil society (that is, it is not part of government) and that it is non-profit (and thus it is not part of the commercial sector) (Willets 2001). Other characteristics shared by NGOs include their mandate, the activities implemented by them and their financing. Viewed historically, the term NGO and its variants are neologisms. As will be discussed in Chapter 2, early Western humanitarian organizations were usually known as committees or societies and later the term "voluntary agencies" (VOLAG) was adopted. The term NGO can be traced back at least as far as Chapter X, Article 71 of the UN Charter of 1945, which specifically mentions NGOs in making consultative arrangements for areas in which they have expertise, and this gradually became the most commonly accepted term internationally.

Today, there are many other names for these organizations, including charity, philanthropic or non-profit organization, private voluntary organization and, to add specificity, non-governmental humanitarian agency. These terms are defined slightly differently by specific authors and organizations (Frandsen 2002), usually to communicate what they feel to be a more accurate description. Fowler (1998), for example, identifies many different types of NGO according to their size, purpose and relationship with other organizations. In practice, NGOs may be based in a country affected by disaster or conflict (often known as "local NGOs") or be "international" (INGOs) by maintaining a home office in a (often rich) country. Examples of local NGOs include the Afghan organizations Afghan Development Association, Afghan Health and Development Services and the Sanayee Development Organization; international NGOs include MSF, Save the Children and CARE (Cooperative for American Relief Everywhere), along with many other similar organizations. These organizations may focus on specific aspects of relief, reconstruction or long-term development but in practice most remain pragmatic, and even "opportunistic," about where and what type of work they undertake. For instance, MSF, one of the organizations most strongly associated with emergency relief, undertakes a range of activities in the approximately 70 countries worldwide where it operates. Federated organizations can hold different positions among their different elements (e.g. MSF-France has developed different policies from MSF-Holland and MSF-Spain). In Afghanistan, the lines between relief, reconstruction and longer-term aid have often been blurred and the occasionally useful division that separates these concepts is less instructive in such cases.

In defining NGOs, humanitarian principles including independence and neutrality are important. The difficulty lies with the extent of the application, the definition and the collective understanding of these principles. With these principles in mind, NGOs can be distinguished by the extent to which they differentiate between politics and humanitarianism (Barnett 2005). Many have suggested that the less the humanitarians separate politics from their work, the more their role is blurred (Ferguson and Gupta 2002, Stoddard 2003). In other words, the distinctiveness of NGOs is lessened because of the instrumentalization of politics. This has been especially true in countries affected by high-profile conflicts, such as Afghanistan. The specific nature and role of NGOs are further complicated by the growing presence of other organizations involved in providing relief, reconstruction and development assistance, such as the UN's specialized agencies, including UNICEF and the UNHCR, international organizations including the Red Cross, bilateral governmental organizations and commercial entities. This leads to a wider point in which, given the research findings in Afghanistan discussed in this book, the exact role of NGOs can be questioned. This will be explored further in the light of our research in the final chapter.

Partnership: The notion of partnership is integral to the work carried out by aid groups, given their relatively small size and resources. A partnership is usually some sort of alliance or cooperation between two organizations, but may have different characteristics, including asymmetries in power (Fowler 1998). Elements of mutual trust, shared perceptions and reciprocal support are also commonly seen (Postma 1994). This asymmetry can lead to friction and sour relations between organizations. For this reason, the label "partnership" is often used in a top-down fashion; for example, when a donor calls its relationship with an NGO a partnership, but not the other way around (Lister 2000). As was mentioned earlier and will be elaborated on in later chapters, this imbalance can also lead to different dimensions of partnership, including co-option of aid organizations (Brinkerhoff 2002). Within the concept of partnership, two allied ideas are particularly important: politicization and proximity.

The notion of politicization is usually seen as part of the subservience of humanitarian principles and actions to dominant power interests. This is especially prevalent in the lead-up to the invasion and occupation of countries such as Afghanistan and Iraq. The growth of aid and the larger amounts of donor funds given to aid organizations are seen as an integral part of this process (Barnett 2005). Indeed, this process works in tandem with the forces of "marketization" and "securitization" (Jacoby and James 2009). Tornquist (1999) suggests that politicization can come into being on the basis of specific issues or interests as well as through ideology or collective interests. The forms of politicization occur either through the state or as a result of "self-management" (Tornquist 1999, p. 158). This idea of aid organizations being part of a wider political and military effort, in effect becoming willing participants, is critical to this research and will be returned to later in this book.

In the military–humanitarian relationship, proximity manifests itself in multiple ways. Garwood offers clarity on the issue of closeness or "defining [NGO] proximity to military forces" (2006, p. 11) by suggesting four variables. First, there is "geographical proximity," which can be measured by physical distance or the quantity of aid workers and military personnel in a given area. Second, there is "actual operational proximity," which is "the extent to which [an] NGO is co-operating or coordinating with military forces" (Garwood 2006, p. 11). Third, and an extension of the second, is the "perceived operational proximity" in which an aid group is thought to be cooperating with the military. Finally, there is "proximity of identity," which is the "extent to which NGOs are confused with military forces" (Garwood 2006, p. 11) and relates closely to the "blurring the line" debate. A closely allied concept is the notion of visibility, which can manifest itself in at least two ways, through reputation and through physical presence, which has been shown to be mutable depending on context (Gioia et al., 2000). This will be discussed further in Chapter 7.

Humanitarianism: The concept of humanitarianism relates to the assistance provided to others in times of disaster and war to reduce their suffering and improve their wellbeing. It is often distinguished from the highly contested term "development." Some see this as the furtherance of hegemonic economic aims (Rist 2014), while others connect it to a process designed to promote rights and "freedoms"

(Sen 1999). This latter understanding posits that the policies and actions associated with development aim to reduce poverty and reduce vulnerability, decrease exclusion and foster resilience. From this perspective, humanitarianism can be seen as the part of a "developmental" response to violent conflict or the occurrence of disasters when local coping mechanisms are overwhelmed. When these situations are prolonged, they are said to require interventions such as education, income generation and participation with an objective to "build back better." These cases blur the perceived differences between humanitarianism and development. This is the lens through which the "security–development" nexus has arisen and why it is difficult to divorce these concepts from emergency responses. It is through this that the experiences of the decade and a half since 2001 have "firmly entrenched" these linkages (Beswick and Jackson 2014, p. 2).

Three important additional elements are critical to the understanding of humanitarianism. First, violence and conflict are closely tied to its practice. As will be explored further in Chapter 2, modern Western humanitarianism was born out of conflict. Without conflict, it would not be necessary (except for relief supplied in the wake of naturally caused hazards) and the tension in the relationship between an aid organization and the military would not exist. Second, the idea of action is an integral part of humanitarianism. While theory can be found within its practice, along with corresponding debates and tensions, it is inherently pragmatic and practice oriented. It is about responding to cases of urgent human suffering and need in areas and contexts where the local capacity is overwhelmed. In this way, the activities of specific organizations such as the Red Cross and certain NGOs are commonly seen as a critical element in defining the concept (Weiss 1997). Third, legal and moral principles are central to its practice. Unlike development assistance, humanitarianism is based on international law. According to the Geneva Conventions, humanitarianism must be practiced in a way that is impartial (Slim 2001a). As such, it is not confined to a narrow set of principles but is pragmatically oriented. A key tension explored in this book is that the dissonance between "principles and pragmatism" (Frerks et al., 2006, p. 1) is inherent in aid practice and the scholarship of humanitarian assistance. Pragmatism here refers to the imperative to make the practice of humanitarianism relevant and meaningful for the intended primary beneficiaries (those suffering from violent conflict and other causes). An additional element of importance is the notion of "humanitarian space" or what is sometimes referred to as "humanitarian operating environment." Although the concept of humanitarian space does not have a common definition, it is often understood as the "access and freedom for humanitarian organizations to assess and meet humanitarian needs" (European Commission's Directorate for Humanitarian Aid, cited in Guttieri 2005, p. 1). The military influences this space by the types of strategies it follows.

Worthy of further consideration is who uses the term "humanitarianism." When used by aid workers, it is limited to the actions of their staff members and those directly engaged in assistance activities, with little regard for subsidiary goals (besides, perhaps, making a living). When used by the military, it is broadened in scope to include its own activities that are targeted toward civilians even when its primary goal is said to be "winning hearts and minds" as a part of a larger military strategy. Another term is used in military circles where there is any activity of a civilian nature is "civil–military operations," which might typically fall into the category of humanitarian activities or projects. The much-debated concept, especially following the North Atlantic Treaty Organization's (NATO) operation in Kosovo, of humanitarian intervention relates to the overwhelming application of force for what are deemed to be reasons of humanity, such as preventing or stopping widespread killings (Roberts 1993, Lin 1995 and Holzgrefe and Keohane 2003). The latest United States military doctrine (TRADOC 2014) keeps humanitarian aid as a key element of its core (albeit in last – 11th – place).

Military: The military is the primary, although not the only, representative of "security" in places undergoing violent conflict. The strategies it is obliged to follow can be seen as the "continuation of politics by other means," following the often-quoted phrase of the Prussian General Carl von Clausewitz (1780–1831). This places it firmly at the center of politics, particularly when Western militaries engage in occupation and militarized forms of governance. There is, of course, not just one "type" of military, and a spectrum of military forces and people engaged in security or belligerent action can be discerned. These range from peacekeeping forces constituted and approved by the UN Security Council to armed groups with mixed political and criminal motives (James 2008). Within this spectrum are traditional military forces constituted by states to further their domestic and foreign policies (Smith 2006) and, as such, they try to be exacting and reduce uncertainty in their operations as much as possible. All countries, save a few exceptions such as Costa Rica, have militaries. In Afghanistan, the most elaborate and well-resourced militaries are members of NATO. These are the forces which make up the bulk of the international military presence in Afghanistan and are the focus of the research described in this book.

Military personnel are governed by their own state laws and by IHL (also known as the Laws of War or the Law of Armed Conflict). These laws are made up of a body of international agreements including the UN Charter, the Geneva and The Hague Conventions and the Nuremberg Principles relating to war crimes and crimes against humanity, stemming from the experiences during and since the Second World War. These include prescriptions on the behavior of military personnel, such as the use of deception in battle, the wearing of uniforms and the distinction between those directly involved in conflict and those who are not. The distinction between combatant and civilian is important to understanding the nature of the military. Insecurity, the blurring of the line between aid and the military and the reduction of humanitarian space are all issues that are now germane to both the research and practical aspects of interaction between the humanitarians and the military and will be explored in later chapters.

Book structure

This book is divided into two broad parts. In the first part, a review of the historical background of the military–humanitarian relationship will be undertaken. In Chapter 2, the underlying historical context of the research topic will be examined. It will be shown that, when the relationship is looked at historically, three drivers – technology, strategy and ethics – were important in bringing humanitarians and the military together. In Chapter 3, issues related to security, international development, management studies and other social sciences will be considered. This focuses on three key research issues, each of which have constituencies that are for or against close cooperation between humanitarians and the military. These three issues are: the tension between structure and agency; programming and policy ethics; and the security–development debate. From this analysis and presentation of the case study a number of assumptions about the military–humanitarian relationship will be revealed which are explored in later chapters. To provide a firm theoretical grounding for this research, a framework will be offered which corresponds to the structure of the book outlined here. Specific areas of analysis are organized into a structure of causes leading to the tension within the military–humanitarian relationship.

In the second part of the book, the Afghan case study will be presented. In Chapter 4, a historical narrative is presented focusing on security and development in Afghanistan from roughly the nineteenth century to 2001. In Chapter 5, a closer examination is made of the period from 11 September 2001 to the end of 2014. Three specific areas are described. First, the role of insecurity and strategy in shaping the relationship between humanitarians and the military is discussed. The second area examined is the political developments and the structure of international assistance (the "aid architecture"). Finally, the humanitarian situation and response are outlined, with specific attention to several key manifestations and tensions of the military–humanitarian relationship in Afghanistan. In Chapter 6, the research findings are presented. This discussion is structured according to the key research areas and the assumptions first introduced earlier in this chapter.

The research findings are the result of primary research carried out in Afghanistan (as well as several Western capitals) and extensive secondary research. Organizational friction, for instance, was found to be a common but not always detrimental element of the military–humanitarian relationship. In relation to humanitarian security, the research revealed that the military rarely put relief workers in direct danger, although the latter can be part of or even create insecure environments. Humanitarian principles, it was found, are not a fixed set of propositions but change according to temporal and situational context. Finally, it was found that many humanitarians are not "being" co-opted, they come ready and willing to help achieve wider political and military goals. In fact, some NGOs take funds from donors in an attempt to influence the policies of those particular donors. This suggests that aid organizations change their policies and actions depending on the context, thus raising the possibility of transcending the simple arguments "for" or "against" and leading to a more refined understanding of the relationship between humanitarians and the military.

In the final chapter, the findings are analyzed and the assumptions are again reviewed with regard to the findings and what they say about the policy arena and the practice of humanitarian action. By questioning these assumptions, the underlying policy issue is addressed. We argue that while in some cases different approaches are made by humanitarians toward the military, there is a need to transcend the issue of whether humanitarians should be simply "for" or "against" the military. In support of this analysis, a framework for understanding the context and organizational policy options will be developed based on a flexible approach most commonly followed by humanitarians.

Conclusion

This first chapter has introduced the military–humanitarian relationship. Using recent history in Afghanistan, the underlying policy question was posed: why should NGOs have a close or distant relationship with the military? Relief workers are faced with a choice of working closely with the military or keeping a pronounced distance. Building on the research of others, a distinction has been drawn between two approaches. The first approach supports close relations between humanitarians and the military and is considered "integrated" in terms of policy and practice. The second approach is generally opposed to close relations and is "segregated" by taking a more critical and principled approach. To begin to answer this question, five assumptions were introduced in this chapter, based on a set of propositions in the literature, policy making and commonly held opinions in the field. These are:

- the relationship between humanitarians and the military is new
- differences between humanitarians and the military cause inter-organizational friction
- a close relationship with the military is dangerous for humanitarians
- principled positions are well established
- official aid leads to co-option and politicization.

These serve as an important base line for the research framework discussed in detail in Chapter 3. Several key concepts have been defined, including NGOs, partnership, humanitarianism and the military. Finally, the book structure has been described and the main findings summarized.

2

The military–humanitarian complex: a historiography

Introduction

Since the first recorded battle in history, distinctions have existed between those who fight and those who deal with the consequences of fighting (Cioffi-Revilla 1991, Hallett 1998, Morgan 2005) and remain one of the most important aspects of the laws of war (Crowe 2014). Yet, these spheres –humanitarian and military – have never been as distinct as they might appear. In fact, the relationship between civilians and the military during and after war has been closely intertwined – in some cases, humanitarians and the military have been one and the same. When present, these distinguishing features have been at some times unmistakable and at other times weak, yet they have never been universally respected. To help explain how this relationship evolved over time, this chapter examines three closely interlinked stimuli – technology, strategy and ethics – which both created the need for humanitarians and prompted the military to undertake "humanitarian" tasks.

The first stimulus, technology, took time to develop, but then accelerated exponentially during the last century and a half. In particular, this section will look at three technologies which have had the most profound impact on humanitarianism in war: arms and military hardware, medicine and the media. The first types of arms and military hardware (such as metal-bladed weapons, chariots and siege engines that relied largely on manpower) dominated warfare until the wide-scale introduction of gunpowder into the West after 1500. In time, Western militaries made significant advancements in organization, transport, telecommunications and other technology, making more effective use of this Eastern import to greatly increase their destructive capabilities, leading in turn to related advances in medicine. In the treatment of the sick and wounded, the line between humanitarians and the military blurred, especially during the modern era of industrial warfare and high-intensity conflict. Mass media also had an impact on the military–humanitarian relationship through subtle forms of popular and "manufactured" influence which altered the way war was perceived and carried out (Minear, Scott and Weiss 1996).

Strategy, the second stimulus, changed and evolved in reaction to technological developments as war became increasingly destructive. Strategy can be defined in a myriad of ways; here it is used as both a descriptor of a type of warfare and the corresponding ways it is addressed (through planning, direction and execution). In this case, two general strategies, high- and low-intensity conflict, led the military to interact with humanitarians in different ways. In high-intensity conflict, for instance, some approaches, such as linear formations and the extensive use of fortifications, were an important element of warfare for more than a millennium. Modernity brought nationalism, vast standing armies and "total" war. Alongside this trend, the use of low-intensity conflict strategies which deliberately targeted civilians increased (Callwell 1976, Beaumont 1995, Evans and Newnham 1998, Boot 2002). Humanitarian action became an important part of the reaction to such developments, helping to drive forward further codification of the laws of war.

This helped to provoke a third stimulus, ethics. In this section, the codification of these ideas into classical and neo-humanitarian will be reviewed. While the clearest examples are the Geneva and The Hague Conventions, cultural norms of restraint among the nobility, faith groups and humanists are also important in driving forward a shift from relief just for soldiers to a more general concern for civilians. Starting in the 1860s, the founders of modern humanitarianism encountered issues which have remained constant ever since. These include deciding to what degree to speak out about atrocities, determining the role of religion in humanitarian work, achieving organizational and programmatic effectiveness, working with the media and negotiating independence.

Technology

Technology is a useful starting point for this discussion because it is the critical element in organized violent conflict and influences the other stimuli discussed in this chapter. Technology often follows an exponential curve in terms of its increasing complexity and utility. Following Moore's Law, computing power is perhaps the best-known example, but the pattern applies to many other examples, including those technologies associated with the military.

Figure 2.1 shows the increase of weapon destructive power and dispersion in history. This reveals two important phenomena. First, that there was an exponential rise in the destructive power of arms over recorded history. Combatants altered their strategy by, among other things, becoming more dispersed. Second, for every weapon, a defensive device was made and for every device, a new weapon was made. During the time of Classical Greece, for example, arms consisted of swords, thrusting spears, the javelin and, for defense, shields, helmets and the cuirass (Hanson 2000). From the tenth century onward, fortifications became common and in reaction there was a greater use of siege engines and weapons like the catapult, which became more sophisticated. Relatively soon after this, the crossbow and longbow became standard weapons. The advent of gunpowder transformed war, but the uptake was relatively slow as compared to later advancements such as the rifle and

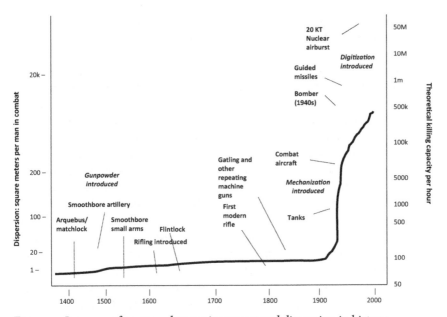

Figure 2.1 Increase of weapon destructive power and dispersion in history

Source: Adapted from Dupuy 1984, pp. 288–9.

Note: Dotted lines indicate approximate introduction and killing capacity. Solid line represents dispersion.

aircraft. The complexity and expense of technology, however, had a limiting effect on war. Heavy cavalry, for example, was costly in both procurement and upkeep and required considerable resources for it to be employed (Phillips 1984).

During the late nineteenth century, the rifling of firearms increased their accuracy, advances in engineering standardized their performance and industrialization increased their availability (Dupuy 1984). Where once bladed weapons had been seen as the critical battlefield tool (Napoleon, for example, regarded the bayonet as vital to winning wars), breech-loading rifles and breech-loading rifled artillery became key, resulting in a great increase in the destructive power of militaries (Wylly 1907). During the American Civil War, for instance, brass bullet casings replaced those made of paper, making rifles more efficient and easier to handle on the battlefield (Richie 1999). The conical rifle bullet used with the first repeating rifles, which gained widespread use in the 1850s, caused casualties at a hitherto unparalleled level (Dupuy 1984). During the Crimean War (1853–56), one officer lamented, "the means of destruction of people are getting stronger with each day; and it would be no wonder if they invented some sort of machine that will kill a thousand people in one go" (Kerr 1997, p. 178). Despite this, such advances – particularly an early version of the machine gun (created by medical-doctor-turned-inventor Richard Gatling in 1861) – were seen as "humanitarian" because "fewer men would be employed to kill just as many of the enemy, and the losses from disease would, in consequence, be much reduced" (Smith 2002, pp. 1–2).

Logistics, organization and ancillary advances such as the railroad and communications also contributed significantly to increased battlefield destructive power, particularly from the late 1800s onward. The Second War of Italian Independence, of 1859, was the first war in Europe in which railroads could dramatically extend the reach of armies (Wylly 1907). The telegraph – dubbed the "stepchild of war" by Martin Van Creveld – also became a major influence during this period and was used to dispatch trains for the first time in the 1850s (1987, p. 28). Together, these innovations created a synergy from 1870 on, where "war henceforth was a matter of movement, depending on good roads and railways; and of supply, destructive firepower and organization" (Pick 1993, p. 111). By the First World War, these combined technologies had become commonplace. The use of warplanes developed from providing aerial reconnaissance to dog-fighting and dropping bombs, and chemical and biological weapons were employed using modern methods. Destroying the industrial capacity of states, by breaking the will of people through technology, became the aim of high-intensity conflict (Grayling 2006). By 1945, the potential existed for the complete destruction of societies through the delivery of strategic (via plane, submarine or fixed missile silo) or tactical (via artillery and man-pack) nuclear devices. Since the 1940s, however, no significant inventions for small and light weapons have been made. The cyclic rate of arms, for example, reached a plateau with the invention of weapons such as the Kalashnikov (1947) and the Uzi (1955). Other weapons like hand grenades, landmines and artillery have also reached their highest destructive power. Instead, advances now focus on digitization, unmanned deployments and long-range force projection. In sum, the rapidity of technological advances continues to allow war to be carried out in ways which surpass contemporary ethical constraints.

Technological advances have long been one of the key impetuses for medical interventions into the battlefield – the second aspect of the technological stimuli for closer relations between humanitarians and the military. While medical care in war is largely a modern phenomenon, there are examples throughout history of health professionals joining militaries to tend to the wounded. The ancient Greek writer Xenophon, for instance, mentions doctors on the march with the Spartans alongside "soothsayers and flute players" (Salazar 2000, p. 71). The Roman legions trained and maintained their own medical corps, and surgeons commonly accompanied monarchs into battle during the Middle Ages (Gottfried 1986, Gabriel and Metz 1992).

During the Crusades (eleventh to thirteenth centuries), the chivalric orders such as the Order of St. John and the Knights Templar maintained *hospitalia* along the common routes between Western Europe and the Levant (Singer 1928). By most accounts, the chivalric orders admitted anyone, except those with incurable diseases like leprosy, and performed basic surgery using opium or mandragora as an anesthetic (Riley-Smith 1999). Not long after its founding, however, the Order of St. John became involved in defensive military operations where it occupied frontier posts. It was no doubt felt that to do so without a military element at the time would have been "foolhardy" (Forey 1992, p. 19). Conversely, the Knights Templar began as a military order which then began to undertake humanitarian activities (Slim 2001b). To further their Christian military aims, they undertook fundraising, recruitment and tasks such as supporting hospitals. As such, they possessed a dual role of protection and assistance, much as humanitarian (and some military) organizations do today. Indeed, the Order of St. John was revived during the mid-nineteenth century, making substantial contributions to the development of first aid and ambulance assistance (Haller 1992, Pearn 1994). In a genuine sense, then, these "extraordinary hybrid military–humanitarian orders [can be seen] as the starting point of international humanitarian charity in the Western tradition" (Slim 2001b, p. 333, see also Brauman 1996, Benthall 1993).

In the eighteenth century, a fuller understanding of disease and advancements in chemistry began to revolutionize medicine, beginning with militaries benefiting greatly (Gabriel and Metz 1992). The French Army, for example, instituted regular medical screening of recruits as early as 1726 (Gabriel and Metz 1992). Despite this, even as late of the wars of the 1860s, the majority of soldiers were still lost to disease rather than through enemy action (Kirk 1996, Lee 2003). The British military expedition in the Crimea, for instance, was still inefficient enough to obstruct the flow of adequate supplies, food and staff (Cope 1958). A surgeon during the campaign explained that medical equipment was "meagre in the extreme," food for patients was scarce and dirty water was used in an attempt to kill maggots that infested the patient's wounds (Reid 1911, pp. 40–41). To help alleviate the suffering of soldiers, the Irish Order of the Sisters of Mercy and professional health staff such as Florence Nightingale went to the region under British government authority. Through their advocacy and provision of medical care, these humanitarians improved the sanitary conditions that had contributed so significantly to morbidity (Pyemont 1855, Chambers and Madgwick 1968).

During the American Civil War, the Union (of Northern states) also suffered more than half its deaths off the battlefield (Bollet 2002). Many soldiers preferred to avoid doctors altogether and relied on home remedies and available narcotics or alcohol (McPherson 1990). Despite the poor conditions, important medical advances were introduced, including the first regular use of anesthetics and the development of trauma care systems (Gillet 1987, Blaisdell 1988, Trunkey 2000). Americans, led by private groups such as the Women's Central Association of Relief, feared that soldiers would face a "sanitary debacle" like the one experienced in the Crimea (Haller 1992, p. 24). President Lincoln approved the establishment of a Sanitary Commission to address these concerns as a complementary organization that was to do what the government could not do. Its duties included procuring medical supplies, sourcing nurses, establishing a permanent ambulance system, providing relief to the displaced, offering advocacy for health and hygiene, collecting donations and helping families locate wounded soldiers (Haller 1992, pp. 24–5). These are all tasks intimately familiar to modern humanitarians.

The conditions found in these wars of the mid-eighteenth century gave rise to what Coupland calls the "Solferino Cycle" – after the Second War of Italian Independence's eponymous battle of 1859 (1999, p. 864). In their aftermath, the technological advancement of arms and military hardware triggered not only a refinement of weapons but also an improvement in the treatment of victims. They were, for instance, instrumental in the founding of the Red Cross and its program of placing civilian volunteers in and around combatants (Moorehead 1998, Hutchinson 1996). To do so, they achieved an ethical accommodation (a "moral militarization") that was "highly ambivalent" to the violence around them in a way close to the chivalric orders before them (Slim 2001b, p. 335). Discussed later in detail, these early modern ("classical") humanitarians relied heavily on their independence from the political-military concerns around them and on maintaining the understanding that they would not speak out against what they witnessed.

By the First World War, medicine on the battlefield had – through innovation, trial and error – advanced significantly. Blood transfusions started in 1917 and anesthetics, antiseptics, dressings and instruments all became "freely available" during the war (Keegan 1976, p. 237). Following the Second World War, global efforts were made to eradicate diseases, address problems such as famine and extend medicine into hard-to-reach places (Chabbott 1999). Beginning in the 1960s, emergency pre-hospital care became a major focus, building on the work of organizations such as the Order of St. John. In the United States, elaborate schemes were made to handle mass-casualty incidents and build the capacity of paramedic services (Dick 2003). France made similar efforts with its Service d'Aide Médicale Urgente and the Service Médical d'Urgence et de Réanimation (Taithe 2004). Many NGOs were founded specifically to deliver medical aid and many more implemented health-related programming as part of a larger portfolio that included human rights promotion (Drori and Keiko 2006).

During the Nigerian (Biafran) Civil war (1967–70), a group of young French doctors working for the International Committee of the Red Cross (ICRC) became appalled by the human suffering they witnessed. Recognizing the power of medicine (treating children who were "like dry plants finally watered"), they felt the need to speak out (Bortolotti 2004, p. 43). They were well connected and included the media-savvy Bernard Kouchner (Chandler 2001, Taithe 2004). Their vision was that, in addition to providing medical assistance, it was necessary to intervene (*le droit d'ingérence*). After leaving the Red Cross, they founded Médecins Sans Frontières with the explicit aim to interfere where necessary and protect civilians, regardless of international borders. Around the same time, Western military medicine also advanced. By specializing in preventative medicine, advanced life support and trauma care, medical providers were able to reduce casualties both on and off the battlefield. With its spare capacity in peacetime, the military began to see the provision of medical care as a key area in which to carry out humanitarian action – frequently as part of more general attempts to "win hearts and minds" of local people (Sharp, Luz and Gaydos 1999).

Here, media reportage, the final key element in the development of technology in shaping the military–humanitarian relationship, was key. Both civilians and soldiers have long known that the ways in which their actions are portrayed are vital in "manufacturing consent" for their objectives among leaders and the general public (Chomsky and Herman 2002). Much before the "CNN effect," in which television helps drive policy, the Athenian general and historian Thucydides "reported" extensively on the Peloponnesian War (431–404 BC). The first modern war reportage likely dates from the British Peninsular Campaign (1808–14), covered by *The Times* correspondent Henry Crabb Robinson. William Howard Russell, who worked in the latter half of the nineteenth century, is widely considered to be the first war correspondent. His dispatches are thought to have put immense political pressure on the British government of the time (Furneaux 1944, Haller 1992). During the Crimean War, *The Times* ran stories of the soldiers' suffering and set up a public relief fund to provide assistance to the British military.

Starting in the late 1890s, sensationalist "yellow journalism" competed to increase readership and sales for the two big American news agencies owned by William Randolph Hearst and Joseph Pulitzer. Both, for instance, were instrumental in securing public support for the intervention in Cuba which helped to cause the Spanish–American War of 1898 (Smythe 2003). To meet the needs of national mobilization during the First World War, similarly extensive media campaigns were used not just by governments but also by humanitarian organizations. By using emotive words and images, compassion became an industry. National Red Cross societies staunchly supported nationalism and war fervor through their media campaigns. This approach to humanitarianism, which closely aligned succor with foreign policy goals, became what Hutchinson has labelled the "militarization of charity" (1996). In a similar vein, Rozario demonstrates a link between the images of war and modern humanitarianism as practiced by the early Red Cross and goes as far as to hold that "sensationalistic mass culture" served as a necessary pre-condition for modern humanitarianism (2003, p. 418). Taithe concludes that the Red Cross at the time "definitively enslaved the humanitarian agenda with national and military ones. The Red Cross then served to blur the boundaries between war and peace because it mobilized for war and disasters in peace" (1999, p. 179). The First World War certainly provided a global platform on which the Red Cross could grow as an organization helped along by mass media. The decision of humanitarians to remain largely part of national agendas, with notable exceptions such as Oxfam during the Second World War, lasted from the 1940s until the late 1960s. During this period, the link between mass media and war became profound. Little fell outside the purview of government and the use of mass media was part of the political–military strategies of the large ideological blocs of the Cold War.

The widespread availability of television, and later satellite communications, was to speed the process of mass communications and its impact on humanitarianism. The instantaneous spread of information, including pictures and "raw" or unprocessed data, had a significant impact on the way people viewed the world and made decisions. The implications of this change have been covered elsewhere (Ryan 1998), but the impact on war and humanitarianism is noteworthy in that "the news media influence the pace, scale, locus, and duration of action mounted by humanitarian actors" (Minear, Scott and Weiss 1996, p. 45). Increased media attention created more funding, which in turn brought organizations greater capacities and a stronger willingness to respond.

The Nigerian civil war, again, serves as an important event in this discussion. It is widely regarded as the first televised humanitarian crisis where mass media influenced both the conduct of war and the humanitarian response (De St. Jorre 1972, Cervenka 1971). It was the first time that humanitarians deliberately acted as a "spokesman" for the suffering (Waters 2004). Decolonization, Cold War political divisions, the manipulation of humanitarian activities and the use of the image of the "starving African child" interplayed to heighten the humanitarian response. Media coverage in Biafra, and the later conflicts in Bangladesh and Ethiopia, had a significant impact on Western audiences, resulting in massive fundraising and large-scale humanitarian responses (Minear, Scott and Weiss 1996). These formed the basis from which the "Band-Aid" phenomenon was to exert such a powerful influence during the 1980s (Benthall 1993).

A decade later, the power of 24-hour international television news and the Internet was used extensively by NATO to justify its airstrikes on the former Yugoslavia. Daily press briefings, embedded journalism and social media began to combine to create the so-called "CNN effect" (Minear, Scott and Weiss 1996). The interventions in Bosnia, Eastern Congo and Somalia were all preceded by significant media attention and widespread "calls for action" (Olsen, Carstensen and Hoyen 2003, p. 124). While the tendency for leaders to point to public concerns as a justification for their actions may be an attempt to "obscure other, more self-interested, motivations underpinning Western humanitarianism" it seems that a multitude of influences interplay to set the necessary conditions, but not necessarily "trigger," humanitarian action. (Robinson 2005, p. 345). In sum, there is, as Minear, Scott and Weiss observe, an "undeniable mutuality of influence" between mass media, war and humanitarianism (1996, p. 45).

Strategy

Strategy, a second stimulus of the military–humanitarian relationship, consists of the planning, management and control of military operations. In different types of warfare, two basic strategies were used; high- and low-intensity conflict. This section will trace both of these through the historical development of military strategy and its impact on the military–humanitarian relationship. Before proceeding, though, it is important to note three points concerning the high- and low-intensity distinction. First, they are not mutually exclusive and may be used in conjunction or separately. Low-intensity conflict may precede high-intensity conflict or vice versa. Shared aspects of the two include the co-option of humanitarians and interaction with the media. Second, the link between strategy and politics, the context in which war occurs, is critical in both strategies. Clausewitz's famous dictum, that war is the "continuation of politics by other means," is instructive in that it links organized violence to more general goals (cited in Smith 2005, p. 33). Finally, these strategies are exclusively the domain neither of the global North nor of modernity; each has been used throughout history by militaries in the developed and developing worlds (Duyvesteyn 2005).

In classical Greece, high-intensity conflict consisted mainly of infantry (*hoplites*) formed in structured ranks (*phalanx*) engaged in frontal assaults on open spaces (Hanson 2000). Battles usually pitted army against army in fields or farm lands devoid of civilian populations (McGlynn 1994). By the time of the Crusades (eleventh–thirteenth centuries), there was more tactical planning and control using divisions of maneuver and reserve (Smail 1956). During the development of military strategy in early modern Europe, these changes produced greater military efficiency that led in turn to increased destructive capacity. A key strategy during the Middle Ages (lasting until the fifteenth century) that brought civilians close to warfare was the use of siege against fortified castles and towns (Dupuy 1984). Europeans learned much about fortifications from their ventures into the Middle East and, as these developed, attacks on the people and property that existed outside city and castle walls increased. Over time, however, high-walled buttresses were rendered obsolete by cannon and artillery.

The reliance on civilians for logistical support was an important element of siege warfare and the prolonged periods of deployment that it entailed (Best 1994). As time passed, towns in Europe became increasingly prepared for war. This included economic measures to improve their ability to supply provisions to passing troops and the manufacture of their own weaponry to arm their inhabitants against hostile forces (Eltis 1989). This put civilians directly in the line of combat and made them vulnerable to disease, theft and exploitation (Black 2006). By the 1700s, monarchs relied on, and went to great lengths to gain, an early form of public opinion, looking "to their people not only for bodies, cash and kind, but for sympathy and moral support" (Duffy 1987, p. 303). Bands of citizen-soldiers, formed into ill-disciplined militias, became the primary form of high-intensity combat unit (Black 2002b). As a result, the distinction between belligerents and non-combatants was vague. In 1572, for example, Catholic civilians, not soldiers, were responsible for the deaths of most Huguenots in France (Black 2006).

From the late 1700s to the twentieth century, organized high-intensity conflict outside state control became delegitimized. As Mary Kaldor explains, "once state interest had become the dominant legitimation of war, then claims of just cause by non-state actors could no longer be pursued through violent means" (1999, p. 17). As such, a distinction between political and military leaders developed (Smith 2006). The emergence of "total war," however, ensured that this separation did not lead to greater protection for civilians. Epitomized by Napoleon's efforts to mobilize French society in its entirety, this involved mass conscription (known as levée en masse), the manipulation of information and the pursuit of total victory through speed, envelopment and annihilation. By some estimates, an unprecedented amount of resources (upwards of 80 per cent of Britain's GDP, for instance) were deployed during the subsequent Napoleonic wars from 1803 to 1815 (Mann 1993).

Conscription swelled the military ranks and, because they were no longer billeted among the local populace, a suitable structure of barracks and supply was devised (Showalter 2002). This was achieved mainly through bureaucratization, the extension of a taxation state, the establishment of garrison towns and the creation of a permanent "regiment" system (Keegan 1993). These advances permitted armies to be self-reliant (for example, in terms of food and transport) for the first time without having to rely on the nearest civilian population (Best 1994, p. 257). The standardization of uniforms from the late eighteenth century onwards also helped to separate soldiers from civilians (Kaldor 1999). Organizational skills, military logistics and increased professionalism also became the norm for high-intensity campaigns – a phenomenon that paralleled the rise of nation-states in the West (post the Peace of Westphalia, 1648). This provided elites with what Michael Mann (1988) has termed "infrastructural power" – defined as the "incentive *and* the means with which the central power was able to dominate ... [thus enabling] the capacity to penetrate civil society and to implement logistically political decisions" (Centeno 2003, p. 86).

In the process, high-intensity war gradually shifted its focus to include the civilian as a central element in the strategy making. Skirmishes thus replaced linear columns, cover and concealment became paramount (through tactical field fortifications such as trenches and hardened fighting positions) and tactics involving speed and maneuver became more sophisticated. Developments between the First and Second World Wars made this most pronounced. These developments made the "old line-and-column tactics at first obsolete, then suicidal" (Lind 2004, p. 12). The battle "field" was no longer confined to a single geographic location but might be spread across hundreds or thousands of miles, including urban areas. Because of the available technology, these could no longer be effectively defended except by further changes in strategy.

Before the modern era, armies were more likely to represent a burden and a threat to civilians through looting, insecurity, the spread of disease and the destruction of property. Total war and industrialization, however, meant that societies themselves, through industrial output, became the backbone of military might. Thus the civilian became increasingly the target of military attack. To win militarily, it became necessary to break the will of the people and their productive capacity (Grayling 2006). Media attention and the control of resources (including those deemed "humanitarian") were central to the high-intensity war efforts. In the unprecedented destruction wrought by the Second World War, Allied military forces incorporated non-enemy civilians into their strategy on pragmatic as well as humanitarian grounds. The military might face main supply routes clogged with refugees, and hungry civilians who harassed soldiers on patrol, and resistance might have been fomented if occupying forces did not devote resources to civilian welfare (Black 2006).

This military attention to civilian matters underpinned the response to the massive humanitarian crisis toward the end of the Second World War. During that time, Western governments became heavily and actively engaged in efforts to assist civilian populations. Keen to maintain order in areas they occupied, Allied armies formed "Civil Affairs" units, often at a divisional level (a "division" typically consists of 10,000 or more soldiers). These turned soldiers into political governors by giving them supervisory authority over humanitarian and reconstruction issues ranging from education to elections (Ziemke 1990). A pattern was set in which governments saw humanitarian activities as an extension of military efforts. During the Second World War, government control boards, for example, directed almost all American relief outside the Red Cross (Curti 1963). This made the co-option of humanitarian organizations a reality of the Second World War, and nearly inevitable after that, setting the modern precedent for a "common project" (Lipson 2003, p. 11). While they were intimately associated with government efforts of the time, some humanitarian organizations, however, managed to maintain a degree of independence. Save the Children was established to assist German children despite a British blockade, while Oxfam transferred relief supplies to Greeks blockaded by American military action (Chabbott 1999, Black 1992). Following the Second World War, responding to need was sharpened during the wars of decolonization. Many large mainstream humanitarian organizations generally accepted that principled positions would face tension and accepted the direction – and the resources – of state officials.

The bi-polar rivalry between the Eastern and Western blocs during the post-Second World War era brought new levels of destructive potential, rendering a direct high-intensity conflict mutually catastrophic. Great Power strategy thus moved towards low-intensity "proxy wars", again blurring the lines between the humanitarian and military spheres. Between 1945 and 1991, roughly 75 per cent of all conflicts were considered to be "low-intensity" (Van Creveld 1991, p. 20). Such an approach proved to be a viable strategy in contexts as diverse as the Sudanese Darfur, Nepal, Iraq and Afghanistan, where it has become a standard means of waging war (Smith 2005). Whereas high-intensity approaches often rely on technology and material resources, with an emphasis on destroying opposing forces and their ability to fight, the low-intensity rubric relies on "the people" to advance political change. In this way, perception, political images, propaganda and the selective use of force are crucial. Humanitarian space also tends to be more open, allowing for a greater presence amid generally higher levels of security (Taber 1965, p. 153).

Despite its contemporary prevalence, low-intensity conflict has existed throughout history. Rebellions against a superior or occupying force with greater material resources led to war becoming a grassroots affair "in which the people in the streets and house and fields – all the people, anywhere – are the battlefield" (Smith 2006, p. 3). This was apparent during the revolutions in the Tyrol (1809), Russia (1812) and Spain (1803–13) (Hahlweg 1986). Napoleon's fight to control the Iberian Peninsula, for instance, gave rise to the first use of "guerrilla" warfare (or "small war") from 1807 to 1814. An element here was a tendency of the superior force to use "counter-insurgency" strategies to win the support of the local populace. Conversely, ravaging, which consisted of pillaging, destruction and laying waste to land, also took place as either an accompaniment to a period of higher-intensity conflict or as a discrete strategy of its own (Strickland 1996). In this way, civilians such as the peasantry were brought directly into the breach of battle as the control of agriculture, water and education became a key weapon of war. Working on and with such resources, it became inevitable that humanitarians might alter the military balance.

The growth of Western power outside its borders paralleled the beginning of the provision of humanitarian assistance in low-intensity conflicts. Early on, the French carried out military interventions in a way that presaged the later *sans frontiérisme* movement. The rescue of French aristocrats from the slave revolt in Saint-Domingue (present day Haiti) in 1793, for example, provides a case in point. The French also landed troops in Lebanon following unrest that resulted in the deaths of roughly 20,000 Christians in 1861 (Ferre 1995). By the late nineteenth century, military operations to re-establish order, evacuate civilians, support collaborationist regimes or oust disobedient governments had become nearly commonplace. In this way, the stage was set for military adventures in asymmetric battles that pitted European forces, equipped with modern weapons and organization, against indigenous fighters in what was to become the "Third World" (Black 2006).

In the 1960s, the low-intensity strategies adopted by North Vietnam in its war with the United States obliged the more powerful protagonist to devise civil–military approaches which addressed both humanitarian and security needs simultaneously (Boot 2002). Programs in which soldiers helped to construct or rehabilitate social infrastructure such as schools and health facilities were an important aspect of some of the work done by Army Special Forces and Marines (West 1972, Cassidy 2004). Underlining that the "plan and strategy must be adapted to the character of the people encountered," it was hoped that people's "hearts and minds" could be won and thus a military victory could be secured (United States Marines 1940, p. 1.8). In Vietnam the United States military thus gradually took over most humanitarian roles that had previously been done by voluntary agencies (the case of Catholic Relief Services is discussed further below). Civilian contractors recruited through the American Agency for International Development (USAID) worked on economic projects, while the army handled other aspects of civilian interaction as part of its Civil Operations and Rural Development Support (CORDS) program (Fisher 2006). Testifying before the United States Senate, the director of CORDS and later Director of Central Intelligence, William Colby (1970, p. 5), stated that "development is a necessary counterpart to the military efforts of our forces in this new kind of war [in Vietnam]." This followed models developed by the British government in the Malayan emergency a decade earlier.

With special operations forces (where Civil Affairs were placed organization-ally) taking on a greater role in America's approach to conflict, the likelihood of overlap with humanitarian organizations became inevitable. The end of the Cold War, with its many "new wars," only accelerated this process (Kaldor 1999). For example, in 1991, immediately following the first Gulf War, more than one mil-lion ethnic Kurds fled Iraq into neighboring countries. At the time, it was felt that the humanitarian organizations were unable to respond quickly enough because of insecurity and inaccessible terrain. The resultant American military-led relief effort, dubbed Operation Provide Comfort, brought together armed forces from 14 countries and more than 30 NGOs, thereby setting a pattern for later humanitar-ian action in Bosnia, Somalia and Afghanistan (Seiple 1996, Sharp et al. 2001). In addition to operations, documentation, training, meetings and informal networks were established, "demonstrating a widespread sense of common project within the field" (Lipson 2003, p. 11). Following this pattern, Western approaches to disasters and conflict have started to involve a wide range of both civil and military actors – archetypal examples of which include the NATO intervention in Kosovo in 1999 and the international response to the 2010 Haitian earthquake.

Ethics

Notions of "development," the codification of the rules of war and the widespread acceptance of charitable values were the final and critical stimuli driving the military–humanitarian relationship. While these emerged for a range of complex, contextual reasons, their ethical components include the restraint of belligerents in the use of force, a distinction between military and civilians and, eventually, the acceptance of humanitarian actors within active and post-conflict zones. This section will firstly trace the origins and codification of ethics in war from the ancient world to the present. In particular, it will look at the development of Western normative values, the influence of the nation-state and the impact of ethics in war to demonstrate that they developed over time as the nature of war itself changed. Secondly, it considers the origins of what might be termed "classic" and "neo" humanitarianism, a common pattern is the inhumanity or amoral conduct in war, followed by an attempt to prevent, mitigate or regulate the use of violence (Leader 1998). Two periods considered here, the 1860s and the 1960s, with their respective wars in Solferino and Biafra, were significant catalysts in the development of modern humanitarianism and its relationship with the military. The reactions to these two wars gave rise to two main streams of humanitarian thought and practice that are categorized here as "classical" and "neo-humanitarianism."

The moral basis for humanitarianism in times of conflict can be found in the ancient world (Best 1994). Natural law, which holds that the basis for ethics can be found in nature and applied universally, has provided a key founding basis for such norms, with writers such as Aristotle, Plato and Thucydides offering moral commentaries on warfare (Gorman 2000). Yet, the main constraints on conflict behavior were mostly economic rather than ethical (Liddell Hart 1970, Kennedy 1988). During the Peloponnesian War, for instance, "the destruction of olive groves was virtually the first act of an invading army" (Walzer 2000, p. 170–71). This strategy ruined the ability of enemies to wage war, but also heavily affected civilians in the process (orchards are much more difficult to replace than looted food stocks). Indeed, the looting of livestock and the plundering of food stocks were a "normal part of the reward of hard campaigning" (Hindley 2003, p. 6–7).

New developments in technology and the perception that war was becoming excessively brutal (and this contrary to Christian ethics), however, led to early attempts to restrict the conduct of combatants, *jus in bello*. Broadly coinciding with parallel rules developed by the great Muslim jurists of the early medieval period, these sought to limit the impact of war on non-combatants. The cutting down of fruit trees was prohibited under the Peace of God in 1041 and the Council of Narbonne in 1054 (Strickland 1996). In 1139, the Church banned the crossbow as "hateful to God and unfit for Christian" use (Phillips 1984, p. ix). This edict represents the first documented case of arms control, but was limited in application in that it was meant only for Christian-on-Christian combat (Dupuy, 1984). Within this category, ideas of chivalry "marked knights from mere ruffians and bandits and also from peasant soldiers who bore arms as a necessity" (Walzer 2000, p. 34). This had its roots in a general sense of "honor" that was frequently alluded to in the classical period (for example, the Roman leader, Gaius Fabricius (second century BC), held that it was "preferable to lose with honor, rather than to triumph without it") (Hensel 2007, p. 5).

During the Renaissance, writers such as Francisco de Vitoria (1492–1546) and Hugo Grotius (1583–1645) built on the work of earlier Christian and Muslim scholars to argue that sovereigns (ruling, as Francisco Suarez (1548–1617) propounds, not by divine right, but by the consent of the masses) should act in concert to prevent war's excesses. This should, it was suggested, be accompanied by limiting offensive war to just interventions defined by natural law and reason rather than simply by religious difference – a key premise of the modern Church's discourse on warfare today (Duncan 2003). Taken together with the earlier work from further East upon which they build, these propositions represent the philosophical underpinnings of much of what the West currently defines as the legitimate use of force in the international arena. They contain, in other words, the *jus ad bellum* stipulation that sovereign states (not private armies) directed by a legitimate authority can, once all other means of redress are exhausted, use proportionate violence in response to aggression, with the aim of returning to a peaceful status quo. They also led to the gradual codification of more sophisticated *jus in bello* limitations – notably, a responsibility to distinguish between soldiers and civilians, to deploy a level of force commensurate with the tactical goal sought (thereby prohibiting certain weapons) and to adhere to generally agreed rules regarding the treatment of prisoners of war (Frost 2004).

As war became more mechanized during the nineteenth century, these ideas grew in influence. Issued in 1863 by Abraham Lincoln, the Lieber Code (General Order 100), for example, put ethical limits on war and sought to curb the excesses that might occur during martial law and occupation (Guelzo 1997, Moorehead 1998). Section one dealt with military jurisdiction, necessity and retaliation. Section two protected civilians and property and spelled out punishments for violating the rights of the "inhabitants of hostile countries." The final section covered deserters, prisoners of war, hostages and "booty on the battlefield." Apart from delineating specific guidance on conduct, the law also spelled out a vision of war itself, as found in Part 1, Article 29, which states:

> Modern times are distinguished from earlier ages by the existence, at one and the same time, of many nations and great governments related to one another in close intercourse. Peace is their normal condition; war is the exception. The ultimate object of all modern war is a renewed state of peace. The more vigorously wars are pursued, the better it is for humanity. Sharp wars are brief. (Lieber 1863)

International arms restrictions followed in 1868 with the St. Petersburg Declaration against the use of explosive bullets (Christopher 1999). Whereas the Lieber Code was internal, the St. Petersburg Declaration applied to all state signatories (made up of Western European governments) who agreed that such weapons were "contrary to the laws of humanity." The statements of St. Petersburg were reaffirmed and expanded twice in The Hague in 1899 and 1907 to cover the treatment of prisoners of war and restrictions on sieges and certain types of weapons. Around the turn of the nineteenth century, the proponents of the codification of humanitarian ethics were thus "more numerous and vocal than the pessimists" (Best 1994, p. 46).

The work of Henri Dunant was especially important in creating these conditions. Having witnessed the aftermath of the Battle of Solferino in 1859 and helped to organize relief efforts for several days afterwards, he wrote a small book entitled *Memory of Solferino*. First published in 1862, it described his experience and called for humanitarian action in war through the use of a civilian volunteer corps (Dunant 1986). The book is significant in that it included a call to action and led to subsequent lobbying among the upper classes of Switzerland, his home state (Moorehead 1998). Rieff explains the impact of Dunant's book by saying "the conference at Geneva [which became the first Geneva Convention] succeeded in translating the reaction to the book into a body of law" (2002, pp. 68–9). This led to the deployment of field medical staff and generated "policies and laws that impose limits on the design, production, transfer, or use of weapons" (Coupland 1999, p. 864). While it would take many other meetings (in The Hague, Geneva and others) and resolutions to codify the normative ideas of limiting war, the first meeting in Geneva was historic.

This body of "laws" formed the basis for what is now known as "classical humanitarianism" – a set of operating principles first articulated by Gustave Moynier, a founder member of the Red Cross, in 1875. He suggested four programmatic criteria for the Red Cross consisting of "foresight, solidarity, centralization and mutuality" (the last summing up the idea of neutrality). These were confirmed and expanded on in 1921 and 1946. Nonetheless, it was not until 1955 that Jean Pictet, Vice President of the ICRC (1971–79), formalized the principles as they are known today within the Red Cross as the Fundamental Principles: humanity, impartiality, neutrality, independence, voluntary service, unity and universality. Interestingly, at this early stage, "Rifle Associations" were used in the forming of the early Red Cross societies in Western Europe, which aimed at assisting soldiers, not civilians.

The philosophical roots of classical humanitarianism were founded well before Dunant and the Red Cross, though. Several philosophers, including Christian Wolff (1679–1754) and Emer de Vattel (1714–67), argued that interfering with a state's sovereignty was contrary to natural law (Holzgrefe and Keohane 2003). While these have been criticized (giving rise to alternative forms of humanitarianism, discussed further below), a conservative approach is seen as one of its strengths. By finding a "delicate and uneasy balance between recognizing military necessity and asserting a moral imperative," the Geneva Conventions and the Red Cross have been able "to survive and gain almost universal ratification" and acceptance (Leader 1998, p. 198).

The key issue with classical humanitarianism is that, to be implemented correctly, it must acquiesce to whichever political–military powers control access to those in need. The perception of neutrality is critical. Without it, humanitarians could be seen as co-opted by one or more of the protagonists. While practicing classical humanitarianism, humanitarian organizations have often been faced with nothing less than hard choices. Perhaps the most infamous example of these arose as a result of the Bosnian war of 1992–95 in which around 200,000 (mostly Muslim) people died. Many lost their lives in detention centers established by the Serbian-controlled Yugoslav People's Army, which established authority over around 60 per cent of Bosnia-Herzegovina during 1992. Access to them was extremely limited, with the ICRC being the only organization to gain regular entrance. One such facility was created in the northern Bosnian town of Bosanski Samac in April 1992, where an indeterminate number of detainees were abused and some were murdered (Kent 2003). The ICRC is believed to have visited in May and, following the war, was called upon to testify to the International Criminal Tribunal for the former Yugoslavia in a case against three individuals charged in connection with these offenses. A former ICRC interpreter offered to give eyewitness evidence and prosecutors informally called him to appear. The ICRC, however, argued that such a submission would jeopardize its ability to fulfil its mandate. It claimed that its ability to gain access to detainees relies on a relationship of trust with the authorities holding those prisoners and, if the former employee did testify, subsequent access would be denied (Brauman 2013). On legal advice, the Tribunal was forced to accept this argument and the interpreter did not testify (the three men in question were successfully prosecuted in 2003 and were sentenced to 17, 8 and 6 years' detention, respectively).

In contrast to this steadfast attachment to Pictet's Fundamental Principles, neo-humanitarianism stems from consequentialist ethic – a "naturalist doctrine that an action is just if its consequences are more favourable than unfavourable to all concerned" (Holzgrefe and Keohane 2003, p. 20). This therefore obliges humanitarians to speak out, or even side with a particular set of values and actors, if there is a moral case to do so. Notions of sovereignty and neutrality – so crucial to the classical approach – are given credence, but are subsidiary. Instead, the new approach hinged on two suppositions: that third parties had the right to intervene in conflicts (*le droit d'ingérence*) for humanitarian reasons (even if a government was unwilling) and that there exists a right to bear witness to what they saw. This marked an important shift from a needs-based analysis to one based on the rights of those affected by violence (Chandler 2001).

To achieve this, it might be necessary to take up obviously partial positions. During the Biafra war, for instance, the only way to get aid to millions of starving people was to break the government blockade illegally. The ICRC observed the law and phased out its activities without speaking out publicly, thereby – in the minds of some – becoming "accomplices in the systematic massacre of a population" (Benthall 1993, p. 125). By contrast, a few organizations, such as Oxfam, felt they must do something and covertly brought assistance to the Biafrans (Black 1992). Proponents of the new humanitarianism such as Bernard Kouchner, a co-founder of MSF, and Aengus Finucane, founder of Concern, became highly influential, marking the start of the *sans frontiérisme* movement (Allan and Styan 2000).

This nascent solidarism also appeared in Vietnam during the 1960s. There, the American government used its relationship with non-governmental organizations, such as Catholic Relief Services (CRS), to gain a military advantage. The partnership between CRS and the United States administration was "based on a set of common values and mutual interests" (Flipse 2002, p. 247). By the mid-1960s, a major part of CRS's program in Vietnam consisted of food distributions to the South Vietnamese Popular Forces on behalf of the military. When this was made public in 1967, the ensuing scandal led to the program ending the following year. CRS, like many other NGOs, remained very conflicted. But in some ways "the hope of a 'neutral' humanitarianism was dissolved, and charity was politicized," setting the scene for a new generation of relief agencies to maintain an often contradictory combination of outspokenness, on the one hand, and a continued closeness with Western governments, on the other (Flipse 2002, p. 266).

The end of the Cold War saw an increased willingness on the part of Western militaries to mount operations with humanitarian objectives, and so neo-humanitarians found ready partners for the "new" low-intensity wars of the 1990s. Close cooperation in Somalia (Maren 1997) and Rwanda prompted many humanitarian organizations to call for a military-based humanitarian intervention in Kosovo and a growing sense among some that the classic principles of neutrality, impartiality and independence "have become myth[s]" to be referred to, but set aside in the face of more pressing operational concerns (Mills 2005, p. 161).

Perhaps the best-known example of this occurred during the aftermath of the Rwandan genocide starting in April 1994. There, a relatively small section of the ethnically Hutu majority killed as many as 1,100,000 people from the minority Tutsi ethnic group in around 100 days, prompting a major Tutsi-led military offensive which displaced around two million, mostly Hutu, refugees. The scale and rapidity of the exodus was enormous, with 800,000 Rwandans entering the refugee camps around the town of Goma in the region of Kivu, eastern Zaire in four days alone in July 1994 (Boutrone 2006). Conditions were appalling and, by the end of July 1994, 2,000 refugees were dying each week – mainly from diarrheal disease. Media coverage was enormous and donations to the UN High Commissioner for Refugees (UNHCR) exceeded $1 million per month during this period. An estimated $2 billion were spent in the first two weeks of the operation, with more than 200 aid organizations operating in Goma alone. Western policy, strongly backed by these NGOs, was to encourage repatriation back to Rwanda, but grave concerns over human rights under the new Tutsi administration meant that the camps continued to grow throughout 1995 (Soussan 2008).

These camps became increasingly controlled by Hutu militia, who used violence and intimidation to ensure they received the lion's share of the NGOs' distribution network. Backed by the Zairean dictator, Joseph-Desiré Mobutu, they also actively sought to prevent repatriation and to ensure that the camps were as permanent as possible. Many were believed to have been guilty of genocide within Rwanda (known as *genocidaires*). Attempts were made to screen genuine refugees from members of the Hutu militia, but without adequate security forces these were of limited effectiveness. Organizations working in the Kivu region became increasingly unhappy with the idea of apparently rewarding people of such culpability and an apparent lack of international commitment to driving through their general preference for rapid repatriation (MSF 2010). In November 1994, MSF-France published a report calling for a military deployment (what it called "an international police force") to enforce law and order in the camps, to separate the guilty from the innocent, to disarm the militia operating in the camps and to bring the perpetrators of the Rwandan genocide to justice. When this was not forthcoming, MSF-France "decided to withdraw from the refugee camps as the context of the genocide presented in their opinion a situation contradictory with the principles of humanitarian assistance" (MSF 1995). At that time, the organization was working with over 2,000 national staff and 25 expatriates in Goma alone. It was providing aid to an estimated 300,000 refugees in three field hospitals as well as many other health posts and dispensaries. In the resulting insecurity, it also withdrew from four hospitals on the Tanzanian–Rwandan border, where it was assisting an estimated 55,000 refugees. Over a dozen other NGOs also followed suit and left (Passant 2009).

Conclusion

This chapter has looked at the historical development of the military–humanitarian relationship. This analysis revealed that warfare has developed in such a way that stimulated the need for modern humanitarianism. This was particularly apparent in the second half of the nineteenth century, when the technology of war evolved significantly and spurred changes in military strategy which in turn led to new ways of looking at civilian responses. These conflicts mixed soldiers with civilians as a strategy, drafted the latter into military duties and caused massive population displacement (Ramsbotham and Woodhouse 1999). Further, the birth and growth of modern Western humanitarianism put civilians into greater proximity to soldiers, where they were working and living within the same milieu. Relief workers intervening directly in areas with active combat, combined with the military taking on a greater role in looking after civilian victims of war, blurred the lines between the humanitarian and military spheres that had hitherto existed more distinctly.

In times of war, humanitarian and military medical personnel might work on the same patients. High-intensity military strategies came to involve both bombing for "humanitarian" purposes and the use of civilians in nearly every aspect of battle. In conflicts characterized by low intensity, there are a number of influencing factors that bring humanitarians into a close relationship with the military. Where there are fewer combatants and the distinction between civil and military is even less clear, the relative security may attract external humanitarian actors. The primary Western military objective of trying to "win hearts and minds" also leads to close cooperation with humanitarians, rendering the latter open to co-option or manipulation.

This relationship was driven forward by three closely linked stimuli – technology, strategy and ethics. Table 2.1 summarizes these in relation to the historical timeframe that makes up the focus of this chapter. The former, specifically arms and military hardware, medicine and the media, stimulated changes in strategy which in turn led to the need for a more extensive codification of ethics. Advances in weapons contributed to greater attention to the victims they produced (Coupland 1999). Medicine and its *le droit d'ingérence* blurred, and at times eliminated, the distinctions between humanitarians and the military, while mass media gave reasons for both humanitarian and military action – both representing and manufacturing public consent.

Table 2.1 The development of the military–humanitarian relationship

Time/stimuli	Technology	Strategy	Ethics
Greco-Roman times	Iron (sword and shields) and chariot; physicians accompany soldiers into battle	Field-based column (phalanx)	Classical philosophy (e.g. Plato and Socrates)
Middle Ages	Long-bow and armor, siege engines and complex castle making; cavalry (stirrup) and beginnings of modern weapons using gunpowder; international travel	Siege (offense) and fortifications (defense); regal and communal mobilization; ravaging routine part of warfare	Religion, 'Just War' doctrine, the Crusades and the establishment of the chivalric military orders
Enlightenment/ revolutions	Advancements in modern weapons make fortifications obsolete; development of organization and roads improved logistics and mobility	Large armies (*levée en masse*) supported by technological advances. Beginnings of modern low-intensity warfare	Birth of humanism and nationalism; influential thinkers include Grotius, Kant, Wolff, Vattel and Bentham
Late nineteenth century	Further advancements in weapons (bullets and rifling), travel (railroad) and communications (telegraph); poor medical coverage for soldiers; first global media coverage	First modern/total wars, skirmishes slowly replace columns, colonialism; generally poor treatment of soldiers on and off the battlefield	First legal codification of normative views; birth of classical humanitarianism
World Wars	Major advances in weapons (e.g. delivery systems and nuclear weapons) and military medicine; radio and picture media	Global total, combine-joint operations and multi-spectrum war based on full population mobilization; civilians become direct targets	Age of extremes yet outlawry of war (1930s) and further codification ethics as a result of WWII; humanitarianism subjugated to national interests
Cold War	Consolidation of new weapons from 1940s on; first television coverage of humanitarian emergencies	Bi-polar balance; proxy war in developing world characterized by national liberation struggles and use of strategic/tactical use of populations	Ideological polarity; adoption of codified ethic; birth of neo-humanitarianism
Post-Cold War	Digitization and globalization speed up	Single-polarity with the rise of regional powers; global war on single issue; "humanitarian intervention"	Neo-humanitarianism predominates

Military strategy is an important stimulus because it determines how armed forces carry out their operations which, in turn, exert a profound impact on the work of humanitarians. The historically dominant strategy has been high-intensity conflict. This traditionally pitted army against army, but has increasingly involved civilians through "total" war. From the Second World War onwards, Western militaries developed civil affairs sections to deal with the aging concept of total war. With a generally clear distinction of those involved in combat and where neutrality was accepted, humanitarian space was limited. Low-intensity conflict grew in importance during the twentieth century and became the more prevalent strategy. At the same time, past distinctions between civilians and combatants have become more blurred. In order to operate in low-intensity conflict, Western militaries have thus taken on roles and duties previously the reserve of humanitarians, thereby widening the space available for such work.

Ethics, and the codification of normative values, are crucial to understanding the military–humanitarian relationship. The establishment of the rules of war and IHL was initially slow but made important developments in reaction to conflict. Key examples include Hugo Grotius's founding of IHL in the aftermath of the Thirty Years' War, Henri Dunant's creation of the Red Cross following the Battle of Solferino and the Geneva Conventions after the Second World War. Rules regulating combat, whether they involve unwritten conventions or carefully specified legislation, have always been intermittently effective. From Classical times to the present, restrictions on involving or attacking civilians have been apparent but have also been regularly and deliberately flaunted. Based on two distinct philosophical viewpoints, these gradually crystallized into classical and neo-humanitarian forms. While the former stresses neutrality and tacit cooperation with the military, the latter emphasizes a readiness to speak out and a willingness to use force. Both forms of humanitarianism have maintained a close, although somewhat different, relationship with the military.

3

Humanitarianism in post-conflict settings

Introduction

Before looking at the military–humanitarian relationship in Afghanistan, it is help-ful to first examine the key controversies and tensions present in such a dynamic topic. Analysis reveals an evolution of thought and practices that has led to the development of a host of key issues. Identifying these issues provides the basis for the theoretical understanding of the complex relationship between humanitarians and the military. Thus the aim of this chapter is to identify and flesh out key con-troversies and tensions which will serve as a foundation for the research questions of this book.

The key underlying issue concerning this relationship is that humanitarians are faced with a choice of working closely with the military or keeping distance. Pugh (1998) offers a relatively straightforward analysis of the case "for" and "against" close relations with the military. Another means of analysis is offered by Ankersen (2004), who suggests that two different approaches to military–humanitarian relations are apparent. The first, "integrated approach sees military and civilians working together, sharing information, and planning jointly, perhaps even exchang-ing personnel," while the second, "segregated approach values the separation of the organizations and prefers a more distant relationship" (Ankersen 2004, p. 8). Building on Pugh and Ankersen, these two approaches will be adopted as a basic means for examining the key controversies in the military–humanitarian relation-ship. In other words, the first approach advocates "for" close relations between humanitarians and the military and is considered "integrated" in terms of policy and practice, while the second approach is "against" close relations and is "seg-regated" by taking a more critical and skeptical approach. This underlying policy issue revolves around three main controversies that will be examined here and analyzed later in relationship to the research findings: debate between structure and agency, dilemmas surrounding humanitarian ethics and the link between security and development. Collectively, these three tensions constitute what has so often been described as the "blurring of the line" between humanitarians and the military. They give rise to a raft of issues, including the security of humanitarian staff and its influence on humanitarian programming. Each of these three tensions will be examined in turn.

The first controversy is grounded in debates over structure and agency, which is a fundamental debate within the social sciences. Issues relating to structure and agency manifest themselves in the humanitarian and military relationship through organizational and institutional studies, including structure and management. Organizational culture, coordination and policy making have also been widely debated before (Byman 2001, Stoddard 2003, Frerks et al. 2006) and deserve attention here when analyzing the interplay of different organizational approaches. Tension is also found in researchers and academics debating whether differences in organizational culture between humanitarians and the military are enough to cause inter-organizational friction and poor relations. Two distinct positions are evident. There is the "traditional" or managerialist–positivist position, which views complex dilemmas, such as those found in Afghanistan, as solvable problems. There is also the critical position, which argues that conflict and reconstruction are ongoing processes that may not readily fit the solutions offered by traditional management. While the critical position often presents valid arguments, the managerialist–positivist offers persuasive prescriptions for those involved in policy and practice.

The second controversy relates to ethics. Particularly important in this debate has been the perceived erosion of humanitarian independence and other humanitarian principles. Generally, this debate rests on the fissure between those who define humanitarianism narrowly and those who wish to broaden its scope and applicability (Jackson and Walker 1999). Weiss (1999) offers a useful spectrum of classifying ethical positions to humanitarians in their approaches to their programming. Within the spectrum of deontological and consequentialist approaches, four positions – classical, minimalist, maximalist and solidarist – will be discussed.

The final controversy centers on the link between the security and development agendas. Although elements of this agenda have been around for some time (Hanning 1970), policy makers have recently combined the previously separate fields of diplomacy, security and development to an unprecedented degree, causing consternation on the part of some commentators. In some contexts, this has contributed to an increased blurring of the distinction between humanitarians and the military, which some have argued has contributed to a less secure working environment. Here, three sub-areas will be examined, each with its own set of criticisms. The first is the inclusion of human rights in humanitarian programming and the role of policy positions such as humanitarian intervention. The second relates to policy coherence and the notion of policy coherence for development. The third is the concept of security, and human security in particular. The impetus to bring coherence to policy in places like Afghanistan has brought the military into close contact with the NGO sector. This leaves humanitarians in the difficult position of whether to choose an integrated or segregated approach to their relations with the military.

Table 3.1 Controversies and tensions in the military–humanitarian relationship

	Structure and agency	*Humanitarian ethics*	*Security and development*
"For" (integrated approach)	Managerialist– positivist position	Consequentialists	• Human rights (humanitarian intervention) • Policy coherence for development
"Against" (segregated approach)	Critical position	Deontologists	• Human rights (critics of humanitarian assistance) • Human security

Table 3.1 illustrates the framework of the integrated ("for") and segregated ("against") policy positions with regard to the three issues. The categories in this framework are not absolute but serve as general groupings to separate and bring some order to an otherwise opaque and contentious set of issues. This structure of integrated and segregated approaches to military–humanitarian relations is used again in the discussion of the research findings in Chapters 6 and 7.

The debate between organizational structure and individual agency

The debate between structure and agency is a classic tension in social sciences, and has useful applicability here because of its ability to add understanding of how humanitarians form their relationships. To this end, a basic explanation is helpful in this discussion. Following Giddens' (1984) grand theory of structuration, structures are rules and resources made up of four elements (discourse, moral, material and the non-material) which enable and constrain agency (Lewis et al. 2003). This is typically done through formal structures, policies, rules and regulations. Agency is the action of individuals and relates to their motivations and capacities to act on free will. Agency involves practical and "discursive consciousness" as well as unconscious motives which "may occur in unacknowledged conditions and have unintended consequences" (Blaikie 2000, p. 132). Allied to this classic tension has been the study of institutions (March and Olsen 1989). Political institutions, including the military as well as NGOs, are "collections of interrelated rules and routines that define appropriate actions in terms of relations between roles and situations" (March and Olsen 1989, p. 160). In other words, the institutions themselves are as much about their relationships as they are about outputs and products. Institutions gained favor from the 1980s onward as "new institutionalism," which was eclectic and saw "some softening of the borders separating approaches" (Peters 1999, p. 1). Institutions, meaning the collection of organizations with their beliefs, standards and codes (Powell and DiMaggio 1991), are a primary venue where the tension between structure and agency is played out. In some cases, such as when there are well-formed organizational rules, structures appear to be dominant, while in others agency is more important in determining relationships between humanitarians and the military. This offers a useful framework within which to examine social systems and organizations which are central to the military–humanitarian relationship.

The study of institutions can been seen to fall into two broad positions. The first, labelled the "managerialist–positivist camp" by Gray (2005, p. 7), views the study of institutions as a science which seeks to objectively quantify the study of organizations and the relationships between them. The usual focus is on structures, how institutions function and how to improve their efficiency and effectiveness. Because of its focus on practical issues, the managerialist–positivist position is closely associated with fields such as business, administration and management studies as well as the military. In contrast, the second position takes a critical theory approach and views institutions as social constructions. Gray explains that this group "might be called interpretivists or constructivists or relativists," noting that these are not exactly the same (2005, p. 6). The usual focus of the critical position is on agency and its qualitative approaches. Institutionalism in military–humanitarian relations will be looked at here using these two opposing positions.

The managerialist–positivist position

Through integrated and closely coordinated institutional arrangements, the managerialist–positivist position seeks to optimize inter-organizational relations for wider goals such as the establishment of post-conflict stability and reconstruction. According to this view, Western militaries have moved toward greater integration with humanitarians. Pugh observes that the military has "provided the drive to institutionalize civil–military relations and the dominant model has been one whereby humanitarian organizations are invited to integrate into a mission" (2000, p. 239). For Cross, arguing that soldiers are militaristic "only because military training has imposed a certain pattern of behaviour" (2003a, p. 88), the military is still more of a social actor than a strictly blunt instrument of policy. This element reflects the "civil–military gap" debate at the national level in which some (Janowitz 1971) see a convergence of the military and civil society rather than a separate uniqueness as described by Huntington (1957). Indeed, Western militaries themselves have been seen as becoming more political (Feaver and Kohn 2001) as Clausewitzian instruments of policy. Some, such as Garb (2005), have argued that transitional countries such as Turkey, Brazil and Thailand have had large political and civil roles for militaries, while Latin American has long struggled to find the right balance between civil society and the military (Stepan 1988).

To understand this position better, organizational field theory is helpful. This holds that organizations form institutional environments which shape "cognitive frameworks through which social reality is understood" (Lipson 2003, p. 2). The social reality informs culture, procedures and other ways of operating. Despite their differences, both military and humanitarian organizations operate in a similar milieu, often with similar goals, organizational standards and processes. Comparable features include information sharing, coordination mechanisms (such as Civil–Military Operations Centers, Humanitarian Operations Centers and similar bodies) and, sometimes, joint assistance projects such as distribution of relief commodities and reconstruction of social service infrastructure including schools and health posts. There are many sources that try to identify and address issues and conceptual–contextual gaps in the military–humanitarian relationship. Minear, for example, is indicative of this when he identifies several key issues such as "managing the interface with regional organizations" and "accommodating structural constraints" (1997, p. 3). As such, this position seeks an improved, more efficacious and usually closer relationship between humanitarians and the military.

According to policy documents (see, for example, DOD 2001), the military's structure – its capacity, organization and, in some cases such as occupation and during peace operations, its legal and moral mandate – make it well suited to carry out humanitarian tasks. Some authors, particularly those associated with the military, see cooperation between humanitarians and the military as a "force multiplication" and as a "new tool for peacekeepers" (Pollick 2000, p. 57). In its approach to managing post-conflict situations, the common military views civil society as a means to fostering stability and reducing its role in non-military tasks. This position supports the route many militaries have taken in developing a capacity to interact with civilians, and with humanitarians in particular (DOD 1993, Garrigues 2007, Parker 2007).

Within this position, views differ on ways of developing a means of dealing with conflict and reconstruction, some following a "conventional" approach while others espouse an "unconventional" approach (Rollins 2001, Cassidy 2004, Kilcullen 2006). This is especially true in situations where conflict is said to be "asymmetric" and of a low intensity, with methods that could be considered people centered (Smith 2005, Fukuyama 2006, Dobbins 2007, Gompert and Gordon 2008). At the same time, however, more has been expected of governments and, thus, the "international community" (Finnemore 2000). The end of the Cold War left militaries, particularly those in the West, with a diminished *raison d'être*. This search for new roles and responsibilities has been termed "substitution theory" by Pugh (2000, p. 231–2) and others (Barry and Jeffreys 2002). Humanitarian intervention and other involvement as third parties to conflict became a new, albeit reluctant, focus. Attempts were made to provide the humanitarian community with policy guidance and, in some ways, a common position. Perhaps the first of these was the 1992 Oslo Guidelines, but there have been others such as the Australian Council For Overseas Aid, UN Office for the Coordination of Humanitarian Affairs, InterAction, the International Council of Voluntary Agencies and various NGOs which have developed their own policies and handbooks, such as UNHCR (1995). Yet this focus came with substantial criticism.

In its approach to security, the military sees its efforts in theoretically holistic terms, although firmly within the Clausewitzian dimension of national security discussed earlier (Haftendorn 1991). According to its own manuals on civil affairs, the United States Army holds that national security is supported by political, economic and information dimensions with a "sociocultural foundation," while military aspects are seen as a cross-cutting issue (DOD 1993, pp. 1–4). For the military, its activities are thus important regardless of the state of combat, and span the spectrum from war to peace. Whereas humanitarians generally view "local" people as those in need and as "beneficiaries" or "affected people," the military's approach toward civilians who "may create unfavorable conditions or contribute to them" concludes that civil affairs personnel "must determine whether the populace will be cooperative, passive, or uncooperative" and then undertake activities that address their posture (DOD 1993, p. 2-2). To do this, the military follows existing political–military institutions, of which humanitarians are a part (Herring 2007), develops new ones such as the Provincial Reconstruction Teams in Afghanistan (discussed in later chapters) and seeks to have integrated policies through partnerships and coherence. Thus the managerialist–positivist approach sees the issues associated with conflict and reconstruction as a problem to be solved through organizations and institutional structures.

The critical position

Supporting the segregated approach against close relations between humanitarians and the military, the critical position argues that the formal institutions important to the managerialist–positivist position (with its focus on organizational theory and the like described above) are social constructions. Issues of organizational culture, conceptual–contextual gaps, dysfunctional decision making and informal institutions are important for understanding this position further, as they offer countering perspectives to the managerialist–positivist position. Each of these will be examined here in turn.

The first issue, organizational culture, is itself a contested concept but most definitions are similar in describing it as a "pattern of shared basic assumptions" and practices which are taught to and used within a group (Schein 1992, p. 12, see also Clammer 2005). Despite the difficulty in defining organizational culture, it has a recognized importance both for theory and in practice (Lewis 2002). For many, organizational culture within and between humanitarian and military organizations is quite distinct and perhaps incompatible. The military is known for its rigid vertical structures with heavy emphasis on planning, resources, secrecy and "force protection" (actions that safeguard the military), whereas humanitarian operations tend to be done on an ad hoc basis with little planning, inadequate resources and uncertain security (Nash 1994, Beauregard 1998, James 2003). This stems largely in the way the organizations are founded and have evolved; most NGOs were founded by individuals or small groups of people concerned with addressing specific issues (Morris 2000). With a social concern as the driving impetus (and not national security), organizational development and strong systems are often a secondary concern (Lewis 2001). Cross (2003b) identifies a number of weaknesses in humanitarian organizations, including a lack of resources, poor responsiveness and inter-organizational competition, as well as poor relations with the military. In such a reality, the agency of individual humanitarians tends to dominate.

Despite their intertwined history and the training programs, conferences and other types of exchange that have grown in popularity since the mid-2000s, a lack of basic mutual understanding between humanitarian and military organizations is often cited as a problem. The military finds it "confusing to seek structures analogous to military command among civilian agencies – that structure simply doesn't exist" among the humanitarians (Beauregard 1998, p. 1). In practice, the military tries to reduce all uncertainty, while NGOs tend to specialize in navigating through unknown situations. An additional criticism is based on common but ill-informed stereotypes that are a "breeding ground for misunderstandings and poor coordination and/or cooperation" (Scheltinga et al. 2005, p. 54). Examples include "us and them" language such as labelling soldiers as "warmongers" and calling humanitarians "tree-huggers" (Ankersen 2004, p. 16). With such different starting points, it is not difficult to see how poor relations are likely to flourish and influence the type of relations humanitarians have with the military.

A second issue relates to the differences found between the projects of an organization and what it actually does. This is, in effect, a conceptual–contextual gap. Following Lipson, the theory of organized hypocrisy occurs when there is a "discrepancy between proclaimed norms and values and actual behavior" (2003, p. 5). Because of the difficulty in achieving stated ends, organizations often say one thing but accomplish either nothing or something entirely different. In such situations, Slim (2004, p. 35) has argued, humanitarians "misrepresent themselves" in the role they play. Torrente (2004, p. 12) writes that "a certain hypocrisy prevails" because organizations try to engage with political–military reconstruction projects while at the same time claiming neutrality "to gain access to populations." According to some (Pfeffer 1997, Lister 2000), the gap or hypocrisy stems from a reliance on the agency of relief workers themselves rather than the structures within which they work.

There are many empirical examples where staff inflate numbers of beneficiaries or describe conditions in terms worse than they actually are. Often, humanitarian organizational literature espouses neutrality as a fundamental principle, while in practice the organizations were part and parcel of Western political–military endeavors in countries such as Afghanistan and Iraq. In such environments, "organizations are rewarded for establishing correct structures and processes, not for the quantity and quality of their outputs" (Scott 1991, p. 167, cited in Lipson 2003). Paradoxical situations occur where some humanitarian organizations become risk averse while claiming to respond to emergencies and at the same time being pressured for results (Goodhand 2001). In such cases, partnerships can form which are based on co-option and politicization and lead to reduced distinction between groups. Brinkerhoff (2002, p. 22) describes these situations where organizations may have little organizational culture and weak policies (termed "low identity") and at the same time have matching goals with the more dominant organization (termed "high mutuality"). In the case of "co-optive" relationships, the lesser partner has difficulty in remaining "consistent and committed to its mission, core values and constituencies" (Brinkerhoff 2002, p. 23). She further explains:

> mutuality refers to interdependence, as opposed to sequential dependence. This implies a greater degree of process integration in the joint value to be produced by a partnership, and contrasts with simpler models of supplier or production contracting. Relative integration necessitates more frequent interaction, communication and decision making, both formal and ad hoc, throughout the stages of programme design, implementation and evaluation. Mutuality means equality in decision making, as opposed to domination of one or more partners. All partners have an opportunity to influence their shared objectives, processes, outcomes and evaluation. Mutuality can be distinguished as horizontal, as opposed to hierarchical, coordination and accountability.

A genuine "partnership," in contrast, has both a high degree of mutuality and organizational identity of both entities. The critical position argues that a dangerously "blurred" distinction between humanitarian and military is present when co-option occurs. This is complicated by the mutable nature of identity itself. Gioia et al. (2000) suggest that this identity is fluid, adaptive and changes to meet new situations. Similarly, Farrington et al. (1993) recognize that when working within organizations people have a way of working around the boundaries set by their organizations. Eventually, people may leave to form new organizations (as was seen in the founding of MSF, shown in Chapter 2). Whereas the managerial position sees NGOs as service providers, the critical position holds that they have "expressive values" that fulfil the desire to aid others. This has led Frumkin and Andre-Clark (2000, p. 141) to suggest that NGOs "need to develop a strategy that emphasizes the unique value-driven dimension of their programs." In other words, it may be argued that people too often work around the boundaries set by their organizations, leading to "slippages" (Lewis et al. 2003, p. 546) between what an organization says and what it does.

A third issue is dysfunctional decision making, which can be the result of a number of pressures on people working for organizations (Janis 1989). According to Walkup (1997), a number of elements contribute to what he terms "policy dysfunction" in humanitarian organizations. Walkup describes a process whereby humanitarians who are already under pressure from external criticism, work demands and inadequate resources develop defense mechanisms such as overwork, detachment, transference and reality distortion. These defense mechanisms impact the organizations to which relief workers belong and lead to "defensiveness" and "delusion," which translate into dysfunctional policy making (Walkup 1997, p. 40). Cross (2003a) points out that dysfunctional decision making is not limited to humanitarians, with different types of psychosis within the military being long established (also see Dixon 1979). In terms of decision making and external relationships formed by NGOs, following the policy dysfunction model, they may make decisions that are dangerous to their staff or they may be unnecessarily hostile in their contact with the military. In general, this dysfunction consists of well-known critiques of humanitarian organizations, including miscommunication, lack of evaluation, resistance to innovation and lack of learning (Walkup 1997). Policy dysfunction leads to a number of problems including situations of competition, on the one hand (Aall 2000), and a lack of capacity, on the other (De Zeeuw 2001). Perhaps one of the worst cases relates to the provision of services to refugees. An example is old-style charity in which assistance is "conceived of in terms of charity [through the provision of goods] rather than as a means of enabling refugees to enjoy their rights," which in turn may lead to physical abuse of beneficiaries (Harrell-Bond 2002).

The final issue relating to the critical position is informal institutions, which result in a lack of structure and reliance on personal agency among humanitarians. Ad hoc committees, casual networks and the other informal institutions that characterize humanitarian response are thought to contribute to poor programming and insecurity (Thomas and Spataro 1998, Fearon and Laitin 2003). In situations where there are structures that can be overridden by the strong personalities often associated with relief operations, organizational culture, gaps between concept and context, dysfunctional decision making and informal institutions result in an uncertain approach to their humanitarian ethics and their policies toward relationships with the military.

Closely related to these problems associated with informal institutions are the comparatively weak structures found in aid organizations and the corresponding strong sense of agency which holds powerful influence for humanitarian organizations. Linking problems that are common in international relations, Gibson et al. (2005) conclude that the failure of international aid is a result of the informal institutions involved in its delivery. They cite three specific situations. The first problem is "public goods and free riding," which "do not generate sustainable solutions" (Gibson et al. 2005, pp. 36–7). Reconstruction of roads and schools are but two examples (and will be returned to again in later chapters). The second relates to "common-pool resources," which may suffer from overuse and exploitation, first described as the "tragedy of the commons" by Hardin (1968, see also Ostrom et al. 2002). In vulnerable countries like Afghanistan, certain resources such as budgetary constraints and natural resources (particularly water and agricultural property) are in short supply, making this problem especially acute. The final problem is what was termed the Samaritan's Dilemma by Buchanan (1977), where humanitarians face a prisoner's dilemma-like choice in which they are "better off helping no matter what the recipient does" (Gibson et al. 2005, p. 39). The necessary conditions for dealing with these problems are effective institutional arrangements such as easy-to-understand rules and accountability (Agrawal 2001), which have been problematic in the military–humanitarian relationship.

The dilemmas surrounding humanitarian ethics

The evolution of two ethical positions – deontological and consequentialist – are central to the discussion of humanitarian ethics. A closer study will be made of the consequentialist and the deontological positions while a third position can also be discerned and will be discussed before moving on to discussion of security and development in the final section of this chapter.

The consequentialist position

The integrated position for close military–humanitarian relations is supported by the consequentialist position. The position has a teleological perspective that looks toward future consequences. This is based on the ethical theory put forward by Jeremy Bentham (1748–1832) that posits that the outcome of a situation provides the validity of the moral judgment for an action (Chesterman 2001, Holzgrefe and Keohane 2003). In essence, it follows a utilitarian perspective where ends justify the means. It is from this position that the ideas and doctrine of humanitarian intervention, *le droit d'ingérence* and its corollaries such as Responsibility to Protect, are grounded (ICISS 2001, Evans and Sahnoun 2002). The concept of turning away or doing nothing in the face of inhumanity has been a consistent dilemma for those dealing in the theory and practice of humanitarianism. Dante's *Inferno* reserved a "special place of torment" for those who maintained a neutral life (Slim 1997b, p. 342). In a similar vein, Edmund Burke's frequently quoted maxim "the only thing necessary for the triumph of evil is for good men to do nothing" (cited in DiPrizio 2002, p. vii) frames the issue in stark terms.

While not always clearly identified, this position is seen by many as an orthodox and pragmatic approach adopted by many practitioners. In this sense, humanitarian consequentialism is a "response to complexity" (Duffield 2001, p. 92) that came about in the 15 years following the end of the Cold War with its "failed states" and the attempt to impose a neo-liberal peace. In contemporary terms, this position is most closely associated with "new humanitarians" such as Bernard Kouchner and Aengus Finucane. These new humanitarians first promoted the idea of a new approach that placed primacy on humanity over state sovereignty (Fox 2001). It sought to end the suffering allowed under the deontological approach seen in Nigerian Civil War of the 1960s. While this new humanitarianism is defined in different ways (Macrae 2002), its key characteristics are its politicization and outspokenness in nature, in contrast to the deontologists, discussed below. Its readiness to use whatever means at its disposal, including closely collaborating with the military, was paramount.

The imperial peace and liberal peace models are a separate element of what Macrae (1998) has termed the "anti-imperialist" critique. The criticism is based on the assessment of two positions. First, because of humanitarian aid, political actors are no longer accountable because it "blocks the formation of social and political contracts between warring parties and the civilian population" (Macrae 1998, p. 310), for which evidence from Africa is especially cogent. Second, humanitarianism itself is "fundamentally unaccountable" (Macrae 1998, p. 310). While attempts have been made to make aid in general more accountable (such as the Active Learning Network for Accountability and Performance), there is evidence of poor performance and corruption in many post-conflict situations, including Afghanistan (Torabi 2007). Yet, as Macrae points out, the arguments may be over-stated and it is unclear how social contracts can be forged and reinforced during periods of violence.

It is worth noting how the issue is further muddied in that the military, too, can claim to follow principles that may be considered "humanitarian." Many argue that the members of the military do have a humanitarian impulse (Cross 2003a). Macrae (2002) labels the military itself as a "new humanitarian." There are not only traditions, customs and codes that protect both the military and civilians (French 2003) but also the laws of war and IHL. Peacekeeping forces, for example, may profess and be under a political mandate to be neutral and impartial. Pugh points out, however, that "deontologists (that is, those who look for a moral or ethical basis) who suspect militarism and humanitarianism to be inherently incompatible can be found in both the military and civilian sectors as are those who take a more political approach" (1998, p. 341). Some promote military involvement in humanitarian matters and state it as a *fait accompli*. In such a vein, Wieloch holds that "NGOs that still deny that [military] troops can do anything humanitarian at all are in danger of perpetuating ill-informed and out-of-date opinions" (2003, p. 33). Within this mandate, the military would provide a secure environment in which humanitarian activities (a common understanding for the imprecise concept of humanitarian space) can take place.

The deontologist position

The segregated approach against close military–humanitarian relations is supported by the deontologist position and is closely associated with Kant and Henri Dunant (discussed in Chapter 2 relation to classical humanitarianism). It is the founding position in which humanitarian principles were first promulgated and situated. In arguing for a deontological ethic, Kant's Categorical Imperative is invoked in which actions are duty bound and considered independent from the consequences. A deontologist position holds that closeness with the military leads to an erosion of humanitarian principles and blurring of the distinction between humanitarians and the military. This separation is essential to maintaining the humanitarian principle of neutrality. Deontologists would not accept the equation that "international military intervention equals protection of populations" (Weissman 2004, p. 206). Deontologists view the notion of "humanitarian war" as an oxymoron and believe that "crusading in international relations has a very doubtful record" (Roberts 1993, p. 445). Weissman argues that in contrast to the consequentialist position described above, "aid organizations cannot call for deployment of a protection force without renouncing their autonomy or appealing to references outside their own practices" (2004, p. 205).

A central critique of the deontological position is the politicization and securitization of aid and its direct influence over humanitarianism. This has been done through the "reinvention of development as a strategic tool for conflict management and peacebuilding" (Goodhand 2004, p. 9). Activities ostensibly geared for peace (namely peacekeeping and peacebuilding) are seen by critics as projects of the liberal world order (Paris 2001). The situation has altered in favor of Western governments and at the expense of effectiveness and the basic tenets of humanitarianism. Duffield explains that "where once relatively independent aid agencies were able to mobilize public concern through the media and put politicians on the spot, we now have a situation in which Western governments have regained initiative and control of the humanitarian agenda" (2001, p. 82). This is done through the influence of the media and the many organizations' being dependent on governmental funding.

For its critics, neo-humanitarianism is part and parcel of this politicization. Few debate the role of politics in aid with its use of and involvement with resources, but the degree of politicization is highly controversial and, particularly in Africa, a strong case can be made for its harming effects. Echoing Clausewitz's dictum that war is a "continuation of politics by other means," neo-humanitarianism has become "politics as policy" (Duffield 2001, p. 96). For its critics, the apolitical position of classic humanitarianism may be untenable, and so too is the maximalist position. Fox (1999) argues that the main sponsors of this position are in fact Western donor governments and so the trend toward new humanitarianism causes more problems than it solves. Some, like Lischer (2003), contend that humanitarians act without considering the consequences of their actions. For Duffield, the ethics of the new humanitarians is heavily problematic and contributes to violence itself: "in holding out the possibility of a better tomorrow as a price worth paying for suffering today, [neo-humanitarianism] has been a major source of the normalization of violence and complicity with its perpetrators" (2001, p. 107). The distinction and line of separation with consequentialists, however, is not absolute – some deontologists (including Weissman 2004) reserve the case of documented genocide as a case for intervention along consequentialist lines. Working in such complex environments, confusion and contradictory messages are an inevitable result (Slim 1997a).

A third position

The difficulty some observers have found with the dichotomy between the consequentialist and deontological positions is that they are too rigid and do not adequately reflect reality. During the 15 years since 2000–2001 significant debate has revolved around the practice of humanitarianism and how to best relate – or not – with the military. Based on conflicts such as that in Afghanistan, the pattern of the relationship is evolving and previous assumptions may be incorrect (O'Brien 2004). Humanitarians are said to be caught between "principle and pragmatism" (Frerks et al. 2006), which creates a gap (or "slippage" (Lewis et al. 2003, p. 546)) between rhetoric and reality that is especially prevalent with principles such as neutrality (Cutts 1998, Duffield 2001). Viewed broadly, the applicability of humanitarian principles in practice has changed over time and is largely dependent on economic and political concerns. Stockton notes that:

> this ethical framework [of humanitarian principles] appears to enjoy significant influence over the practices of the international aid system only during those times when big powers are preoccupied with other matters and in those places where "principles" happen to coincide with the economic interests of the host organization. (2004b, p. 10)

While the deontologist position has critical elements, a third position is evident. This critical position holds that "there are no universally valid foundations for norms" – that it is instead "contextual" (Crawford 1998, p. 121). While there are those who argue against the critical position because it does not provide a way forward (see, for example, Booth 1995), others, like Weiss (1999), have attempted to address this issue.

Weiss (1999) argues that most organizations situate their policies and practices somewhere along a spectrum. He describes four positions along a spectrum in relation to humanitarian principles available to humanitarians in delivery of their programs (Figure 3.1). He is careful to point out that a "blurring of categories is inevitable" and that these are not "moral absolutes." At one end of the spectrum, the "classicists," commonly represented by the ICRC, hold most closely to an apolitical humanitarianism in which the principles of neutrality and impartiality are of significant importance. Next, the "minimalists" and "maximalists" seek to grapple with the notion of politicized humanitarianism, but each in their own way: "minimalists" aim to "do no harm," while "maximalists" have a "more ambitious agenda of employing humanitarian action as part of a comprehensive strategy to transform conflict" (Weiss 1999, p. 3). At the far end of the spectrum are "solidarists" who take clearly partisan positions with those to whom they provide assistance. As will be discussed in later chapters, a prime example is the group of NGOs that helped the Afghan resistance during the Soviet intervention of the 1980s (Girardet 1985, Cooley 2000, Goodhand 2004). In contrast to the classicists, who pursue the

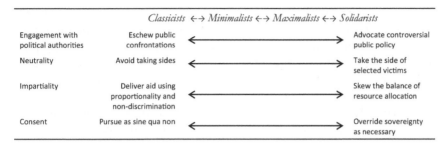

Figure 3.1 Weiss's Spectrum of Humanitarian Operating Principles

consent of authorities, "eschew political confrontations [and] avoid taking sides," the solidarists may be confrontational in pursuit of humanitarianism, aim to "skew the balance of resource allocation [and will] override sovereignty as necessary" (Weiss 1999, p. 4).

There is also an argument that the different humanitarian ethical positions align with different nationalities. For example, Europeans tend toward classical and minimalist positions, labeling their position "Dunantist" after the Red Cross founder Henri Dunant, while Americans are more frequently maximalists and soldarists, earning the "Wilsonian" label for their cooperation with governments (Stoddard 2003). The tensions found within the different approaches described in Weiss's typology form the basis of the debates surrounding humanitarian ethics (Pugh 1998). These are usually described as fixed positions, and not the change suggested in the contingency approach based on contingency theory (Goodhand 2004). This management theory stresses context and individual choice (leadership style) and is helpful in considering the changing situations that form such a large part of the Afghan case study.

In keeping with the segregated and integrated approaches, two dominant positions will be examined here: first, the consequentialist position, which lines up with the maximalist and solidarist camps, and second, the deontologist position, which lines up with the classicist and minimalist camps. In empirical terms, the argument supporting the consequentialist position is buttressed by the Second World War and the Holocaust and the Rwandan genocide of 1994, discussed above, while the deontologist position is supported by the NATO intervention in Kosovo and other places. Thus the deontologist position stands in contrast with the consequentialist position, especially in terms of state sovereignty. Many, including Walzer (1980), argue that sovereignty provides protection against self-determination. Other problems with the consequentialist position include the likelihood of unintended consequences such as making problems worse (Chesterman 2001) and that intervening may be done for neo-imperial reasons (Ayoob 2002). Fundamentally, the consequentialist and deontologist positions roughly correspond to the integrated and segregated positions in terms of military–humanitarian relations. Illustrating moral choices is not an easy task and often the most implausible cases are used, rendering the critiques equally implausible (see, for example, Smart 1973 and Sen and Williams 1982). Empirical examples of the "do nothing" camp are prevalent, especially in relation to the ICRC (such as the Second World War and the Holocaust, see for example Hutchinson 1996 and Moorehead 1998) and the inaction of governments in relation to conflicts, most notably Rwanda (Sellstrom and Wohlgemuth 1996). In Chapter 2 this book outlined how a reaction to the ICRC's inaction in Biafra in the late 1960s led to the founding of the more outspoken MSF and other organizations (Bortolotti 2004). In the post-2001 situation in Afghanistan, a trend toward consequentialist and integrated positions has yielded a position infused with politics and a perceived closeness to Western militaries.

The link between security and development

The link between the previously disparate fields of security and development has gained prominence during the 15 years since 2000–2001. While NGOs have always worked either in, on or around conflict (Goodhand 2004) and, indeed, war gave rise to humanitarianism in the first place (Slim 1996), the emphasis on security in development policy, practice and literature is "proving more and more to be a development-policy paradigm, one that calls for new approaches" (Klingebiel and Roehder 2004, p. 1). These new approaches came about from a number of critiques against humanitarian action. Bryans et al. (1999) suggest that critiques of humanitarianism go back at least to conflicts in Biafra, Eritrea and Cambodia but that they have become "amplified" in three ways (p. 12). First, there is more academic research and attention confirming the findings of the researchers above. Second, there has been internal dissent within humanitarian organizations, which has moved to the political mainstream and the media (Maren 1997). Third, there is less physical security for humanitarians, which has in turn prompted greater concern and attention. In the past, "donor governments have tended to respond to fragile states through a 'silo' approach" (Lockhart 2005, p. 3) which separated diplomatic, military and development responses. Yet this is no longer the case. The blending of security and development agendas can also be seen in the coherence debate, which attempts to merge security and development. These two fields that were differentiated by operational and "epistemic communities" (networks of experts) (Haas 1992) have, arguably, merged in Afghanistan and other recent cases. Security, once seen as the domain of the military and defense community, has become a key component of international development. By bringing "coherence" to government policies, different policy approaches including finance, trade, diplomacy, security and development become joined. The division corresponds to the integrated and segregated dichotomy described by Ankersen (2004).

A understanding the context in which the coherence debate developed is important before proceeding. Until the 1990s, civil–military relations were largely an "empirical and often theory-free approach" that was descriptive and "offered generalizations." As such, the study was dominated by analytical realism and confined to international relations and strategic studies (see, for example, Huntington 1957 and Finer 1962). Within this intellectual historical backdrop, three parallel developments in civil–military relations which coincided with a maturing of development studies in the area of conflict (Lewis 2002, p. 373). First, during the 15 years since 2000–2001, a search for new understanding through research and empirical practice has been redefining the field. Some, such as Ayoob (1991), suggest that orthodox thinking on security and development was dominated by the military and was largely seen as military in nature. The definition of security has thus become much more broad and NGOs have themselves been described as "security actors" (Herring 2007). Second, there are new and enhanced opportunities for interdisciplinary research which bring together fields that would have previously remained siloed. Third, the new research is more theoretically grounded. This was at a time when there was a perceived failure of "aid" and disillusionment with international development, mentioned above (Hancock 1991). These developments led to more scholarly interest in the subject and thus a call for policy development. From roughly 1990 onward, there has been an "avalanche of literature" dealing with peace operations and humanitarianism (Weiss 1997, p. 97).

NGOs became more attractive under the pushes for privatization of the 1980s (Bebbington et al. 2007). More funding was made available for NGOs at roughly the same time as they became more adept at working with the media. This is significant, as it contributes to what appears to be a pattern of co-option and politicization of humanitarians by the military. As a result, the number of NGOs grew exponentially during the 1990s (Macrae and Zwi 1994). By the late 1990s, substantial funding (up to 60–70%) was provided to NGOs by the largest donors to humanitarian emergencies, the European Community Humanitarian Office and the Office for United States Foreign Disaster Assistance (Rigby 2001). With time, the presence and influence of NGOs grew and the field of development took a more active role in conflict situations. This included renewed efforts such as the broad concept of peacebuilding and post-conflict reconstruction (Cilliers 2006, p. 93). Within this complexity, there developed a mutual misunderstanding of humanitarianism by traditional security scholars and of military concepts by development scholars (Finnemore 2000), contributing to widespread debate and a host of issues discussed in further detail below. Picciotto (2006, p. 3) suggests that the remedy for coherence and, by extension, the obscuring boundary between civil and military rests on three "pillars": human rights, policy coherence for development (PCD) and human security. Using this framework, the link between security and development will be examined here further.

Human rights

As in the case of humanitarian ethics, few debate the need or existence of human rights but, rather, their processes and application. The 1948 Universal Declaration of Human Rights, for example, sparked several ongoing debates relating to its universality (some argue that human rights arranged in Western countries should not extend to certain contexts and countries), the original source of these rights (as they are not sourced in natural or religious rights) and the appropriateness of certain rights (such as economic rights). In our discussion here, two particular controversies stand out. The first relates to the extension of human rights into the area of humanitarian assistance. The rapidly changing context of the 15-odd years since 2000–2001 has witnessed considerable action and debate in this area. Some hold that humanitarianism ignores human rights (Leader 1998). This results from particular types of programming (such as "needs based" approaches that focus on the provision of goods) and organizations that focus on single issues (such as landmine removal or reconstruction projects). Others, such as Rieff (2002), argue that the blending of humanitarian action with the human rights agenda has created more problems than it has solved. By expanding their mandate to include human rights, the argument goes, humanitarians have undertaken tasks for which they are ill suited. In scores of conflicts since the 1990s, humanitarian aid has been substituted for political action. For this reason, some argue for a back-to-basics approach and that NGOs should focus on prevention, mitigation and resolving the "effects of violent conflict" (Goodhand and Hulme 1997, p. 5, also see Jackson and Walker 1999). Further, humanitarians, some argue, have little room for independence to set their own agenda (Edwards and Hulme 1995, Hudson 2000) and are prone to be part of political–military actions worldwide.

The second debate relating to the extension of human rights through humanitarian intervention supports the integrated approach for close military–humanitarian relations. The roots of this approach are grounded in the consequentialist position described above. There are strong legal arguments that support intervention, including Chapter VII of the UN Charter and the Genocide Convention of 1948. Evans and Newnham argue that while "there is no legal right of humanitarian intervention comparable to the traditional rights of states, there is growing international consensus that the Westphalian system is too restrictive" (1998, p. 232) and thus intervention can be permissible. This liberal argument holds that permissible cases of humanitarian intervention must be "proportionate international use or threat of military force, undertaken in principle by a liberal government or alliance, aimed at ending tyranny or anarchy, welcomed by the victims, and consistent with the doctrine of double-effect" (Teson 2003, p. 94). Following Walzer (1977), double-effect deals with the unintended consequences of the application of force and holds that the use of force must have good intentions and outcomes as well as being proportional. Discriminate use of force is thus important with regard to attacks against civilians which characterize modern conflict. Violence can pose an "anonymous" threat, in which danger comes from many sources but is not directly targeted toward humanitarians, and "presentational," in which specific attacks are made (Lee 1993). This difference is critical and will be returned to in later chapters.

In contrast, the critics of humanitarian intervention point to at least three fault-lines. First, that humanitarian intervention may be undertaken for the wrong reasons and be open to abuse (Farer 2003). This was a strong argument during the NATO intervention in Kosovo in 1999. Second, more harm may be caused than good when pursuing a human rights agenda. Notwithstanding the doctrine of double effect, this argument rests on the potential realities of warfare such as collateral damage. Finally, there is a relativist objection which holds that the world is too small for one country or a group of states to encroach on the sovereignty of others. The problem is further compounded in the twin contradictions found in the UN Charter: peace versus justice and sovereignty versus human rights (Chopra and Weiss 1992). In other words, as in the drafting of state constitutions, at the founding of the UN tension was deliberately left unaddressed for later cases to decide. As the debate continues, perhaps Parekh gets close to the truth in concluding that "although humanitarian intervention is justified under certain circumstances, it is too limited, too late and too superficial to be of lasting value, and needs to be embedded in and undertaken as part of a larger project of creating a just and non-statist global order" (1997, p. 49).

Policy coherence for development

An often-cited critique is that difficult and complex political problems are thus often addressed through technical solutions carried out by humanitarians (Goodhand 2001, Luckham et al. 2001). In an attempt to address this concern, the view that coherence can have a positive mutually reinforcing influence on international development is encapsulated in the notion of PCD. For the Western countries represented by the Organisation for Economic Cooperation and Development (OECD), "successful poverty reduction requires mutually supportive policies across a wide range of economic, social and environmental issues," thus the stated aim of PCD is to "enhance understanding of the development dimensions of member country policies and their impacts on developing countries" (OECD 2002, p. 1). As described by Picciotto, PCD comprises four separate types: "internal coherence" within a single project or program; "intra-country coherence" between "aid and non-aid" forms of assistance; "inter-country coherence" between countries; and "donor–recipient coherence" between rich and poor countries "to achieve shared development objectives" (2005, p. 312). The second and third forms of coherence relate most closely to the military–humanitarian relationship. Picciotto describes these as being "at the heart of PCD ... [going] well beyond aid and requir[ing] a 'whole of government' approach" (2005, p. 314). In this way, war and poverty – the key concerns of security and development – are seen to be in a "dynamic and mutually reinforcing relationship" (Luckham et al. 2001, p. 3). Policy coherence in practical terms gave rise to the combined civil–military Provincial Reconstruction Teams (PRTs) in Afghanistan (Jackson and Haysom 2013) and later in Iraq.

Many Western governments are increasingly bringing coherence to their collective policies, especially in light of their own renewed security concerns. Sweden's "Shared Responsibility – Policy for Global Development" Bill, adopted by its parliament in December 2004, was designed to make international assistance more coherent but does leave out key issues such as arms exports (Reality of Aid 2006). Similarly, the Canadian government's "3-D approach" is indicative of the coherence in bringing together defense, diplomacy and development. Other prominent examples include Australia, Denmark, Japan, the United Kingdom and the United States. Coherence has also been adopted by the UN, most notably through the "integrated mission" concept that melds military peacekeeping forces with civilian peacebuilding agencies. There are also implications at a policy level. The United Nations Development Programme's (UNDP) *development* report for Afghanistan in 2004 was subtitled "*Security* with Human a Face: Challenges and Responsibilities" (UNDP 2004, emphasis added). Similarly, the OECD's "Principles for Good International Engagement in Fragile States" identifies the "political-security-development nexus" as a key principle because "failure in one risks failure in all others" (2005, p. 3).

While some see the blending of security and development agendas as a natural progression of policy, others view it as problematic. In this debate, some NGOs have played an important role in highlighting inconsistencies in government policies (Picciotto 2005). Calling for the military intervention in Somalia, Kosovo and Haiti are examples of this (de Waal 1995). Since 11 September 2001, however, humanitarians of almost all stripes argue that development and humanitarianism should be separated from the other forms of government policy, particularly the military. Duffield (2001), a critic of the securitization of development, sees humanitarians and the military as part of the West's same system of carrots and sticks. He describes the "strategic complexes" of "state–non-state, military–civilian and public–private" actors "pursuing a radical agenda of social transformation in the interests of global stability" (2001, p.12). These complexes have an ability to adapt and transform to changing situations, which has led to vexing problems for scholars and practitioners alike. Hills (2003, p. 48) argues that the military's interaction with humanitarians "cannot and should not be fully operationalized." The Reality of Aid project, an advocacy effort consisting of 40 civil society networks around the world, persuasively contends that "in the post September 11 2001 security-centric era, poverty and violent conflict in the South are viewed increasingly as 'threats' to the security of the West. Development assistance is once again increasingly seen through the lens of northern foreign policy interests, as a tool for rich countries to defend themselves against these 'threats'" (Reality of Aid 2006, p. 9). Stemming from these concerns, there are very real security concerns based on the assumption that close relations with the military put humanitarians in danger (Fast 2007).

Yet there are two issues in this assumption giving rise to tension: first, that there ever was a time when official development assistance was not tied in some way to political motivations (Buur et al. 2007). At least far back as the dependency theorists (see, for example, Hayter 1971, Freire 1972 and Cardoso 1979), there are many who argue that aid has always been infused with political motivations. Second, that there was a brief period following the end of the Cold War during which development was delinked from politics and other concerns. Given the amount of criticism during the interventions of the 1990s, such as the "humanitarian intervention" in Kosovo, this is hard to believe. Former British Secretary of State for International Development Clare Short was dismissive of opposition to coherence and a close relationship between security and development: "Since the cold war, aid people have tended to say 'we don't touch armies...'. But this is the world we're in. All the time we are having to interface [relate] with the military" (Wrong 2001, p. 3). This was reflected by many in Afghanistan who simply saw relations with the military as a pragmatic necessity; not a question of "if" but of "how."

Human security

Before discussing human security, clarity of the concept of security is important because it is yet another area that brings the two together and is of relevance to the theory and practice of humanitarian action. Historically, security had a narrow definition focused on military and defense issues. Buzan et al. (1997) describe two competing schools of "traditionalists," who view security as narrowly focused on politico-military issues, and "wideners," who view security as including larger developmental issues and more akin to human security. With this understanding, at least three concepts of security are prevalent. First is physical security, which is characterized by military and defense concerns and can also be thought of as protection from abuse (the common humanitarian sector). Physical security, especially in areas of insecurity, is a common concern of both humanitarians and the military from a policy and practical point of view. The nature of conflict has continued to evolve with the low-intensity element becoming more complex. No longer fighting on separate geographic "sides," combatants mix with civilians in "wars within wars" (French 2006) and carry out a range of military missions on separate city "blocks" (Krulak 1997). Despite more attention on NGO security, indications are that conditions have become worse for humanitarians (UNHCR 2006).

Second is collective security. Haftendorn identifies three types of security, each relating to a "different philosophical tradition as well as to a specific historical interpretation of international relations" (1991, p. 4). National security is grounded on political realism and Hobbesian notions of anarchy which pit states against each other. As such, national security holds that states' behavior is driven by survival and that they deploy or balance power to constrain other states. International security, in contrast, flows from the Grotian ideal that rules (laws) and institutions can govern inter-state relations. While states act on self-interest, they use collaborative strategies; thus this was the dominant security model which governed Cold War politics. Global security, again in contrast, stems from the Kantian concept that an enlightened political order can emerge from a global community with shared principles, values and ideals. The UN and IHL are manifestations of this type of security. Clearly, there is evidence of each of these security types during the twentieth century. The mainstream notion is that national security still dominates the international arena, but it is debatable what paradigm now leads all others.

Third is the concept of human security, which has gained increased currency but has yet to replace the other concerns. The notion of human security developed from the debates over how to best address conflict and the uncertain link between security and development. It is critical for understanding the military–humanitarian relationship because of the recent emphasis on human security in countries like Afghanistan. The earliest concept centered on the entitlement of "freedoms" (Sen 1999) and included government "which does not oppress its citizens but rules with their consent" (Frechette 1999). Prior to the Second World War, there was little concern for human rights and other concerns of development, with few exceptions (Keck and Sikkink 1998, p. 83), yet discussion of freedom and rights became common language from the 1940s onward. United States President Franklin Roosevelt's 1941 State of the Union address, for example, described the post-war order as based on "four freedoms" (freedom of speech and expression, freedom of worship, freedom from want and freedom from fear) (Rosenman 1952). There is no widely accepted definition of human security but, as formulated by the UN, it initially encompassed seven elements: economic, food, health, environmental, personal, community and political security (UNDP 1994). An instructive description of human security as policy is offered by Archbishop Desmond Tutu: "[it] privileges people over states, reconciliation over revenge, diplomacy over deterrence, and multilateral engagement over coercive multilateralism" (cited in Picciotto 2006, p. 1). Further, human security "describes a condition of existence in which basic material needs are met, and in which human dignity, including meaningful participation in the life of the community, can be realized. Such human security is indivisible; it cannot be pursued by or for one group at the expense of another" (Thomas 2001, p. 161). Thus human security appears to support segregation and a separation between humanitarians and the military.

The concept of human security is also important in that it is intended to alter the traditional orthodoxy of state-centered politics. While it has gained popularity among academics, policy makers and practitioners alike, it is clearly a manifestation of the merging of security and development, with the same potential downsides. On the one hand, it is not easy to see how human security differs from the concept of international development. On the other hand, aligning security and development is seen as problematic. For some, human security is "far removed from liberal notions of competitive and possessive individualism" (Thomas 2001, p. 161). Paris (2001) identifies several problems with "human security" as it is currently used. First, human security has been used as a "rallying cry, a political campaign, a set of beliefs about the sources of violent conflict, a new conceptualization of security, and a guide for policymakers and academic researchers" (2001, p. 102), and thus its definition it is too broad to be useful. Second, and a result of the first, the concept makes it currently an unwieldy tool for analysis. In the 20 years since 1995 there has been a marked decline of international wars and a corresponding increase in civil wars (Human Development Report 2005). At the same time, there have been increases in human security in almost all areas (UNDP 2006, Pinker 2011, Human Security Report 2013).

Further, the melding of security and development agendas is closely allied to neo-liberal approaches because it "attributes universal legitimacy to a conception of freedom based on private power … [and] presents a set of essentially local, Western norms as universal" (Thomas 2001, p. 167). "Global governance" institutions including the UN, International Financial Institutions and Western governments pursue neo-liberalism and expect it to be pursued (Duffield 2001). These institutions have traditionally used global economic integration and liberalization while allowing for little or no alternative (Thomas 2001). Following this argument, more subtle forms of influence and coercion increasingly are used which combine military and civilian practices and policies. Military institutions use the terms associated with development, such as sustainability, transparency, accountability and even humanitarianism, to promote a worldview and lend it "false legitimacy" (Thomas 2001, p. 167). Because these terms lack broad consensus, the military is able to label its operations "humanitarian" and "developmental" to suit its own goals, operations and doctrine in places like Afghanistan (ISAF 2006a). Thus the concept of human security is highly contested and this has contributed to a period of "soul searching" (as O'Brien (2004, p. 187) noted more than a decade ago) and unclear policies for humanitarians.

Conclusion

Humanitarianism in post-conflict settings is a confounding topic because it is often portrayed in ahistorical terms, which can lead to inaccurate conclusions. Recent conflicts suggest that the pattern of the military–humanitarian relationship is evolving and previous assumptions may be incorrect. The implications of these changes are unclear and require further analysis. This chapter has looked these changes, controversies and tensions. As a means to navigate through these, a distinction was drawn between two approaches. The first was an integrated approach which is essentially for close relations between humanitarians and the military, while the second was a segregated approach which is fundamentally against close relations between humanitarians and the military. It is worth noting again that this framework has general (not absolute) categories to separate and bring some order to the debates, which can be opaque on this issue. Within this framework, three principle areas of controversy were examined. Table 3.1, presented earlier, illustrated this framework.

The first key controversy related to structure and agency. The classic tension relating to structure and agency, and the place of institutions in the relationship between humanitarians and the military were examined. Two distinct positions are evident: the managerialist–positivist position and the critical position. The managerialist–positivist position views complex dilemmas, such as humanitarian crises and post-conflict reconstruction, as problems to be solved. Good inter-organizational relations, signified by strong networks, are seen as a way to meet needs on the ground and build stability and peace. In contrast to the managerialist–positivist approach, the critical position sees the problems associated with conflict and reconstruction as a continual process that may defy formulaic solutions. Weak structures lead to poor and dysfunctional decision making, thus contributing to ineffective programming and jeopardizing humanitarian security. While the critical position often presents valid arguments, the managerialist–positivist approach offers persuasive prescriptions for those involved in policy and practice.

The second key controversy centered on humanitarian ethics. Following Weiss (1999), a spectrum of ethical positions are available to humanitarians in their approaches to programming. At one end of the spectrum are classical and minimalist humanitarians, who are essentially apolitical, seek to "do no harm" and tend to prioritize the humanitarian principles of neutrality, impartiality and independence over others. At the other end of the spectrum are maximalists and solidarists, who are generally willing to take political positions and tend to prioritize the principle of humanity above others. Broadly, these two ends of the spectrum are either deontologist or consequentialist positions which mark another distinctive tension. While the choices can be difficult, the consequentialist position offers a compelling case for action along maximalist and solidarist lines.

The final key controversy examined was the link between security and development. Within this controversy, three sub-areas were examined, each with its own set of criticisms. The first concerned the inclusion of a wider human rights agenda in humanitarianism and the role of policy positions such as humanitarian intervention. The second related to what is commonly termed PCD. Increasingly, policy makers have combined the previously separate fields of diplomacy, security and development, causing consternation by some commentators. Finally, the notion of security, and human security in particular, was examined. Like the wider coherence debate, the human security literature broadens the concepts of security and development to the point where each is poorly understood and even more poorly implemented. In some contexts, this has contributed to an increased blurring of the distinction between humanitarians and the military which, some have argued, has contributed to an increasingly less secure environment for humanitarians. It is unclear how military interests, which often espouse ideas of democracy and good governance, fit into this new approach.

Part II

Afghanistan case study

4

Humanitarian and military involvement in Afghanistan prior to the 2001 invasion

Introduction

Afghanistan's experiences with war and resistance, development and crisis, ideology and big-power politics have had powerful influences and serve as a backdrop to the military–humanitarian relationship. The country's history has been well covered elsewhere and the features of it political history are summarized in Table 4.1 (Gregorian 1969, Dupree 1980, Rubin 1995, Rashid 2001, Ewans 2001, Tanner 2003). The purpose of this chapter is not to provide a similarly general account of Afghanistan's past, but to focus on the history of the military–humanitarian relationship prior to the 2001 invasion. It uses the framework developed in Chapter 3 in analyzing the recent history of Afghanistan within the context of military–humanitarian relations. Three elements – technology, strategy and ethics – were established as historical drivers contributing to a close relationship between humanitarians and the military. This chapter traces five periods which will be examined in light of these three elements. First, the period before the Second World War was characterized by feudalism and the first experiences of breaking isolationism through contact with Western powers. This meant, for example, that some technologies such as advanced weapons were adopted but others, such as the railroad, were not.

Second, the period from 1946 to 1973 can be seen as a "golden age" where dams, transportation, education and other efforts following "five year plans" were constructed. This advanced certain sections of Afghanistan, but fomented divisions and a reaction against the introduction of Western practices and technologies. Third, the period from 1973 to 1989 is marked by the Soviet invasion and the launch of a country-wide resistance. During this time, infrastructural projects continued and the start of foreign-led humanitarianism began. Mujahideen resistance movements also skillfully employed military technology and strategies which brought them into close contact with humanitarians. In contrast, the Soviet Army employed conventional military strategies, thus distancing itself from the populace and in the end failing to achieve its objectives. At the same time, Afghan and international humanitarians adjusted their ethical concerns and adopted a solidarist approach; a politically charged position aligning humanitarianism with political and military

Table 4.1 Important political events in Afghan history

1880–1901	*Reign of Abdur Rahman Khan.* Following the First (1839–42) and Second (1843–80) Anglo-Afghan Wars, the king used British assistance to bring in a Western-style military and security apparatus – but not the telegraph and the railroad, to stem the ability of Western powers to influence the country. Suppressed ethnic groups and consolidated control of the state.
1901–19	*Reign of Habibullah Khan.* The third and final -Anglo-Afghan War in 1919 ended in military stalemate, but provided a means for Afghanistan to gain sovereignty over its foreign affairs, which had been under British control.
1919–33	*Reign of Amanullah Khan.* Amanuallah sought further reforms including overturning many traditional practices which contributed to conservative opposition to his rule. In 1929, Inayatullah Khan ruled for three days before being chased from the throne by the Tajik Habibullah Ghazi, who war in turn quickly replaced by the Minister of War, Mohammed Nadir Shah, who ruled until his assassination in 1933.
1933–73	*Reign of Mohammed Zahir Shah.* Initiated a steady move towards Westernization. During the 1950s and 1960s the country underwent what many describe as a "golden age" in which many large-scale infrastructural projects were initiated and economic growth benefited urban areas.
1970s	*Political turmoil.* After a coup d'état led by his cousin and Prime Minister Mohammed Daoud Khan, Zahir Shah became an exile in Italy (until his return to Kabul in April 2002). The start of the Democratic People's Republic of Afghanistan under Daoud saw Soviet influence stepped up in both the civilian and military sectors.
1978–79	*Political crisis.* Under President Nur Mohammand Taraki, anti-traditionalist reforms were enacted under the Saur Revolution. Resistance was formed, dividing urban and rural Afghans, and within ethnic factions (Khalq and Parcham) of the government. The first Afghan refugees began leaving the country. After Taraki's assassination (September 1979), President Hafizullah Amin tried to restore order but was unsuccessful. Soviet elements assassinated Amin on the eve of the invasion. International organizations (including the ICRC and NGOs) were prohibited from working in Afghanistan.
1979–89	*Soviet occupation.* The 1980s were characterized by a piecemeal Soviet occupation and stiff resistance by the Mujahideen, who were given extensive military and humanitarian support by Western and Arab states as well as by Pakistan.
1989–92	*End of communist rule.* Following the Soviet departure in 1989, the communist government continued under Mohammad Najibullah for nearly four years.
1992–96	*Warlordism.* Following the resignation of Najibullah within days of Moscow's withdrawal of its aid (April 1992), Burhanuddin Rabbani gradually assumed nominal control. Factionalism was rife, leading to widespread anarchy and the destruction of Kabul and other parts of the country.
1996–2001	*Taliban.* Following its rapid military successes from Kandahar under the leadership of Mullah Mohammed Omar, the Taliban succeeded in establishing control over nearly 90 per cent of the country by 2001.

concerns. They not only assisted Afghan refugees, but also worked inside occupied Afghanistan in providing relief. This brought them in direct contact with Mujahideen fighters and foreign military advisors.

Fourth, the period from the Soviet withdrawal in 1989 to 1996 was marked by anarchy, internecine warfare and a return of warlordism (a period where military leaders exercised political control over parts of the country). Humanitarians adopted a minimalist approach and their activities were used as a substitution for Western political and military action. Finally, the five-year period of Taliban rule from 1996 to 2001 was characterized by a return of stability but at the cost of repression and a further deterioration of conditions for Afghans. During this period, humanitarianism assumed a maximalist approach in reaction to Taliban policies.

Technology

Technology as a driver of the military–humanitarian relationship in Afghanistan fits a similar pattern as in Western countries. In an analysis the influence of technology on this relationship, three patterns emerge. First, Afghans have been highly selective in the adoption of technology. For a variety of reasons, including geographic location, the outlook of it leaders and a highly traditional, rural-based society, the influence of technology as a driver in the military–humanitarian relationship has been at a slower pace than it was in the West. Second, and related to the first, foreign influence has played a significant role in the introduction of technology and thus as a stimulus of the military–humanitarian relationship. This has been profound enough that to each element of technology (arms and military hardware, media and medicine) it is possible to add the prefix "Western." Finally, violent conflict itself, linked to these elements of technology, has been a stimulus that has brought humanitarians and the military together. In examining technology's influence on the military–humanitarian relationship, this section follows the model developed in Chapter 2.

The first element of technology is arms and military hardware. Given the fractious nature of Afghan history, it is not surprising that the country's internal divisions and geographic location as a landlocked buffer state between empires made it a prime area of military and economic interest (Hopkirk 1991, Stockton 2004a). The earliest efforts to bring about Western-style change in Afghanistan were undertaken to acquire improved military capacity and achieve internal security. Following the Second Anglo-Afghan War, the British used military assistance to prop up Abdur Rahman Khan, who developed the Afghan military as leverage against his brothers and to quell resistance from the Hazaras and others (Nyrop and Seekins 1986, Vogelsang 2002). He adopted advanced arms and military hardware and created an extensive internal security apparatus. At the same time, he resisted other projects like the railroad and telegraph which might have extended European colonial reach into the country (Gregorian 1969), particularly from the British and Russian empires. In the light of Abdur Rahman's military oppression and religious zeal, many parallels can be drawn between his rule and that of the Taliban. Following the end of the Second World War, Afghanistan's importance as a buffer state was reconstituted within the framework of the Cold War. By that point, under the nominal rule of Mohammed Zahir Khan, Afghanistan was largely controlled by the king's independently minded uncles (Dupree 1980). When Zahir's cousin, Mohammed Daoud, became prime minister in 1953, he sought foreign assistance for reforms which ensured the country's status as a client to Soviet interests in Central Asia (Rubin 1995, Saikal 2004). In keeping with local traditions of conservatism, Daoud "remained a firm opponent of the liberalization in Afghan society" (Rubin 2002, p. 3). In 1956, however, he bought $25 million worth of Soviet arms, including tanks and helicopters, while also receiving military technical assistance in the north of the country (Rubin 2002, p. 3). This was also at a time when the strength of Afghanistan's military was seen as lacking, compared with neighboring countries, and this drove the country closer to Moscow, especially when Daoud assumed full control of the country in 1973.

Political events of the late 1970s spiraled into civil unrest, followed by invasion and war. For the Soviets, Afghanistan was the first major conflict it had fought since the Second World War. They used a number of new weapons and tactics which combined sophisticated air–ground maneuvers (including the most advanced attack helicopter of the time), telecommunications, logistics, planning and coordination. The resistance gained attention after 1983 when assistance was significantly stepped up by the Americans, Saudis and Pakistanis. Initial United States help came before the Soviet invasion in July 1979, but consisted of only $500,000 for psychological operations, medical supplies and cash support (Coll 2005). However, large shipments of standard infantry weapons such as mortars and heavy machine guns, and eventually sophisticated Stinger surface-to-air missiles, followed. Ultimately, the Mujahideen came to rely heavily on foreign military assistance (as well as humanitarian aid described below), with arms and military hardware being made in or supplied from a diverse range of countries including China, Egypt, Poland and Switzerland (Coll 2005). One Mujahid is reported to have said at the time, "Western aid has changed us from the hunted to the hunters" (Richards 1990, p. 203). In this way, following the pattern established in historical battles from Solferino to Biafra, the destructive power of weaponry and the attempt of medical practitioners (discussed further below) to address the effects of war were stimuli for bringing the humanitarian and military sectors together. The cycle of war and suffering did not end with the Soviet departure and, following years of civil war, the Taliban seized control of Kabul. Its triumph can be seen as a reaction not only to foreign influences over the country as a whole but also to the power of elite Pashtuns whom the West had long courted. Its leadership rejected many elements that did not fit its vision of Islam; however, this was highly selective and it welcomed many technologies of war.

The second element of technology was medicine. While the practice of military medicine can be traced to the Anglo-Afghan Wars (Doyle 1982), the link between this and civilian humanitarianism can be traced only to the 1980s. Following the Soviet invasion, some aid organizations were expelled from the country. The war witnessed humanitarians providing medicine to both Afghan "civilians and combatants" (Baitenmann 1990, p. 71). As fighting intensified, casualties outstripped the health infrastructure of the country. Estimates vary from roughly 560,000 Afghan battle deaths to 1,000,000 as the conflict moved into remote areas where advanced medical practices were largely unknown (Lacina and Gleditsch 2005). Working closely with the Mujahideen, solidarist humanitarians established "clandestine health relief" projects in many rebel-held areas, especially areas bordering Pakistan (Girardet 1985, p. 215). The Panjshir valley, for example, became renowned for its ability to resist the Soviets and was known to host French relief workers. This involved close coordination with Western donors and Mujahideen commanders, logistical operations and the fielding of several hundred expatriate medical staff who worked directly with the Mujahideen by establishing a relationship in Pakistan and then crossing into Afghanistan. As one observer noted at the time: "working clandestinely, and at great personal risk, they have not only tried to treat some of the country's often horrifying war casualties (85 per cent civilian) but also commonplace maladies ...." These organizations played an especially important role (Girardet 1985, p. 215). Examples included MSF, Aide Medical Internationale, Médecins du Monde and the International Medical Corps (the last of these created because of the conflict in Afghanistan).

Later, during the 1990s, humanitarians continued to provide emergency medical relief and community health activities such as education and the training of birth attendants. When the Taliban came to power, the political nature of humanitarianism became pronounced. Medical relief workers discovered what they perceived to be a "clash between the Muslim fundamentalism of the moujahidin and rational modern medicine, a clash which would prove dramatic and far-reaching after the extremist Taliban movement took control" (Cooley 2000, p. 101). Medical service for women and women working in mixed-gender field hospitals became especially problematic when the Taliban tried to institute its gender policies, which segregated men and women in public life. Some humanitarians maintained access to vulnerable populations through quiet "green tea" diplomacy (Goodhand 2004, p. 46) but, as will be discussed later, other NGOs maintained strong and outspoken positions that led to poor relations with the Taliban. Relations with the anti-Taliban Northern Alliance continued as they had under the Mujahideen rule, and medicine remained as a primary means for humanitarians to carry out programming.

A third element of technology was the use of the media. Prior to the Soviet intervention, mass media in Afghanistan such as radio and newspapers were rudimentary and not a significant driver of military–humanitarian relations. During the 1980s, international news agencies and Western journalists were largely barred from government areas, thereby pushing them towards the resistance and its clandestine informational networks (Borovik 2001). This led to a somewhat contradictory situation where, on the one hand, there are detailed accounts of journalists' traveling in rebel-held locations, thus maintaining awareness of the Afghans' plight and contributing to support for the resistance (Gall 1983, Girardet 1985). On the other hand, however, because of the danger and complex logistical arrangements needed to tell the story, Western media often ignored the Soviet-Afghan war (Roberts 2003). For much of the 1990s, the international media was similarly focused on other global crises and, for many in Afghanistan, their plight had become a "forgotten disaster." The share of attention it did receive was closely linked to the level of donations to NGOs and, indirectly, to Western government policy (Kolhatkars and Ingalls 2006). In addition, its shifting front lines and general insecurity made reporting from the country particularly dangerous. In Taliban-held areas foreign journalists were allowed to enter, but were under heavy restrictions, especially following the prohibition of photography in 1996. In areas controlled by the Northern Alliance, journalists were more welcomed (Al-Qaeda exploited this fact to murder the military commander Ahmad Shah Massoud on 10 September 2001) and likely to be given crafted stories by Western-educated officials, but the group lacked real international leverage until 2001 (Clark 2004).

Strategy

In Afghanistan, strategy has long been a stimulus of the military–humanitarian relationship, particularly from the 1980s onward. Following the analysis of Goodson (2001) and others, the dominant factor in Afghanistan's recent history has been violent conflict. The country has been known throughout history as a place of battle, conquest and overthrow. Writing of his experiences in colonial India, Winston Churchill observed that the Pashtuns, the dominant group in Afghanistan, "are always engaged in private or public war. Every man is a warrior, a politician and a theologian. Every large house is a real feudal fortress. ... Every family cultivates its vendetta; every clan, its feud. ... Nothing is ever forgotten and very few debts are left unpaid" (1941, p. 149). In many respects, the country has never witnessed a sustained period without political tension and violence. Between themselves, Afghans have never fought "to the knife" (Grau 2004, p. 130), but tended to fight seasonally, and inferior forces usually faded in the face of stronger opposition. Afghans made exceptions to this pattern for foreign invaders, at which time they followed a "custom of joining in associations for mutual defence" (Elphinstone 1842, p. 4).

The 36 years since the Soviet invasion in 1979 have been especially trying for Afghans. The late 1960s and 1970s brought unprecedented change to Afghanistan. Foreign influences, including Marxist ideology, were particularly important. Returning university students, a small middle class and a large, poorly disciplined army added to political volatility. An even more significant factor in insecurity was the continually weak state structure. With only one government administrator per district (Ferris 2006), the control of the central government extended little beyond the major cities and along a few key roads. Although statistics are hard to come by, visitors were warned of the dangers of travel. Special permits were needed for some areas, and firearms were known to be maintained by some Western researchers. By the late 1970s, political tension was on the rise and, in April 1978, the Soviet-backed People's Democratic Party of Afghanistan launched a coup d'état. This regime proved to be fractious and violently oppressive, which "triggered a large-scale rural rebellion against the new government" (Gibbs 2006, p. 240). Initially, there was scant reaction by the United States, even after its ambassador was kidnapped in 1978 and killed in a gunfire exchange during a botched rescue attempt the following year. By some accounts, this was seen as a green light for further Soviet intervention. Although the American diplomatic mission withdrew, a plan to help anti-communist elements was developed, thereby signaling the end of a period of Russian détente with the West (Gibbs 2006).

The Soviets had a successful history of counter-insurgency, as demonstrated in the Ukraine, in the Baltic States and in Central Asia against the so-called Basmachi. In those cases, massive military interventions were matched by political changes, such as land reforms and industrialization. In Afghanistan, however, land was distributed among families and the preponderance of subsistence agriculture made the latter very difficult (Cullather 2002). Further Soviet involvement failed to stem the civil war, despite efforts to develop large-scale infrastructural projects in hydropower and irrigation (Girardet 1985). The level of insecurity and fighting made expansion of these programs difficult and new efforts were not undertaken. After a reaching peak of $435 million in 1979, direct Soviet economic aid lessened and many civil projects were "abandoned," while military assistance reached nearly $1 billion a year (DIA 1983, p. 32). With this, the government mostly adopted conventional military approaches in response to the resistance. By some estimates, the Soviets would have needed one million troops to pacify the whole country with the Red Army. With up to 80 per cent of its forces being organized along conventional lines, the military "did not wish to conduct counter-insurgency, which it left to the KGB, but to follow its book for war in Europe" (Ferris 2006, p. 21). When soldiers from Central Asia showed an unwillingness to fight, out of sympathy for the local populace, the Red Army relied on European recruits, who proved more aggressive toward Afghans. Out of custom and later frustration, it followed a now familiar pattern where it maintained high-intensity military strategies that made its victory less attainable. This included blowing up sluice gates to destroy irrigation and agricultural capacity and often deliberately attacking civilians, thereby ensuring that it won every major military battle, but ultimately lost the political struggle (Chayes 2006).

Whereas the Soviet Army attempted to apply massive force along conventional military lines, the Afghan resistance embraced the local populace, accepted outside assistance and skillfully employed a low-intensity conflict strategy. Relying on lightning strikes and avoiding pitched battles, the Mujahid fighter was often difficult to distinguish from the refugee (Centlivres and Centlivres-Demont 1988). Numbers of the former grew exponentially after the Soviet invasion, to a point where only 15 to 20 per cent of Afghanistan could be considered to be under central government control (Isby 1989). Although the movement was not an organized group as such, its commanders, such as Ahmed Shah Massoud, were considered to be among the most efficient guerrilla strategists of recent times (Kaplan 1991). While Afghans had a long tradition of waging low-intensity campaigns against invaders, a major problem throughout the Soviet period was infighting among the Mujahideen. The resistance was fractured and as diverse as the country itself, with the "Tadjik-inhabited highlands of northern Afghanistan often bear[ing] little resemblance to the Pashtun areas of the southeast" (Girardet 1985, p. 10). From within the Mujahideen, rudimentary political administrations developed during the 1980s, but many of the typical social services provided by resistance movements worldwide, such as schools, clinics and economic programs, were not present. Because these parties lacked the means to provide such services, international humanitarian assistance filled this gap.

There was also a realization by outside actors that no single group could legitimately claim to represent all the Mujahideen factions. Alliances were formed along two lines; the first was "liberal" or those that the West considered to be politically and religiously moderate, while the second was "fundamentalist" or those regarded to be adherents to traditional views (Kushkaki 1988, p. 164). In Peshawar (Pakistan), a group of the most powerful Mujahideen political parties and armed groups formed in the early 1980s. Predictably, differences emerged between the leaders in Pakistan and those who focused on making on-the-ground gains against the Soviets (Coll 2005). Just as in its approach to the war in Vietnam, the United States government tried to meld these disparate organizations together in an attempt to develop a coherent and results-based policy that brought in the intelligence services and the humanitarian sector. As one United States government advisor explained: "We've taken a lesson from Mao. The Soviets are trying to kill the fish [rebels] by draining the sea, and we're trying to keep the sea full" (quoted in Baitenmann 1990, p. 76). Direct American humanitarian aid to Afghans inside their own country did not start until 1985, but by the end of the war it had contributed over $600 million (Goodson 2001). This assistance was spent not only on traditional sectors such as health, education and agriculture, but also included support to build the bureaucracy of Mujahideen political parties (Rubin 1995).

When the Soviets finally withdrew in 1989, continuing tensions within and between these factions gave rise to a new warlordism which, in the sudden absence of a common enemy, quickly became a full-scale civil war and an ongoing humanitarian crisis. It took three years for the government to fall to the Mujahideen commanders. Under such conditions, "every ethnic or tribal group in Afghanistan became a political fracture" (Ferris 2006, p. 24). While American and other foreign military assistance ended after the Soviet withdrawal, Pakistan maintained an active influence in Afghan affairs. In addition, certain groups such as Arabs and Chechens continued to be drawn to the country's civil war. Kabul, which had been largely spared from destruction under Soviet occupation, became a battle zone in which large sections of the city were reduced to rubble. In other parts of the country, criminality and lawlessness were endemic. The ensuing violence helped give space for the creation and expansion of the Taliban.

The early Taliban had common backgrounds in the Mujahideen. Coupling this experience with an aggressive military strategy, it sought to reform Afghanistan into an integral state. Following the atrocities of the civil war, Afghans accepted this with a "mixture of fear, acceptance, total exhaustion, and devastation" (Rashid 2001, p. 4). After first assuming power in Kandahar in November 1994, it went on to take Herat in September 1995 and Kabul in September 1996, bringing relative security to areas long affected by conflict. In the pursuit of Massoud's forces, the Shomali plain north of Kabul, once a lush and highly populated rural area, was left a wasteland. In its attacks on Bamyan, Mazar-i-Sharif and other northern towns, the Taliban met stiff resistance which led to a shift in strategy. Since the Northern Alliance had "implanted itself among the population, using it as a source of provisions and fighters", the Taliban carried out attacks against local civilians and, as it did so, its intolerance grew along with its military gains (Calas and Salignon 2004, p. 71). This strategy was partially successful militarily but failed to address human security and effectively provided a reason for continued humanitarian programming. At the same time, it appeared as though "the Taliban's cooperation with, and reliance on, Arab and other foreign fighters" was growing (Byman 2005, p. 193).

Following the 1998 United States embassy bombings in East Africa, targeting these networks of Arab and foreign fightersbecame a "primary policy objective" for Washington (Rashid 2001, p. 177). The subsequent United States missile strikes inside Afghanistan had several outcomes. First, the attacks brought together the Taliban and foreign Muslim fighters and in this way solidified the resolve of these groups (Coll 2005). Second, they led to a heightened insecurity for humanitarians in the country. Under these conditions, most foreign humanitarians and UN staff left the country. In March 1999, a United States government document spelled out a policy that advance security warning would not be given to humanitarians (Jalalzai 1999). The American government has an established record of secrecy in this regard, including the failure to notify its humanitarian "partners" in Northern Iraq in 1991, despite advance knowledge warning of violence. Third and finally, they set the stage for further confrontation between the Taliban and external political powers. Although resistance to the Taliban never ceased, the Taliban continued to make military gains, controlling roughly 90 per cent of the country by 2001. It also became more widely known internationally, although only three countries (Pakistan, Saudi Arabia and the United Arab Emirates) officially recognized the Taliban government. In successive years, it tried to obtain the Afghan seat at the UN, but failed, based on its record of human rights and its association with Al-Qaeda (Guillaume

2000). Because it was based largely on Pashtun ethnicity and a particular interpretation of Islam, its victories were based on a shaky political foundation in so diverse a
country as Afghanistan. The major Western powers provided increasing amounts of
assistance to counter the help received by the Taliban from external sympathizers.
At the same time, the Taliban became increasingly isolated internationally.

Ethics

In Afghanistan, the ethical impulse to limit the impact of war and to improve
the lives of those affected has been the third and final stimulus contributing to a
close military–humanitarian relationship. As in other cases, the ethical position of
humanitarians ebbed and flowed over time with the political and military climate.
At different times, the range of positions described by Weiss (1999), including
classical, minimalist, maximalist and solidarist humanitarian approaches, were all
practiced in Afghanistan. This section looks briefly at the historical roots of development before tracing the evolution of humanitarianism from the 1980s onward. The
effect of this is closely related to global and local politics as well as practical considerations such as organizational mandate, the type of programming undertaken and
the degree of security available to humanitarians.

The first attempts at Western-style "development" were undertaken to expand
and maintain state security during the rule of Amanullah Khan (1919–29). With the
rise of European liberal internationalism in the early twentieth century, however,
development programming was undertaken to bring a degree of Westernization
to Afghanistan. Following the Second World War, Soviet-style "Five Year Plans"
were adopted to bring a comprehensive and far-reaching approach to industrialization. External assistance was thus largely driven by Great Power rivalry, with a
geographic split appearing between the Soviet-influenced areas north of the Hindu
Kush and the Americans' prioritization of southern Afghanistan. By the 1960s, there
were thousands of foreign development advisors in the country (Lieberman 1980).
Other countries, including China, West Germany and Czechoslovakia, provided
a variety of other projects, including construction of public buildings and Kabul's
electric trolleybus system. The building of large infrastructures, particularly dams,
was generally pursued by the United States and the Soviets. Although there was an
Afghan civil society (for example, the Women's Welfare Society in Kabul, which
was established in 1946), its role was de-emphasized in favor of centralized, state-
run initiatives (Cullather 2002, p. 536).

By the early 1970s, this approach had not been able to make up for internal divisions and the weakness of the state. Daoud's ascendancy, discussed above, paved
the way for deeper Soviet involvement, leading to further divisions and turmoil by
the end of the decade. Afghans have traditionally felt weary of government and this
became particularly pronounced with the rise of a communist-inspired social movement later in the decade. Communism was embraced by the youth, and students in

particular were more willing to challenge traditions and experiment with new ideas. This mix of infrastructural development and ideology played an especially important role in shaping the path Afghanistan took. However, "words like 'revolution', 'democracy', 'modernization' and 'progress' are regarded with repugnance by most rural Afghans" (Girardet 1985, pp. 182–3), who related such ideas to negative foreign influence and repression. According to one Afghan asked about this period, "they made their first mistake from the start by saying that God did not exist." This greatly upset conservative Afghans and led to greater levels of political violence.

Those who could escape the Soviets settled mainly in Pakistan, and in the process that country provided the earliest assistance. This aid took three forms (Baitenmann 1990). First, there was advocacy and fundraising among donor institutions and the general public (for some, Afghanistan became a *cause célèbre*). Second, direct assistance was provided for the vast refugee camps that sprang up in Pakistan and Iran. Third, there were cross-border activities, such as the medical assistance described earlier in this chapter. Pakistan was to serve as the base for humanitarianism in Afghanistan from this period until 2002 following the fall of the Taliban; by the mid-1980s, there were over 35 NGOs providing relief in Pakistan (Hatch Dupree 1988).

The Soviet invasion gave the Afghan cause an instant appeal as "Afghan aid committees sprang up throughout the world" (Hatch Dupree 1988, p. 251). These early relief workers contributed to a number of solidarist NGOs which were formed, including the London-based Afghan Support Committee (1981) (which became Afghanaid in 1983), the Swedish Committee for Afghanistan (SCA) (1980) and the consortium of Danish NGOs known as DACAAR (1984) which were to be among the larger and more influential NGOs in later years.

The UN, and UNHCR in particular, played an early and critical role when the Pakistan government requested its help in May 1979 (Hatch Dupree 1988, p. 251). For the first years, Pakistani officials were somewhat ambivalent about their assistance; the country was not a signatory to the refugee treaties and many saw the situation as transient. Refugees were thus kept in temporary-status "tented villages" even after shelters were made of mud-brick (Hatch Dupree 1988, p. 248). In contrast, many international humanitarians focused on longer-term activities related to health, education and income generation (Hatch Dupree 1988). With over three million people displaced in the early 1980s, sizeable programs were established in the "refugee arc" along the Afghan–Pakistan border (Hatch Dupree 1988, p. 250). The large but less substantial numbers of refugees in neighboring countries including Iran, parts of Western Europe and North America received international assistance.

During the Soviet period, a human rights ethic was a key motive for providing assistance. For many, the occupation and its atrocities were the main impulse and so they were willing to adopt a solidarist approach even if political ("anti-communist") viewpoints were part of it. For American leaders such as the Democratic Congressman Charlie Wilson and the Republican founder of the

International Medical Corps, Dr. Bob Simon, concerns over the plight of Afghan civilians were mixed with national interest and a determination to resist Soviet expansionism (Miller 1995). Many French humanitarians were of a Left Bank tradition which was politically liberal and was likely to eschew alignment with Western interests (Cooley 2000). These developed a strongly solidarist approach, aligning directing with Mujahideen factions to gain access to vulnerable populations and war wounded. Explaining their position, one French humanitarian put it this way:

> Our view is that humanitarian considerations are far more important than the *'raison d'etat'* of a particular country. For the moment, we are working mainly in areas where other agencies do not go. But they too should realize that there are millions of people, far more than the present world refugee population (estimated at 10–12 million), who receive no help whatsoever because their governments do not accept them. (Girardet 1985, pp. 215–16, italics original)

The earliest assistance came in the form of cash handouts directly to commanders and elders, but, over time, also food and non-food items. "Clandestine health relief," described earlier, played an especially important role in this regard (Girardet 1985, p. 215). At its height, there were an estimated 50 NGOs involved in cross-border activities (Baitenmann 1990). As Hatch Dupree concluded, "the diverse roles pursued by the VOLAGs are exerting a significant impact on Afghanistan's present, in Pakistan and inside Afghanistan" (1988, p. 261). While there were NGOs that crossed into Afghanistan to provide assistance, initially more established organizations made a conscious decision not to do so. Often for fundraising reasons, they preferred to restrict their operations to refugees only. As an American CARE official argued: "We are not into clandestine relief" (quoted in Girardet 1985, p. 210). Over time, however, this changed as they aligned with the Mujahideen political parties, took advantage of increasing aid flows and sought to mitigate the pull of the refugee camps by addressing the needs of vulnerable people inside Afghanistan (Girardet 1985). A strong case can be made that this strengthened the Mujahideen, but it also contributed to divisions among the Afghans and created competition over the "spoils of aid" (Donini 2004, p. 122, Baitenmann 1990). As Rubin argues, the solidarist approach "was effective in delivering the aid to those in need, but it not only failed to create a national political center, it contributed to political fragmentation by strengthening the autonomy of commanders" (1995, p. 67).

Along with attempts to improve health, education provides a case which mixed security concerns with humanitarian objectives. During the war of the 1980s education was used as a tool for political–military indoctrination and manipulation by both sides. This education of Afghans in the Soviet Union was widespread, with roughly 20,000 students attending schooling, cultural events, summer camps and exchanges (Girardet 1985, p. 140). In Pakistan, the education of Afghan refugees also took on a dual role of developing children and achieving a political–military objective. Depending on human and financial resources, military training was frequently incorporated into school curricula (Centlivres and Centlivres-Demont 1988). This included, along with standard subjects and religious instruction, military skills such as tactics and weapons handling (Rastegar 1991). Text books developed by the University of Nebraska included the counting of dead Russian soldiers as mathematical problems. Some felt that this approach was just as important as the military hardware the Mujahideen were supplying (Kolhatkars and Ingalls 2006). Teachers who did the training were paid by NGOs and members of different Mujahideen parties who would often enter classrooms once or twice a week. Far from being unwilling or co-opted bystanders, humanitarians took a direct role in the campaign to oust the Soviet-backed government as part of their solidarist approach (Donini 2004, p. 125).

Following the Soviet withdrawal in 1989, Weinbaum observed that "the next generation of Afghans will be a more difficult people to govern ... Exile has established higher expectations about government that will make resettled Afghans less easily satisfied, more critical, and more distrustful of those exercising authority" (1989, p. 304). As before, nearly all the relief and reconstruction efforts were undertaken by the UN and NGOs (Goodson 2001, p. 101), yet the realities of the previous decade – an intimate relationship between the Mujahideen and NGOs, a relatively weak UN, a highly vulnerable Afghan populace and the whims of donor governments – were hard to shake off. The end of the war brought a "second generation" of humanitarians with a greater emphasis on bureaucratic dispassion (Goodhand 2004, p. 14). A period of "considerable soul-searching" followed which shifted humanitarian positions from solidarity to a classical or a minimalist approach with a focus on service delivery (Donini 2004, p. 125). The UN activity increased exponentially, with the relief convoys under "Operation Salam" receiving increased funding, but the resumption of development aid was not possible because of insecurity and a lack of international commitment (Aga Khan 1990, Van Brabant and Killick 1999). Humanitarian funding did, however, continue at $200–300 million a year (Goodhand 2004). Despite this, mediation efforts to bring peace between the warring factions all ended in failure. When the communist government under Najibullah fell in 1992, the country was plunged into civil war under the Mujahideen commanders, none of whom built "schools, hospitals, water supply systems or anything remotely related to civic development" (Rashid 2001, p. 213). In response, Afghans "turned to poppy [production] which was a traditional crop anyway" (Goodson 2001, p. 101).

These conditions helped give rise to the Taliban and its brand of "stability." Pakistan provided nearly all the Taliban government's $10 million annual budget. Assistance also came from other sources in the Arab world, mostly through informal channels. Under these conditions, NGOs became "a de facto shadow government running many of the social services that the Taliban and their predecessors were unable or unwilling to provide" (O'Brien 2004, p. 187). Women and children were the primary beneficiaries of this assistance, with the SCA alone educating more than 150,000 children (of whom 30,000 were girls) (Rashid 2001). CARE was said to have provided water to 400,000 people in Kabul, and roughly half the population of Kabul relied on international food assistance (O'Brien 2004). Whereas humanitarians had switched to a minimalist position to deal with the chaos of the early 1990s, under the Taliban a maximalist approach was taken by a "third generation" of humanitarians" (Goodhand 2004, p. 16). Many responded vehemently to the harshness of the regime and took up an outspoken and critical position, pressuring the government on gender and other human rights issues. As a result, the Taliban saw no distinction between humanitarians and Western states. Each had their own intractable position and so, almost from the start, the Taliban and aid workers were at loggerheads. François Calas and Pierre Salignon describe the situation this way:

> The mullahs lacked the means to achieve their totalitarian ambitions. Contrary to their wishes, they were unable to oust the Western aid organizations in favour of Islamic NGOs which, although closer to their conception of solidarity, were poorly endowed with resources. By exploiting the regime's weaknesses, the humanitarian organizations managed to preserve a minimum of freedom to work in a way that more or less respected the principle of impartiality, although this was constantly challenged by shifting conditions. (2004, p. 76)

Since the Taliban's social polices affected women in particular, "a number of donors invested in NGO community-based education initiatives, especially in those rural areas where it was possible for local communities to negotiate access for girls despite official policy" (Johnson and Leslie 2002, p. 866). This inevitably reduced their capacity to intervene in urban areas. Consequently, humanitarians were "torn between the principle of equality and the humanitarian imperative", leading to a division between some who felt that the best response was to withdraw and others who believed that it was better to find means to constructively engage the Taliban (Kreczko 2003, p. 241). In both instances, the gender issue galvanized the UN, donors and NGOs to develop a tailored response. In January 1997 the UN sponsored the International Forum on Assistance to Afghanistan in Ashgabat. This effort merged political, security and humanitarian concerns into "one mutually supportive and coherent strategy" known as the "Strategic Framework" (Macrae and Leader 2000, p. 44). By the UN's own assessment, this was a "quantum leap" forward because standard practices had been a failure in bringing a stable peace (UN 1998, p. 7).

Conclusion

This chapter has traced the evolution of three elements – technology, strategy and ethics – that have contributed to the relationship between humanitarians and the military. These have exerted an influence over all five periods examined here. First, until 1945 Afghanistan was characterized by feudalism, warlordism at the local level and ties to the British Empire as a buffer state. Based on military and security reasons, Afghans adopted some technologies such as advanced weapons but not others, such as the telegraph and the railroad. The second period, from 1945 to 1973, was seen as a "golden age" where massive infrastructural projects were undertaken, including dams, transportation, education and other efforts following "five year plans." This advanced parts of Afghanistan, but fomented divisions and a reaction against change. The period from 1973 to 1989 was marked by the Soviet invasion and the launch of a country-wide resistance led by the Mujahideen. During the 1980s, development achieved in the previous period was halted, although Soviet projects initially continued, and foreign-led humanitarianism began. The Mujahideen were ultimately successful by employing available technology, using low-intensity conflict strategies and fostering close relations with humanitarians so as to obtain the social services which they generally lacked. Under these circumstances, Afghan and international humanitarians adopted a solidarist approach. The fourth period, from the Soviet withdrawal in 1989 to 1996, was marked by anarchy, internecine warfare and a return of warlordism. As a consequence, humanitarians adopted a minimalist approach and their activities were used as a substitution for Western political and military action which might have been used to bring about an end to suffering. Finally, the five-year period of the Taliban, from 1996 to 2001, can be seen as a return of stability in certain places but at the cost of repression and a further deterioration of conditions. During this period, humanitarianism assumed a maximalist approach in response to Taliban policies. This history shows a mix of approaches adopted by those engaged in providing aid and their respective relationships with security actors, which were to take on a larger dimension with the massive US-led intervention from 2001 onward.

5

Afghanistan: overview of conflict and assistance from 2001 to 2014

Introduction

This book thus far has introduced the military–humanitarian relationship and argued that the key question of whether an NGO should have close or distant relations with Western militaries is predicated on five basic assumptions – historical context, inter-organizational friction, insecurity, principled positions and co-option and politicization. In Chapter 2, the history of the military–humanitarian relationship was examined, suggesting that three drivers – technology, ethics and strategy – meant that humanitarians have had a historically close relationship with the military. In Chapter 3, three further issues were revealed that influence the military–humanitarian relationship. These were the tension between organizational structure and individual agency, humanitarian ethics and the link between security and development. In Chapter 4, attention shifted to the case study, examining the history of Afghanistan by deploying the three drivers of the military–humanitarian relationship first discussed in Chapter 2.

The purpose of this chapter is to describe the situation in Afghanistan from 2001 to 2014 with a focus on international actors. It will be shown that, apart from the military–humanitarian relationship, close and overlapping interests continue with the linkage between security and development, policy coherence and a belligerence that does not recognize the separation between humanitarian and military spheres. These interlinked issues contributed to the military–humanitarian relationship's being a highly contentious issue in Afghanistan. This chapter discusses the context from late 2001 to the end of 2014 by focusing on the proximal causes and manifestations of tension within the military–humanitarian relationship.

First, the recent conflict will be discussed, along with a focus on strategy and ongoing insecurity. Second, the characteristics of the war, the insurgency and the "coherent" combination of aid and force will be discussed. Third, political developments will be analyzed. The aid architecture that arose following the Taliban will be examined and located with donor imperatives, state-building objectives and development programming. Finally, it will be shown that the overlap between development and security concerns led to tension between NGOs and the military – examples include soldiers' wearing civilian clothing and blurring the distinction between humanitarians and the military, the numerous security incidents that involved humanitarians in Afghanistan and the merged security–development agenda that gave rise to the PRTs.

Insecurity and strategy

For Afghanistan, the impact of the attacks on 11 September 2001 was profound. They marked the beginning of the end for the ruling Taliban regime and the start of a state-building effort that is not yet complete. They also led to a new phase in the military–humanitarian relationship, with each component being increasingly vocal and active in the areas of relief, reconstruction and development. In Afghanistan, there was a consistent pushing of the military of different nations, sometimes with different objectives, into activities traditionally carried out by NGOs (Halliday 2002, Chayes 2006). With no clear blueprint, NATO borrowed from previous conflicts. This led to experimentation and hybridization, largely based on three factors – the characteristics of the war, the role of force and the humanitarian response.

The nature of the war in Afghanistan during the period examined here was not "new" but it did have elements that made the approaches to it somewhat different. In previous chapters it was shown that conflict can be seen to take place across a spectrum of different intensities. High-intensity conflict is characterized by the use of technology, conventional tactics and force-on-force battles. Low-intensity conflict is associated with guerrilla tactics and a heavy emphasis on political–military strategies. Afghanistan from 2001 to 2014 showed characteristics of both, generating four significant implications for military–humanitarian relationships.

First, the nature of the insurgency threat, technology, terrain, past experience by both the Soviets and the interventions of the 1990s influenced greatly the initial military involvement in Afghanistan (Larsdotter 2005). In the weeks following the 2001 attacks on the United States, three initial steps were taken by the international forces. Advising and equipping the anti-Taliban opposition were undertaken with a relatively small amount of forces on the ground (Moore 2003, Ryan 2007). The building of logistical support facilities was critical as well, first in the Central Asian republics of Uzbekistan and Tajikistan and later in Afghanistan itself. At the same time, preparation of the battlefield, especially in terms of intelligence and strategic air strikes, provided momentum for the eventual capitulation of Taliban forces (Berntsen and Pezzullo 2006). This involved gathering information on which NGOs were operating in the country. In Afghanistan, there were conventional-style troops and key points such as military facilities, airfields and the homes of leaders (the "centers of gravity") that could be attacked using a high-intensity strategy. The United States-led Coalition Force began operations on 7 October 2001 with air operations and the insertion of intelligence and Special Forces personnel who worked alongside the anti-Taliban Northern Alliance (Shura-yi Nazar) with an objective of eliminating Taliban rule in Afghanistan and to capture Al-Qaeda adherents. Because a large conventional assault was not used (necessitating a large-scale invasion), a low-intensity strategy was followed in which soldiers wore civilian clothing and maintained a heavy reliance on air power. The front lines could be carpet-bombed with B-52s, while specifically identified homes could be targeted and "taken out" with precision-guided munitions and special operations direct action.

Second, the conflict in Afghanistan was expansive in its scope in policy and application (Jones 2009). While support of the anti-Taliban resistance in Afghanistan started well before 11 September 2001 in response to increasing attacks against United States overseas interests (Coll 2005), the so-called Global War on Terror was not underway in earnest until the first American military action in Afghanistan. Given the strong emphasis the United States placed on this strategy, it was almost immediately recognized that a stabilization force was needed to pacify and support the historically weak Afghan state. In the past, an occupying force would have assumed these responsibilities but the United States and its allies showed an unwillingness to commit their resources to such an effort, especially when planning and executing the invasion of Iraq (Tanner 2003). Within this context, the post-2001 period has been marked by the competing concerns of pursing the remnants of the Taliban through direct-action counter-terror missions (known as "kinetic operations") and providing a degree of assistance and stability to the new government through the UN-mandated International Security Assistance Force (ISAF) (Saikal 2006).

Third, attempts at peacebuilding which combined security and development objectives played a central role at a time when violence continued under a growing insurgency. Part of the reconstruction effort was the disarmament, demobilization and reintegration (DDR) process that began in April 2003. Supported by the Japanese, and managed by the UNDP, it was called the "New Beginnings Programme." Initial estimates of the number of Afghan soldiers to be included as part of DDR ranged from 60,000 to 200,000 fighters (Jones et al. 2005) and, in the end, 62,376 Afghans were demobilized (UNDP 2006). However, there are estimates that between 500,000 and 800,000 Afghans were under arms when the invasion took place (Sedra 2002, p. 39). To extend the program, a process of disarming illegal armed groups was started when formal DDR activities ended in 2005. Many of the normal problems present in other countries that have undergone a demobilization process, such as Liberia and Mozambique, occurred, including reporting of erroneous troop numbers and turning-in of shoddy weapons for monetary rewards while keeping the best and buying more (ICG 2005, Bhatia 2007).

Fourth, violence in the period since the fall of the Taliban regime has proved intractable, which had a significant impact on the security of humanitarians. As will be discussed later in this chapter, there was also a low level of enthusiasm from local Afghan commanders who were uncertain of the future and did not want change to come about or to relinquish power (Jalali 2007). For a number of reasons that will be examined later, the security situation worsened during the post-Taliban government. As time progressed, the government began to solidify and the insurgency's strength grew, as did the intensity of the conflict. This incorporated a greater use of propaganda, mass-casualty bombings, increased poppy production helping to support the insurgency and skirmishes to draw in international military forces. From 2003 onward, when international military forces adopted a counter-insurgency strategy, "winning hearts and minds" became more important. An emphasis on "security, restoring essential services and meeting humanitarian needs of the local populace while fostering long term development of indigenous capacity, fostering a viable market economy and promoting rule of law and democratic institutions" emerged (Johnson et al. 2011, p. 2). This was confounded by poor ability of international forces to distinguish between civilians and anti-government fighters (Kilcullen 2009).

Influenced by developments in Iraq, this strategy evolved into what became generically known as counter-insurgency. Supported by the United Kingdom, Denmark and the Netherlands, it was formally put on ISAF's agenda at the Riga Summit in 2006 (Williams 2011). ISAF's "new" role in Afghanistan went well beyond traditional military–civilian agreements and positioned the military in a leading role to promote economic growth, political stability and development (Lawry 2009, Jakobsen 2010, Patterson and Robinson 2011). While the objective remained to stabilize the country, counter-insurgency defined success not as "the destruction in a given area of the insurgent's forces and their political organization ... [but] the permanent isolation of the insurgents from the population, isolation not enforced upon the population, but maintained by and with the population" (Turcan 2011, p. 6). Since counter-insurgency legitimatized the use of non-traditional military methods to win the hearts and minds of the local population, bottom-up approaches were given particular emphasis by ISAF, and psychological operations were tasked not only to analyze the local population but also to influence public opinion through the media to align citizens' interest with military objectives (Frerks et al. 2006, Turcan 2011).

Counter-insurgency had experienced limited success, due to the military's inability to meet the combined demands of security, governance, economic and humanitarian issues (Beljan 2013). The election of President Barack Obama in late 2008 brought a new perspective to the conflict, at least within the United States government. Within the new administration, there was a debate between those who sought to continue a solely counter-insurgency-focused approach and those who wanted to emphasize counter-terror. In the end, Obama chose a compromise between the two. In 2009, United States General Stanley McChrystal thus re-emphasized interagency coordination with civilian actors. Civil–military coordination was, however, problematic, "due to incompatible planning, training, and conduct of operations and differences in organizational culture ... This unique civil–military integration in the difficult security environment of Afghanistan posed serious challenges in the absence of clear doctrinal guidelines on how to conduct joint, combined civil–military efforts, to include governance and developmental programs" (Beljan 2013, p. 3). In an attempt to bridge the "civilian gap," money was used as a "weapon system" to advance counter-insurgency objectives through the United States Commander's Emergency Response Program (Patterson and Robinson 2011). This funding was used to respond quickly to local needs to reduce violence and "improve security through the purchase of loyalty or information, improve governance, protect forces, build capacity, or improve the relationship between the Afghan population and government" (Fischerkeller 2011, p. 5). There is, however, an extensive literature that indicates that counter-insurgency projects have been stymied by corruption, local power dynamics and poor governance and thus not only have been ineffective in addressing economic and humanitarian needs but, in some cases, have brought further conflict and insecurity (Williamson 2011).

Supporting McChrystal's call for interagency coordination, President Obama also increased civilian staff embedded in military units (Beckwith 2012). Countries that supported counter-insurgency followed the call for civilian surge, nearly doubling troop levels including PRT (Jackson and Haysom 2013). By 2011, the 27 PRTs in Afghanistan were under the leadership of 14 nations. Some – like Italy, Spain, South Korea, Norway, Sweden and Finland – opted for peace-support operations, while others stuck to a traditional counter-insurgency strategy (Jakobsen 2010, Fishstein and Wilder 2011). Various PRTs thus took different approaches to the civilian surge, some having an independent mandate while others were under military hierarchy (Date 2011, Williams 2011). The ratio of civilian/military could range from 3–5 per 80 military staff to 30 per 100 soldiers, depending on the leading PRT nation (Ryerson 2012). Despite ISAF's supposed common mission, the varied structures and leadership of the PRTs created an inconsistent approach to counter-insurgency. Most nations that implemented "pure" strategy were mainly based in the south and east of Afghanistan and consisted of the biggest troop contributors and donors, resulting in a louder voice than smaller nations and troops based in the calmer north and west. The political influence of "big" nations and insurgency activity in the south have taken a lot of media attention and presented a regional experience almost as a national position (Fishstein and Wilder 2011). PRTs in highly insecure areas (mostly in the south and east) argued strongly for counter-insurgency, since they are one of the very few actors who can deliver aid in these conditions (Ryerson 2012).

Despite the increase in troops, funding and civilian support, insurgency activity had increased over the years and, in 2010, a Taliban Reconciliation and the Afghan Peace and Reintegration Program was introduced in the hope of reducing insecurity (Zyck 2012, FCO 2010). It aimed to reintegrate "former" Taliban fighters, increase the local rule of law and strengthen Afghan security forces (UN 2013). By 2011, 1,948 fighters had received assistance for their "reintegration" but 90 per cent of these were in the north and west rather than in more insecure areas (Zyck 2012). By 2013, the number had risen to 6,840 and had been accompanied by "Village Stability Operations" that embedded Special Forces in villages to train local citizens as "local police" – a move that surprised many Afghans, since much had been done to remove guns from communities in the previous years (Beljan 2013). The Afghan government also tried to launch a peace process with the Taliban alongside these efforts but, despite preliminary talks and negotiations, the effort stalled when former president Burhanuddin Rabbani, the chair of the High Peace Council, was assassinated in late 2011 (Sheikh and Greenwood 2013).

Amid a consistently volatile security environment, NATO presented its exit strategy at the Lisbon Summit in 2010. It recognized Afghanistan's needs for development aid, human rights and governance, and reassured the Afghan government that the transition would be condition based and not calendar driven (NATO 2010a). A revised policy under President Obama would eventually bring a surge of ISAF force strength, reaching a peak of roughly 140,000 troops in mid-2011, and a shift toward greater Afghan government responsibility for security. In 2012, NATO declared at the Chicago Summit that by "the end of 2014, when the Afghan Authorities will have full security responsibility, the NATO-led combat mission will end" and ISAF would no longer be responsible for security but would, rather, provide training and advice to the Afghan National Security Force (NATO 2012, p. 1, DOD 2012). The transition entailed four tranches in which the latter would gradually take over; by the end of 2013, 87 per cent of the population in 23 out of 34 provinces were in full transition, but staffing was still precarious and 140,881 out of 157,000 Afghan National Police were being funded externally (NATO 2013, UN 2013). By December 2014, the ISAF mission officially ended and a follow-on mission (called "Resolute Support") remains to assist Afghan security forces through training and other types of support.

Coherence and the role of force

In Afghanistan, many Western governments and international organizations felt that using a "coherence policy" was the way to employ force and achieve reconstruction at the same time. It was adopted in Sweden's "Shared Responsibility – Policy for Global Development" Bill, the Canadian government's "3-D approach" and the UN's "integrated mission" concept that melds military peacekeeping forces with civilian peacebuilding agencies. These competing missions caused tension between ISAF (established under a UN resolution) and the United States-led Coalition Force. This started with the initial intervention. After the fall of Kabul in early December 2001, the military units most closely associated with humanitarians took on a significant role. The Coalition Joint Civil–Military Operations Task Force was, for instance, established for strategic command of civil affairs personnel. As some saw it, this group "served essentially as a military NGO, trying to fill humanitarian aid gaps that seemed to exist among the civilian NGOs that were deployed on the ground" (Williams 2005, p. 204). At the tactical level, following the deployment of Special Forces operational detachments in key areas, the Coalition deployed Coalitional Humanitarian Liaison Cells (CHLC; pronounced *"chicklets"*) in several urban areas around Afghanistan. While these sought open cooperation with NGOs, they did not open "store front" offices as was a common practice in other post-conflict situations. They performed a variety of tasks, including assessments, information sharing, contracting "quick impact" projects and supporting combat operations. These units had a mixed mission and were "operating across the spectrum" of the high-intensity conflict and low-intensity conflict paradigms. They might work alongside NGOs one day and be involved in "kinetic" offensive operations the next. During their initial arrival in Afghanistan, they sometimes operated in civilian clothes and supported USAID by providing logistics and security (James 2003, Morris 2003). This became very contentious and, as will be discussed later, was taken up by humanitarians as an advocacy issue. Depending on their mandate and mentality, some humanitarians cooperated with the CHLC while others kept them at arm's length.

Figure 5.1 represents a typology of the civil–military relationship in Afghanistan. This separates the entities into two Western-led spheres or "realms" – one military and one civilian – but these were often blurred in practice. Within the "military realm" the United States-led "anti-terror" Coalition (officially called Operation Enduring Freedom (OEF)) carried out low-intensity combat operations that included reconstruction and activities to win the "hearts and minds" of Afghans. In support of the Afghan government, ISAF carried out stability and peacekeeping operations in the north and west (and now part of the South) of Afghanistan. Although the number fluctuated, there were approximately 17,000 Coalition troops and close to 9,000 ISAF troops deployed throughout the country in 2006. In 2009, President Obama authorized an additional 30,000 American troops, most to the South, increasing ISAF numbers to 150,000 by 2011, compared to the Afghan National Security Forces total of 266,000 (Welle 2010, ICOS 2011). ISAF's withdrawal started, however, the same year and its numbers were down to 66,000 by May 2012 (ICOS, 2011, DOD, 2012). By 2013, many military units had been redirected from military activities to assist with physical reconstruction, micro-grants for small businesses and advisory roles for public administrators and national troops (Beljan 2013). As part of the Civilian Surge, the United States had also deployed 700 civilians to join ISAF troops and increased Embassy staff from 300 to 1,000 to support USAID and the Departments of State, Justice and Agriculture (Welle 2010, Chemlali and Sadat 2013). In order to improve civil–military coordination, United States Embassy staff were reorganized by function rather than by agency, but two-thirds of civilians were stationed in Kabul, due to security restrictions. In all, despite the years ISAF spent trying to expand beyond Kabul, its imminent end of mission is reducing NATO's overall presence to the center of political power in Afghanistan.

Categorization			Actors
NATO and partner governments	Within military camps	Military realm (ISAF/OEF)	Combat and peacekeeping troops • Afghan National Army • ISAF combat/Force protection troops • Coalition combat/Fortce protection troops
			Psychological operations Within both ISAF and the Coalition
			Facilitating rule of law by strengthening: • Afghan National Police • Judiciary • DDR • Counter-narcotics
			Military outreach to civil actors and civilians • Civil–military coordination • Rehabilitation by the military • Country-specific agencies
	Partly embedded	Civil realm	Foreign affairs and development agencies of donor governments • Political advisors • Development (e.g. USAID, CIDA, DFID)
Inter-govern mental	Outside military camps		International organizations • UNAMA and other UN agencies • IOM and other UN-affiliated organizations
Non-governmental			Civil society • International NGOs • Afghan NGOs • CBOs, *shuras*, etc. • Other civil society
			Private sector • Local contractors • International contractors

Figure 5.1 Civil–military actors in Afghanistan

Source: Adapted from Frerks et al. (2006, p. 55)

As part of the relief and development effort (the "civil realm"), there were a plethora of organizations and entities. In 2004, there were over 2,000 NGOs registered with the Afghan Ministry of Planning, but that number has come down significantly and, by 2008, 1,395 NGOs were officially registered with Ministry of Economy, comprised of 1,094 local NGOs and 301 international NGOs (INGOs) (ADB 2009). By 2010, the number had slightly increased to 1,468 NGOs and 1,716 social organizations (Counterpart 2011). As the military transition advanced, the number of local NGOs increased to 1,707 in 2012, most of which were small "briefcase" organizations or construction companies (Nijssen 2012).

Crossing the two realms were the PRTs. These units were important because they became a fixture throughout Afghanistan and a key locus for interaction between the military and humanitarians. In the summer of 2002, as the mission changed from combat to one of supporting stability, the United States government launched combined civil–military PRTs. Initially it was thought that the PRTs served as a stop-gap measure in areas where the ISAF was not deployed and the nascent Afghan Transitional Authority failed to hold sway. While differences existed between national contingents within ISAF, the PRTs were perceived as the "'tip of the iceberg' attached to a force support structure, including quick reaction forces, air cover, emergency medical evacuation, and logistic support system. A PRT without links to military forces is not conceivable" (Jalali 2007, p. 36).

While initially very slow to deploy, the PRTs were first established in Gardez and expanded to selected cities, although to none in the more volatile South of the country. The PRTs were eventually placed in 32 provinces around Afghanistan by 2006. The approaches followed by the various country contingents differed considerably. In general, they consisted of "carrots" in the form of foreign assistance and "sticks" such as the use of force. The goal of the PRTs was to bring about change in their respective provinces while maintaining their security (through "force protection"). While the American units were widely thought to be heavy handed, other national contingents positioned themselves as a more benign force, particularly the early phases of ISAF. The Dutch contingent, for example, embedded the idea of winning hearts and minds. One of their commanders put it this way: "We're not here to fight the Taliban. We're here to make them irrelevant" (New York Times 2007, p. 1). This was similar to the view of United States Secretary of State Colin Powell, who stated "I am serious about making sure we have the best relationship with the NGOs who are such a force multiplier for us, such an important part of our combat team," drawing heavy criticism for such an overt co-option of NGOs by the United States government (Powell 2001, p. 1; Lischer 2007).

There was also concern about the policy known as the "light footprint." The Senior Representative of the UN Secretary General, Lakhdar Brahimi, stated that the UN Assistance Mission to Afghanistan (UNAMA), formed under Security Council Resolution 1401 on 28 March 2002, "will operate with a 'light footprint,' keeping the international UN presence to the minimum required, while our Afghan colleagues are given as much of a role as possible" (cited in Roberts 2009, p. 17). The United States military initially operated under "force caps" approved by the then Secretary of Defense, Donald Rumsfeld, which limited the number of troops deployed in 2001–2002. This concept was to maintain itself for nearly the entire 12-year period under examination here. Testifying before Congress in 2009 on the surge and ongoing operations in Afghanistan, Navy Admiral Eric Olson explained that the United States would use "as small a footprint as we can get away with."

At least part of the idea was that existing capabilities within the country and Afghans worldwide would assume control of their country and not require the same level of international involvement as had been the case in Kosovo, Timor-Leste and Liberia. Afghanistan was considered beyond the capacity of a single country or body, including the UN, to administer. Even while UN staff were extolling the virtues of the light footprint (for example, during a UN-led coordination meeting in 2002, NGO staff were urged to use standard automobiles in Kabul at a time when the UN was importing large vehicles and the foreign militaries were expanding operations), divergent views were formed. Some argued that the operation in Afghanistan had been "done on the cheap" from the start and had been "given proportionately many fewer peacekeepers and less resources" than other interventions (ICG 2006, p. i). Others held that too much funding had come from external donors and that this overwhelmed Afghan capacities (Nixon 2007). Whatever the truth, it is certainly the case that, as Figure 5.2 shows, the numbers of military personnel in Afghanistan were far below those of many other post-conflict situations.

A further concern was what NATO called a range of "national caveats" which limited the use of force. Germany, for example, prohibited its aircraft from certain types of military operations and its soldiers from patrolling at night. Others, such as New Zealand, placed their soldiers in relatively safe areas such as Bamyan province. Some of these were more passive. The United States, for instance, could

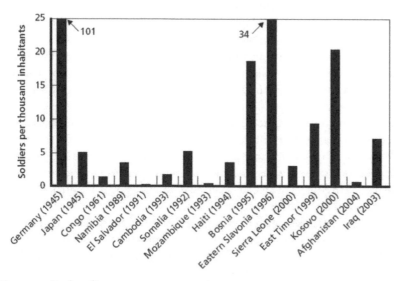

Figure 5.2 Peak military presence per capita

Source: Jones et al. (2005, p. 82)

be seen, initially at least, as having a stipulation against nation building because of the reluctance to commit its military resources to the reconstruction effort (Rubin 2007). This changed over time but hampered the deployment of a force more finely tuned to the needs of the situation. The context in which the Taliban were not completely defeated, the military's hesitant presence outside of Kabul and high hopes among the Afghan people even while large swathes of the country were "left to fester" resulted in a "crucial loss of momentum" (ICG 2006, p. 4). The 2006 NATO summit in Riga was meant to reduce these restrictions, solidify commitment and bring about stability through unity of effort, but this was obstructed by the powerful concerns of national constituents among each member country. Instead, NATO took the opportunity to promote civilian and military coordination further and encouraged the UN to take the lead in creating interagency collaboration to support the Afghan National Development Strategy – an approach reinforced at the subsequent Bucharest Summit of 2008 (NATO, 2008).

This was, however, vigorously obstructed by the establishment of an anti-government insurgency related to, and partially supported by, opium production and popular local and regional discontent stemming mainly from a lack of perceived progress and a frustration with corruption (Karzai 2007). The emergence of armed opposition groups (AOGs) can be attributed to four sources. First, although there had been a relatively swift response by NATO following 11 September 2001, there had been a slow response with regard to foreign assistance. It first went to the comparatively supportive cities and areas of the North. Some saw this as a reward for peace but it could also be seen as a punishment for those areas that were the Taliban strongholds. Under these conditions, the linkage between security and development was relatively strong, and important for understanding the military–humanitarian relationship in Afghanistan. In place of this slowly coming assistance and the vacuum of a weak central government, high levels of insecurity prevailed and thwarted reconstruction. In particular, Pakistan in the East and South and Iran in the West, where insecurity was at its highest, were known for supplying weapons and other support to their favorite groups (Sedra 2002, Rubin and Armstrong 2003, Jones et al. 2005). The drug trade in particular has been cited as an important financial support mechanism for AOGs (Mansfield and Pain 2006, Riphenburg 2006). The increasing poppy cultivation coincided with the worsening security because it was a funding source for the insurgency. As will be discussed later, many NGOs reduced or modified their activities as a result of insecurity (ANSO/CARE 2005).

Second, there was an apparent vacuum left by weak governance. Historically, Afghanistan has had a weak state, with the central government extending little beyond major urban areas. This gave local power-brokers sway over considerable areas of the country and was arguably made worse by a lack of roads and communications. Because of this state weakness, at least in part, the remnants of the Taliban did not fully disband following their defeat in 2001. Instead, they faded as a movement into areas along and across the Pakistan border. Between 2002 and 2004 the different AOGs, including the Taliban, regrouped and prepared themselves for new offensives, becoming a formidable force in southern and eastern areas of the country – especially along the frontier. Increasingly, the insurgency depended on training camps in Pakistan, weapons from Iran and "exchanges" from Iraq to learn tactics to use improvised explosive devices and explosively formed projectiles (Humayoon 2007). Insurgency operations increased as time went on, reaching 7,612 a year by 2011 (ICOS, 2010, 2011).

Third was the grievance of key individuals and the presence of ethnic divides, especially among the Pashtun (ICG 2003). While there was traditional animosity between groups such as the Tajiks and Hazaras, the Pashtuns were seen as a dominant group without which stability in the country would be difficult if not impossible. Elements of the Pashtun learned early that direct engagement against international military forces was not as successful as employing low-intensity tactics and strategies. This included attacking "soft targets" such as ordinary civilians, government workers and humanitarians (Karzai 2007, p. 63). In the process, anti-government leaders were to lose their "fear of the B-52," which was a common worry following the demonstration of air power of 2001. Although it is often portrayed that the Taliban had a single command center, it seems likely that a modified "network" structure was used, giving rise to individual decision makers (Hoffman 2004). As such, there were several AOGs, loosely affiliated and sometimes at odds with each other, which were responsible for insurgent activity. These included a number of different commanders such as Hazrat Ali, Padsha Khan Zadran and Amanullah Khan. Most were small, but groups such as Hizbe-e Islami (under Gulbuddin Hekmatyar) held wider influence and were a larger concern for the Coalition Force. By the end of 2004, this fragmented mélange had coalesced into three main groups – the Taliban, Hezb-e Islami and the Haqqani Network (Cordesman and Chair 2006).

Finally, because AOGs are sub-national groups, they are not signatories to treaties that follow IHL and often did not recognize the distinction between military and civilian. The distinction between civilians and combatants was not always recognized and targets such as schools and other reconstruction projects were open to deliberate attack (Gabriel 2007). In addition to much empirical evidence, this is demonstrated by the Taliban's *Layha*, made available in December 2006, entitled "The rules and regulations of Taliban movement, distributed initially among the 33 members of the *Shura*, the highest Taliban council, at their meeting during Ramadan 2006, from the highest leader of the Islamic Emirates of Afghanistan." Among its rules, Rule 8 states that "a provincial, district or regional commander may not sign a contract to work for a non-governmental organization or accept money from an NGO. The *Shura* (the highest Taliban council) alone may determine all dealings with NGOs." Rule 26 is more explicit in its opposition to NGOs and in communicating its view that combines the civil society with the state:

> Those NGOs that come to the country under the rule of the infidels must be treated as the government is treated. They have come under the guise of helping people but in fact are part of the regime. Thus we tolerate none of their activities, whether it be building of streets, bridges, clinics, schools, madrassas [schools for Qur'anic study] or other works. If a school fails to heed a warning to close, it must be burned. But all religious books must be secured beforehand. (Cited in Euben and Zaman 2009, p. 417)

The position among the Taliban changed, however, throughout the years and some aid groups were able to develop working relationships. The *Layha* has been updated at least three times, reflecting the Taliban's rules of engagement during war. In 2009 Taliban emissaries approached aid agencies to increase their knowledge and understanding of their operations and encouraged them to register with the Taliban to avoid casualties and unnecessary attacks (Jackson and Giustozzi, 2012). The registration "is granted on several additional conditions, including a pledge not to commit 'hostile' acts against the Taliban" and a clear separation of humanitarian and military activities per IHL (Jackson and Giustozzi 2012, p. 10).

The architecture of aid

Amid the backdrop of insecurity and underdevelopment, a complex system of assistance was developed. A description of this assistance architecture is important for at least three reasons. First, it shows the extent to which the landscape has changed from previous attempts at coherence and strategic coordination undertaken during the 1990s. Second, because aid organizations were heavily involved in post-invasion reconstruction, the assistance architecture provided a rationale for their work in Afghanistan. As key implementers of assistance projects, these organizations had a central place in the provision of relief, reconstruction and development in the country. Yet, while NGOs are often described as a "partner," the precise nature of this role is unclear. Finally, the assistance architecture is important because it demonstrates a manifestation of policy coherence between the humanitarian and military spheres, but where security and the responsibilities of the military have a heightened role. For this reason, politics are central to understanding the aid architecture.

The Bonn Agreement reached in December 2001 established the foundation for the post-Taliban era. It was not a peace agreement but, rather, a document that set the terms of regime change. The Bonn Agreement, and the follow-on *Loya Jirga* eighteen months later, consolidated many of the gains made by the Northern Alliance (ICG 2003, Starr 2006). For many, it was a document dictated by the winners. Annex One of the Agreement, dealing with the ISAF, explicitly states that the foreign militaries should be part of the reconstruction effort in the country: "it would also be desirable if such a force were to assist in the rehabilitation of Afghanistan's infrastructure" (GOA 2001, p. 7). This resulted in a security–development framework bringing together three mechanisms: the Afghan Development Forum (ADF), the National Development Strategy (NDS) and the Afghan Compact starting in 2006.

An ADF was held each year, starting in late 2002, until 2006. While its exact purpose changed from year to year, it was meant to allow specific government–donor issues to be resolved, especially for budgeting and strategic planning support. According to the Afghan government, the ADF "is a particularly important meeting" for three reasons:

> (1) donors still fund more than 93 per cent of Afghanistan's national budget (ordinary and development) and are facing increased pressure to fund other contexts (like the Tsunami response), (2) Afghanistan's reconstruction/development efforts need to be accelerated, and (3) the new cabinet needs to share its vision and strategy and also build its relationship with donors. (GOA 2007)

In 2006, the Joint-Coordination and Monitoring Board replaced the ADF, but continued its primary responsibility to oversee the implementation of the NDS, increase aid effectiveness and secure fiscal transparency. This was updated for the subsequent five-year period, 2008–13.

Second, the NDS was created as the overarching framework used by the government to promote development throughout the country. Building on the work of the ADF and the Consultative Groups which address specific sectors such as health, education and social protection, the NDS was planned in 2005–2006 in a phased approach based on widely used developmental models including planned strategy, broad consultation and use of available data on poverty. The NDS consists of three pillars: security, governance, and social and development under which a number of elements and activities along with five "crosscutting" issues are arranged as shown in Figure 5.3. Within each pillar are specific concerns such as defense placed under security and education found under the social and development pillar. Some issues, such as counter-narcotics and border, tribal and *Kuchi* affairs, appear in more than one pillar while some issues are cross-cutting including gender and regional cooperation.

The NDS was created as a "half-way" step for Afghanistan in developing a full Poverty Reduction Strategy Paper, a key mechanism used in more stable developing countries to access funding from international financial institutions. According to the Afghan government, it has been "committed to using the National Development Strategy as its overarching framework to guide the promotion of growth and prosperity for all and the reduction of poverty and vulnerability" (GOA 2007). The NDS was "patterned on the Multi-Year Road Map used to coordinate NATO SFOR [Stabilization Force] and the international community efforts in Bosnia" (Maloney 2007, p. 37). Although the NDS was an Afghan government document, the Bosnian Road Map concept was used after Canadian advisors became frustrated, "after four years of uncoordinated efforts," with the lack of an overall strategy (Maloney 2007, p. 37). This includes a framework for working with both the

New Pillar Structure

PILLAR 1	PILLAR 2			PILLAR 3			
SECURITY	GOVERNANCE			SOCIAL and DEVELOPMENT			
Security	Good Governance and Rule of Law	Infrastructure and Natural Resources	Education, Cultural, Media and Sport	Health and Nutrition	Agriculture and Rural Development	Social Protection	Enabling Private Sector Development
National Security Council	National Assembly	Public Works	Education	Public Health	Agriculture, Animal Husbandry and Food	Refugees and Repatriation	Economy
Interior Affairs	Justice	Transport	Higher Education			Women's Affairs	Finance
Defence	Supreme Court	Communications	Women's Affairs		Rural Rehabilitation and Development	Martyrs and Disabled	Central Bank
Border, Tribal Affairs and Kuchis	Hajj and Endowment	Water and Energy	Youth Affairs			Borders, Tribal Affairs and Kuchis	Information, Culture and Tourism
Foreign Affairs (Mine Action)	Women's Affairs	Urban Development and Housing	Labour and Social Affairs		Counter Narcotics (Alternative Livelihoods)	Labour and Social Affairs	Audit and Control Office
Counter Narcotics	Attorney General	Mines and Industries	Information, Culture and Tourism		Water and Energy	Youth Affairs	Financial Service Providers
National Directorate of Security	Civil Service Commission	Geodesy and Cartography	Border, Tribal Affairs and Kuchis		National Environment Protection	Office of Disaster Preparedness	Chambers of Commerce (AICC)
DDR	Audit and Control Office	National Environment Protection	National Olympic Committee			Red Crescent	
	Anti-Corruption Commission		Science Academy				
	Human Rights Commission						

Gender Equity (Cross Cutting Issue 1) – Women's Affairs (Lead)
Counter Narcotics (Cross Cutting Issue 2) – Counter Narcotics (Lead)
Regional Cooperation (Cross Cutting Issue 3) – Foreign Affairs (Lead)
Environment (Cross Cutting Issue 4)
Anti-Corruption (Cross Cutting Issue 5)

Figure 5.3 The National Development Strategy framework

Source: GOA (2007)

Afghan National Army and the Afghan National Police, as well as the Afghan intelligence apparatus (comprised of the National Security Council and the National Directorate of Security). In 2005, a sub-national coordination mechanism known as the Provincial Development Committees was created, with a corresponding Provincial Development Plan. These mechanisms contained no additional financial support, which meant that they were not as effective as intended (Jalal 2013). By 2010, the NDS implementation strategy had been reformulated around 22 National Priority Programs covering six sectors: Peace, Human Resources, Governance, Infrastructure Development, Private Sector Development, and Agriculture and Rural Development.

Finally, following the formal end of the Bonn Process in September 2005 and elections at the provincial level and in the Parliament, a conference was held in London which established the Afghan Compact. This was seen as a "make or break period" for the country (Mollett cited in BAAG 2006, p. 1). Launched in January 2006, its aim was to address the most pressing problems that had yet to be resolved by the assistance efforts until that point: security, governance, the rule of law, human rights, counter-narcotics and sustainable economic and social development. While it was claimed to be a joint effort, the Compact came about as the result of donor instigation and it is a common feeling in Kabul that the international donors dictated the policy. This is perhaps unsurprising, given that the preceding Berlin Conference of April 2004 had seen aid pledges of more than US$8 billion. At the London Conference in 2006, another US$10 billion was pledged over the following five years.

However, in comparison, this level of funding was less than in many other postconflict situations, such as Bosnia and East Timor (Jones et al. 2005). When military and development spending are compared, the substantial discrepancy is clear. From 2002 until 2009 US$286.4 billion went to Afghanistan but only 9.4 per cent of it went to aid; the rest went to foreign military operations, security-related support and peacekeeping (Poole 2011). As Figure 5.4 illustrates, even though a sizeable portion of American funding is disbursed though USAID, over 56 per cent of it goes through the military and its Commanders' Emergency Response Program, which can dispensed quickly and tailored to battlefield conditions (Fishstein and Wilder 2011, Johnson et al. 2011). To date, it has been primarily spent on transportation and storage (61 per cent), education (9 per cent) and reconstruction (7 per cent) projects, but the fact that the "U.S. military [is equipped] with more financial, personnel, and material resources, and far greater reach than either USAID or the State Department, inevitably makes the military's role strong and potentially dominant" (Fishstein and Wilder 2011, p. 18).

Moreover, due to the geographical presence of the United States military, most funding is spent in insecure areas in the South, primarily Pashtun, which creates a disproportionate aid distribution. In the initial 2000s, most funding went to relatively secure and "cooperative" areas in the North and Center but this was later

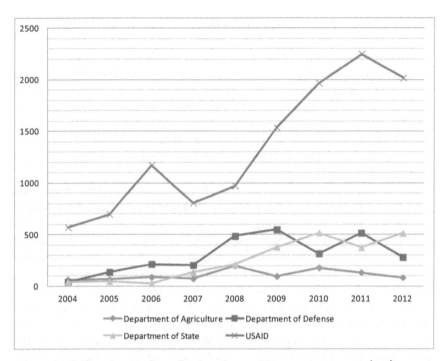

Figure 5.4 Disbursements from the three largest US agencies 2004-12 ($m)

Source: Greenbook, http://gbk.eads.usaidallnet.gov/query/do?_program=/eads/gbk/
tablesByCountry&cocode=7AFG

reversed. USAID, for example, spent 77 per cent of its funding between 2009 and
2010 in the South, Southwest and East of Afghanistan (Fishstein and Wilder, 2011).
This increased in 2011, potentially creating insecurity incentives in volatile areas
while "punishing" secure areas by redirecting funds where assistance activities are
least able to be sustained (NRC et al., 2009).

Although many have highlighted the lack of funds devoted to the central government, which thus contributed to a lack of state effectiveness (Rubin 2007), there was
also an inability by the government to spend what funds it had been allocated. In the
years examined here, the highest expenditure rates consist of 50–60 per cent (by the
Ministry of Finance and the Ministry of Rural Rehabilitation and Development),
whereas many ministries, such as health, have trouble spending more than 25 per
cent of what they receive on a yearly basis. Donors, however, agreed in 2010 to
increase support to 50 per cent and align 80 per cent of aid to national priorities;
these have yet to be reached in 2014. NGOs continued to fill in the gaps, which have
access to additional money not part of the "official" funding channels. Some 70 per
cent of United States development aid went through UN agencies, contractors and
NGOs during the five-year period 2001–2006 (Haidari 2007). Moreover, between

2002 and 2010, 82 per cent of on-budget support was redirected to NGOs through subcontracts and national programs (Sulehria 2013). Overall, 10–15 per cent of off-budget support is implemented by NGOs (Cornish 2007). In 2005 international organizations, such as the UN, primarily funded Afghan NGOs, but by 2011 only 21 per cent of them had received such support (Counterpart 2011).

In addition, two further elements of the assistance architecture were established: one development oriented and one focused on security. First, the launch of a National Solidarity Program (NSP) followed a participatory and community-based approach. The program is lauded by many in Afghanistan because it empowered communities by moving decision making to the grassroots level. Second was the creation of Afghan Development Zones (ADZ) in late 2006, which further joined together security and development. The idea was forwarded by the United Kingdom working in the South of the country and approved by President Karzai in August of that year. They were intended to be areas in which "improvements in security and governance, delivered through an integrated approach by all relevant actors, will create conditions for sustained development" (ISAF 2006b, p. 1). The intention was to speed the delivery of assistance in a coordinated way in the most unstable areas of the country. It envisaged a coherent approach in which development actors collaborated with ISAF once an area was free of kinetic military operations. Concerns were immediately raised that this would leave areas outside the zone without assistance. Some felt that all of the country should be a "development zone," not just specific areas. From a security perspective, the Zones resembled the "strategic hamlets" used during the Vietnam War, where specific areas were designated differently from those open to military strike.

Humanitarian responses and tensions

By the summer of 2001, the humanitarian situation in Afghanistan was dire. Development activities had all but ceased and lifesaving programming made up the bulk of assistance and the main humanitarian concerns were food, displacement and protection. As detailed previously, the security situation was such that humanitarians had to either reach an accommodation with the Taliban in areas under their control or work with the Northern Alliance. Following standard practice, NGOs that had established programs before 2001 withdrew staff as a precautionary measure in anticipation of increased violence following the death of the Northern Alliance Commander Ahmed Shah Massoud that year. As the subsequent bombardment and invasion began, ongoing activities such as food delivery ceased. At the time, estimates were that one and a half million refugees might be created, over two million internally displaced persons and another four million needing assistance in their homes (Oxfam 2001). Severe drought had crippled the country, causing a 50 per cent harvest loss and massive internal displacement (Oxfam 2001). It was also widely believed that there would be significant war-related fatalities and increased suffering inside the country, especially during a prolonged campaign.

Reports of food insecurity proved to be unfounded and initial provision of health care was a top assistance priority. It was not long before humanitarians began to return, even as fighting intensified during the last months of 2001. "It was only days after the attacks that we started planning to establish programs," said an NGO staff member who worked in the country at that time, "initially people were evacuated but we knew that would change." As the offensive advanced and areas became accessible, assistance programs expanded in both breadth and scope. In addition to food, assistance to the displaced and protection activities, other priorities were added, including rehabilitation of schools, expansion of access to health care and establishment of development activities for women and other vulnerable groups. As such, the humanitarian goal was to alleviate human suffering and prepare for reconstruction. Within months, however, stability and state-building objectives had been added.

Similar to the regime change following the Soviet withdrawal in which humanitarians who were close to the Mujahideen were forced to distance themselves to find more space to operate, NGOs faced somewhat of an identity crisis as they tried to establish a new set of external relationships. For many NGOs which had operated for years under very insecure conditions, it was difficult to understand why there were so many changes with respect to programming and security. There was tension not only between NGOs and security organizations but between NGOs themselves. Some that had established programs in the country prior to 2001 felt that they were solely dedicated to helping Afghans and that the newly arrived NGOs were more closely associated with the international political and military presence who – in the view of some – placed greater priority on meeting the bare minimum of their contracts and less on respecting culture, fostering development and helping Afghans, despite the significant size of their budgets.

The influx of both Afghan and international relief workers did, however, have an appreciable impact on the ground and this was accelerated by the arrival of private companies, investment and the return of Afghans themselves. By 2005, roughly 4.6 million displaced Afghans had returned. During the Taliban regime, measles claimed 30,000 lives a year but an immunization campaign in 2002 vaccinated 11 million children and the disease was thought to have been effectively eradicated from the country (Oxfam 2006, p. ii). Economically, GDP growth remained consistently in the double digits over the period looked at here, averaging 11.87 per cent between 2003 and 2014 (*Afghan Statistical Yearbook* 2014). Roads have been paved, airports opened and markets have flourished. Some major investors were attracted, particularly in hospitality, transportation and telecommunications sectors. Although there had always been an urban–rural divide in Afghanistan, assistance did not completely miss the countryside. Crucially for improvement of conditions on the ground, there was declining child mortality (SCF 2007), many women-focused programs were established and school enrolment increased markedly with a net attendance rate of 54 per cent (or 2.3 million students) in 2003 (Afghan President Office 2005). According to UNICEF, primary school education net attendance reached 57 per cent by 2012 (the average remains just 73 per cent in least-developed countries).

Obviously, all was not fixed in Afghanistan. The country's first ever *Human Development Report* in 2004 found that it ranked 173 out of 177 countries – scoring just above Africa's least-developed countries (UNDP 2004). By 2013, it ranked 175 out of 186; although a bit better, it was not by much (UNDP, 2013). Despite the efforts to extend reconstruction to the countryside, rural areas, where the vast majority of the population lived (70 per cent according to some estimates, Goodson 2001), remained damaged and unemployment remained very high. More than 50 per cent of Afghan schools were thought to be "in need of major repair," leaving an estimated two million students in tents or without any shelter; 87 per cent of the population was without access to safe drinking water; and 92 per cent did not have access to adequate sanitation facilities (Oxfam 2006, p. ii). According to the WHO, Afghanistan has an "extremely high prevalence of chronic malnutrition with 39% of all under 5 children" (WHO 2014, p. 1). Each year, health campaigns are scaled back because of insecurity and polio remains endemic.

Given this lack of progress, there was disagreement about how much to collaborate with the government. Humanitarians needed access to help the population and this could no longer be done without this collaboration. As Starr observes, however, even here there was tension:

> From the government's perspective, the NGOs appeared to be undermining civil administration at the local level, even in cases where local officials were trying to do their jobs. NGO staffs made little attempt to hide their contempt for local bureaucrats, whom they regard, usually correctly, as corrupt. They also resented the central government's attempt to monitor and regulate their work. (2006, p. 116)

Perhaps because of massive funding, the large number of actors and the attention devoted to the country, well-founded criticisms against the aid community surfaced. One was the fact that many local NGOs were fronts for small contracting companies attempting to gain access to reconstruction funds. Although exact numbers are not available, many of those that have used the label "NGO" as a façade were founded by legitimate companies to take advantage of the reconstruction boom. With such a wide conceptualization of what an NGO might be, even private security contractors could be called NGOs. There were well-documented cases of contractor corruption and waste (see, for example, Stephens and Ottaway 2005). According to President Hamid Karzai, assistance was "wasted on high salaries, large overheads, luxury cars, luxury houses … that Afghanistan cannot afford at all" (AFP 2006, p. 1). Perhaps the most scathing calls for change came from the former Minister of Planning and MP for Kabul, Dr. Ramazon Bashardost. When the number of registered NGOs jumped from 500 at the end of 2001 to over 2,000 a year later, he called for a mass dismantling of the aid sector (Hewad 2004). This led some to accuse Dr. Bashardost of "indirectly contributing to violent attacks on NGOs through his repeated critical public remarks about their activities and functioning" (DOS 2004, p. 1).

Even before this there was discussion of what constituted an NGO in Afghanistan. In September 2002, the deputy head of UNAMA, Nigel Fischer, publicly asked "What are the roles of NGOs? ... I think we haven't had that discussion" (ACBAR 2002c, p. 1). Around the same time, the Agency Coordinating Body for Afghan Relief and Development (ACBAR) identified a number of problems, including a distance from government, insufficient information sharing, a "lack of [a] clear definition of NGO and its mandate in Afghanistan ... [and a] need for a clear legislation and regulatory system that is inclusive of NGOs" (ACBAR 2002b, p. 1). These pressures led to the creation of a new "NGO law" in 2005 (and amended in 2009) which reduced their number by almost half. Legitimate and properly established organizations were not affected by the new law, but confusion over what constitutes an NGO continued, leading ACBAR to publish a further critical document entitled *A Handbook for Understanding NGOs* in 2007.

Within this context, the intermingling of military, political and humanitarian and development concerns produced three key and closely linked tensions. The first relates to a "blurring of the line" between the armed and civilian spheres. This tension surfaced with the appearance of military personnel out of uniforms, wearing civilian clothing, and continued in various examples over the years. According to ACBAR (2002a, p. 1), "it was felt that further pressure needed to be put on the Coalition Forces to start wearing uniforms at all times in the field in order to distinguish them from humanitarian workers." One manager commented: "What got them [the Coalition soldiers] back into uniform were the photos of SF [Special Forces] in beards. This did more than the letters we sent them [the Pentagon]." Further, it was not just uniforms but also civilian 4x4 vehicles painted white and houses in residential areas in close proximity to humanitarians that sparked controversy. This was important not only in increasing insecurity but also in terms of international law, which requires combatants to be distinguishable (Pfanner 2004). Legally, all warring parties are responsible to protect affected civilians and assure humanitarian channels to assistance. Humanitarian impartiality thus specifies "the beneficiaries of aid and relief [as] those who are in need and who are suffering because of the conflict, not those who might be strategically important in overcoming insurgents" (Williamson 2011, p. 1049).

Since aid "made conditional on military or political cooperation threatens to overlook the humanitarian needs and poverty of politically marginal groups," this is in contrast to the counter-insurgency strategy, which targets population groups that oppose insurgents (Oxfam 2011, p. 18). Moreover, the exchange of humanitarian aid for information can put beneficiaries at further risk from insurgents, thus violating the principle of 'Do No Harm' (Oxfam 2011, NHRP 2010). In the year 2009, for instance, nine Afghans, including at least one community leader, were assassinated each week (Oxfam et al. 2010). Many NGOs have resisted the idea of humanitarian aid as a weapon to achieve military aims and control territory rather than alleviate suffering. They argue that the military reduces the local population "to one of the two conditions: either helpless and generally passive recipients of aid; or brutal, cowardly insurgents" (Ryerson 2012, p. 62). For many, an NGO approach to aid is "not compatible with the short-term imperatives which drive the military's stabilization strategy. The military's use of often costly, ineffective and unaccountable implementing partners is also highly problematic" (Kristovič and Tomić 2011, p. 72).

More generally, military leadership over civilian affairs is not accepted in Western liberal democracies but is "justified" in a peacebuilding context (Welle 2010). By raising these kinds of issues and "questioning the politicisation of aid and the notion of shared goals (commonly ascribed) amongst all 3-D actors, humanitarians are [however] now seen as obstructionist and antiquated by the political and military communities" (Cornish 2007, p. 3). The relationship between NGOs and the military is, as Cornish notes, further strained by the perception that "the US-led effort paid little heed to the laws of war … or to IHL." It is, as Cornish continues, "thus not surprising that there should be a lack of respect for the existing civil/military cooperation guidelines" (2007, pp. 23–4). In contrast, the armed forces generally see the two actors working in the same "business." The "Guide to NGOs for the Military," for example, states that "military personnel also often find themselves cycling out of active duty and entering the service of an NGO doing jobs similar to those they had in the military" (Lawry 2009, p. 49).

There is also a sense that NGOs *need* ISAF. The United States argues that without "COIN [counter-insurgency] and without the military's support, many of the humanitarian agencies – such as Oxfam – that raise such complaints, would not be able to enter the areas once controlled by insurgents" (IRIN 2009, p. 1). Echoing the earlier quote made by Colin Powell, it is "a widely held assumption in military and foreign policy circles … that development assistance is an important 'soft power' tool to win consent and to promote stabilization and security objectives" and they do not understand why humanitarian actors do not collaborate to win the war, which is perceived to be a common good (Fishstein and Wilder 2011, p. 8, Oxfam et al. 2010, Williamson 2011). Many NGOs, however, reject this notion: "NGOs do not represent a 'Soft Power' … The true nature of a Non Governmental Organisation is independent and thus does not support any military or political strategy" (ACBAR 2010b, p. 1). Some feel that the military tries to use their existence for inadequate, unethical and anti-humanitarian purposes. For example "the protection cluster in Afghanistan at some point had to refrain from including all information in minutes of meetings to ensure that information did not end up in the 'wrong hands' (i.e. the international military forces) and prevented staff other than from human rights/humanitarian sections from attending the meetings" (NRC 2012, p.7). The fear of being a tool *for* ISAF rather than working *with* the military also led to the disbandment of the Civil–Military Working Group in 2009 (Currion 2011).

It is important, however, to distinguish between organizational positions and the influence funding has had on positions they adopt vis-à-vis the military–humanitarian relationship. Organizations that have large sources of independent funding (e.g. from private donors) have the luxury to refuse military funding, while those reliant on donor funds from governments are more likely to be pressured to accept conditions, regulations and policies that might be at odds with their operational preferences. This is particularly true when looking at the difference between local NGOs and INGOs. This has been described as "resulting from a confluence of both pragmatism (the groups are desperate for funding and do not have a long cultural history embedded in the neutral and impartial tradition) and the ways in which some groups are thinly veiled money-making ventures in the shape of NGOs" (Ryerson 2012, p. 64). By contrast, several INGOs feel that they do not need the military because they have operated in Afghanistan even prior to the existence of ISAF. They do not generally see the armed forces as unskilled but, rather, as limited in what they can do, since most troops have a rotation period of six months and are dependent on Afghan interpreters (Fishstein and Wilder 2011). Moreover, due to the security situation, military actors tend to live in secluded environments and rely on their interlocutors to interpret the outside world while seldom interacting with it.

The "lack of 'penetration' of local communities and the inability to adequately understand social structures and politics allowed powerful individuals at provincial and district levels to mislead and manipulate ISAF in their disputes with other power brokers" (Fishstein and Wilder 2011, p. 48). The differences between clans within the same tribe can also be stark and military troops often lack this overall picture, potentially resulting in damaging decisions when engaging in aid delivery. NGOs argue that while the military has a lot of information, it lacks the right kind of information for aid delivery, making it prone to abuse (Fishstein and Wilder 2011). Military funding often tries to buy the support of local strongmen who alienate the population and fuel corruption. Projects are often corrupt, of poor quality and implemented without the collaboration of the local government, resulting in citizen distrust and disapproval (Oxfam 2011, Fishstein and Wilder 2011). Moreover, the use of private contractors strengthens the disruptive power dynamics at subnational level and raises issues of accountability. At least some PRT projects, for instance, lacked effectiveness and oversight because the military's role is to disburse funds rather than monitor quality and ensure a degree of community ownership (Oxfam et al. 2010, Aid/Watch 2012, Jackson and Haysom 2013). The Special Inspector General for Afghanistan Reconstruction reported in 2011 that 27 out of 69 projects in Laghman funded through the Commanders' Emergency Response Program were at risk or had questionable outcomes, and that $49.2 million was at risk of being wasted in that province alone (Fishstein and Wilder 2011).

The second key tension surrounded the real and perceived insecurity of humanitarians. The first murder of a relief worker in the post-2001 period was that of Ricardo Munguia, an ICRC engineer killed in Uruzgan province in March 2003.

What is significant is that the ICRC was well known for its "classical" humanitarian approach that stressed neutrality, independence and a refusal to cooperate with Coalition Forces. Although other foreigners had died in Afghanistan following the invasion, including soldiers and eight journalists in a week during the Taliban retreat, Munguia's murder made clear the idea that the country was still a dangerous place. Although nationally the impact was treated as another security incident, in Kandahar it was "like an electric shock," resulting in most NGOs suspending their activities and leaving that area of the country (Chayes 2006, p. 235).

Equally significant was the attack against MSF in Badghis province the following year in which five staff members were killed (first mentioned in Chapter 1). The organization had in fact been a staunch critic of the war, stating that it was not a "humanitarian-aid operation, but more a military propaganda operation, destined to make international opinion accept the US-led military operation" (cited in Monshipouri 2014, p. 144). By contrast, the May 2005 Kabul riots marked a broad attack against the aid community following an incident in which a United States military vehicle was involved in an accident with Afghan civilians. Angry bystanders shouted "Death to America. Death to Karzai" (BAAG 2007, p. 3) and during the unrest that swept through the city, well-known organizations, including the large United States-based NGO CARE, were looted and torched. Since then, the security situation has remained perilous. From 2003 to 2007, 130 aid workers were killed in Afghanistan. This number continued to increase; by 2008, 30 aid workers were assassinated in one year alone and in 2010, 225 were killed, kidnapped or injured in violent attacks (ADB 2009, Oxfam 2011).

Afghanistan continues to have one of the highest numbers of attacks on aid workers of any country in the world, regularly exceeding those in South Sudan, Somalia and Pakistan (Humanitarian Outcomes, 2013). In the first half of 2014 alone, there were over 80 such incidents, according to ACBAR's regularly updated website. Military activities outside the security sector and the military's presence in civilian activities instilled the perception that aid workers are "agents" of the military and tragically "the consent-based, impartial NGO assistance model [that] worked out over decades has been erased" (Save the Children 2004, Cornish 2007, p. 27). The shrinking of humanitarian space due to "blurred lines" creates barriers for community participation because citizen trust for NGO activities gets questioned (Aid/Watch 2012). For example a World Bank, CARE and Ministry of Education Report found that schools supported or constructed by military agents "were perceived by Afghans to be at higher risk of being attacked," thereby reducing school attendance rates (Oxfam et al. 2010, p. 3).

The final key tension was around the existence of the PRTs themselves. As mentioned earlier, these teams served as a linkage between security and development and used a range of approaches to bring about change in economic reconstruction, stability and good governance. The "vision" for the PRTs was for them to foster "enduring security" which is seen as a combination of three factors: sustainable

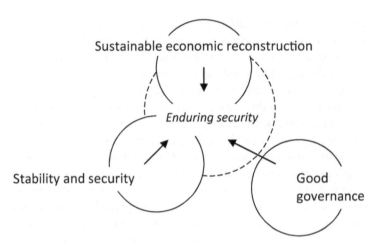

Figure 5.5 The PRT concept
Source: PRT (2004, p. 2)

economic recovery, stability and security, and good governance. As Figure 5.5 shows, good governance was seen as a major constraint because of problems with the local Afghan leadership giving it a position furthest outside the central sphere. Projects were ranked according to difficulty, ranging from the "easy" construction of schools, wells and clinics to the "sensitive" enforcement of counter-narcotics legislation, election support and human rights advocacy and on to the "difficult" objectives of influencing warlords, promoting democracy and obtaining compliance with Kabul's decisions.

From the Coalition's perspective, the PRTs have been a success. American Ambassador Robert Finn voiced the opinion of the Bush administration by saying that "not many initiatives have been as successful in reaching Afghanistan's population" (cited in James 2003). According to the PRTs themselves, they have been "providing considerably increased stability in their area of operations ... [and] even the most sensitive NGOs are developing discreet communication channels with the PRTs" which they are finding "a big plus" (PRT 2004, p. 2; Reconstruction Coordinator Bill Taylor cited in CHC 2003).

Humanitarians, by contrast, have not generally shared such a positive view. While different perceptions have been affected by a "varied local security environment, available resources, and the political priorities of countries contributing troops," the PRTs have been roundly criticized for their mission, structure and lack of effectiveness (Jalali 2007, p. 36). A commonly held opinion has been that they "have failed to tap local resources and have botched construction projects" (Zeller 2003, p. 1). According to Stapleton, "the long shopping list presented by the Coalition of all the skills and resources that PRTs would bring into Afghanistan, mostly never materialized" (cited in InterAction 2005, p. 2). A typical NGO opinion has been that they "have been both unacceptable in principle and inefficient in practice, largely because military participants seem untrained for their humanitarian or 'civil affairs' tasks and are driven by political, military and intelligence motives … epitomizing the Bush Administration's decisions to blur the lines" (InterAction 2005, p. 4). One senior Afghan NGO manager interviewed said that "people don't like to see soldiers doing development…. helping after a disaster is ok, like the floods, and people won't forget that."

Conclusion

The purpose of this chapter has been to describe the recent situation in Afghanistan. It has shown that, apart from the military–humanitarian relationship, the closeness continues with the linkage between security and aid, policy coherence and a belligerence that does not recognize the separation between humanitarian and military spheres. The characteristics of the war, the insurgency and the "coherent" combination of aid and force, combined with a contentious political situation that altered and blurred the purposes so that the military performed "humanitarian" tasks and those involved in aid, often operated as extensions of the political and military apparatus. Examples included soldiers wearing civilian clothing, thereby obscuring the distinction between humanitarians and the military, the numerous security incidents that involved humanitarians in Afghanistan and the merged security–development agenda that gave rise to the PRTs. The overlap between these led to tension between NGOs and the military and contributed to a military–humanitarian relationship that was highly contentious, making it difficult for those involved in delivering aid to Afghanistan to determine an effective path in their external relations.

6

Afghanistan's military–humanitarian complex

Introduction

Following the introduction in Chapter 1 in which the basic assumptions associated with the military–humanitarian relationship were presented, the history of the relationship was examined in Chapter 2. In Chapter 3, three issues were revealed that influence the military–humanitarian relationship. These were the tension between organizational structure and individual agency, humanitarian ethics and the link between security and development. Building on the structure presented in Chapter 3, the findings relating to the basic and underlying causes of tension within the military–humanitarian relationship and the underlying policy issue (whether humanitarians should have an integrated or segregated policy toward the military) will be presented in this chapter. These are decision-making and external relationships related to structure and agency, co-option and politicization of NGOs as an extension of ethical norms and the link between security and development. Five particular aspects stand out here. First, the inter-organizational friction present in relations between humanitarians and the military does not necessarily contribute to negative relations. Second, official policies of NGOs rarely determine the path of military–humanitarian relationships; instead, they are dependent on the agency of specific individuals. Third, the relationship humanitarians have with the military has less of an impact on NGO security than is commonly held. Fourth, humanitarian principles were important to most organizations working in Afghanistan but they were heavily influenced by the politically charged environment. Finally, humanitarians understood that they are part of the stability and state-building process in Afghanistan and, for that reason, those issues relating to co-option and politicization are less significant than is commonly assumed.

Structure and agency: decision making and external relationships

In this section, findings relating to the decision making of NGOs and their relationships with other organizations (the military in particular) will be presented. The notion of international-organizational friction is important here. Following Tsing

(2004), this can be thought of as the thorny relations that develop when organizations are unequal. As discussed in Chapter 1, it is commonly assumed that differences led to friction, causing dissonance between groups. This revealed that, while there were negative aspects to friction on the surface, it was not necessarily harmful or destructive. These relations were usually decided by individual managers based on context, past experience and, on rare occasion, policy guidelines. Relations with the military were sometimes sought to engage on specific programming issues. Internal issues (such as staff experiences and policies) and external pressures (institutional arrangements with other actors) were always influential and gave rise to two types of organizational behavior.

The first resulted from internal decision making by NGOs. Most followed models and common management practices, such as strategic planning and compliance with donor regulations, in management of their programs. Their external relations, however, were managed in a more ad hoc way and usually left to the decision of local or "field" managers. As one experienced NGO manager explained, "I'm not sure how practical common [inter-organizational] documents are but they serve to document policy and can be used as an advocacy tool … which is important in its own right." (See Box 6.1.) Without a policy, the relationship NGOs had with ambiguity in their relationship with the military increased. So to some degree, policies are important indicators of decision-making and because they provide a framework for which humanitarian principles can be applied. Policies will be returned to several times because of their importance in forming the "rules" that guide external relationships (Gibson et al. 2005, p. 33) and their absence indicates a lack of structure and policy dysfunction because policies at the vagary of managers and were opaque to other organizations.

Of the NGO staff members interviewed, only two organizations had formal policies and developed their relations using a managerialist–positivist approach. Contradictions notwithstanding, and while not explicitly stated, the majority of organizations showed a tendency toward integrated policy "for" relations with the military in Afghanistan. Organizations such as the International Medical Corps, the International Rescue Committee, Mines Advisory Group and Relief International were actively engaged with the military. Those organizations with existing policies seemed to be more rigid in their external relations. Organizations such as MSF and ICRC tended toward a critical and segregationist approach "against" close relations with the military. In effect, these organizations maintain an ethos of independence. In most cases, however, if a policy was developed, this tended to be through an opinion piece or policy paper that discussed the issues and raised concerns, rather than as a result of a specific system. There are obvious advantages to this, including not being forced into a decision (having flexibility) and being able to spend resources on other tasks.

Even within a given organization, there are differences, as one former staff member noted: "There are various currents in the organization"; and he added that

Box 6.1 Guidelines available to NGOs working in Afghanistan

- *Guidelines on the Use of Military and Civil Defense Assets to Support United Nations Humanitarian Activities in Complex Emergencies.* In the Oslo Guidelines, as these are known, the November 2006 version is updated from the 1994 and 2003 guidelines drafted by the Consultative Group on the Use of Military and Civil Defense Assets consisting of over 180 delegates from different governments and organizations. Although its focus is on the use of military resources in the delivery of humanitarian assistance, it uses humanitarian standards as its "core principles" and holds that the military be used as a last and temporary resort.
- *IASC Reference Paper: Civil–Military Relationship in Complex Emergencies (28 June 2004).* The Inter-Agency Standing Committee (IASC) is made up of relevant UN agencies and several NGOs involved in humanitarian action. IASC has sub-groups which work on a range of issues such as programming response. This paper serves as a basic reference for organizations to develop their own guidelines.
- *SCHR Position Paper on Military–humanitarian Relations in the Provision of Humanitarian Assistance* (18 October 2004). Building on previous Steering Committee for Humanitarian Response position papers, these guidelines focus on the delivery of impartial humanitarian assistance during violent conflict, with particular reference to UN peace operations. They use scenarios to provide concrete examples on how the positions can be implemented.
- *Caritas Internationalis Policy: Relations with the Military.* Of the several NGO guidelines available, this is well developed and applicable to a very large global organization. Drafted in 2006 following a global meeting in 2004, this document outlines the core and operational principles of Caritas. Among its core principles are two instructive points. These are "subsidiarity: local decision-making is often more accurate and realistic than decisions made far from the scene" and "principles of partnership: a set of relationships formed over time enable trust and engagement with each other" (p. 8). The principle of subsidiarity would seem to support the finding that different approaches are followed by NGOs, while the partnership would be difficult to achieve "over time," given the transient nature of emergency settings.
- *Guidelines for the Interaction and Coordination of Humanitarian and Development Actors and Military Forces in Afghanistan* (2008). These guidelines are an attempt to update and improve previous policy statements made by ACBAR and other NGO consortia in previous years. An attempt was made to have signatories for these guidelines, including representatives from the international military forces in the country, the government and NGOs.

one MSF, in his experience, was top-down while another was more equitable. This invariably led to the inter-organizational friction described below. Of those interviewed, several NGO managers expressed the position that "we don't cooperate with the military," but then went on to describe how they had done so in the past or explained a readiness to share information, especially about security. In response to working with the PRTs, several NGO managers expressed the sentiment that "we used to work with PRTs but not anymore." The implication was that while previous staff had agreed to share information, coordinate and, perhaps, accept funds, the new managers had decided against it, based on their prior experience, perspective in terms of humanitarian principles and worldview. This corresponded with the deteriorating security situation which will be discussed further below. In other words, positions changed, based on the context and particular point in time in which aid workers found themselves. Of the organizations interviewed with formal policies, most tended to follow a "top down" approach (MSF-France was one notable exception). To fill the vacuum, managers exercised greater autonomy and freedom of choice and thus most NGOs showed a preference for people (agency) over systems (structure). One Afghan manager explained that "every country has its own policy but this can be changed at the field level." In the politically charged environment found in Afghanistan, there was thus more likelihood of increased cooperation.

Because of this emphasis on "agency," decisions about NGOs' external relations were made following managers' opinions and were heavily influenced by the "personal baggage" of those managers, such as a tendency not to communicate, mistrust of other nationalities and dislike of the military. Just as members of the military become "socialized into a 'proper' way of thinking" within their units (Piiparinen 2007, p. 149, see also Beauregard 1998), so too were humanitarians when working for different NGOs. In some cases, they might appear to be pro-military or anti-American. As a result, the choices of these managers were heavily influenced by their degree of experience. The more experienced relief workers and, perhaps not surprisingly, those with military backgrounds tended to be more nuanced when speaking of their organization's relations with the military. One NGO Country Director, a graduate of the Royal Military Academy Sandhurst, commented that "there's nothing new in the concept of the military doing development or humanitarianism, but the situations weren't as politicized as before." When viewed within the prism of security, for example, the relationship with the military took on an important role for many humanitarians and some saw the relationship entirely within the security question. Thus another NGO Country Director, who was openly anti-military, expressed a common opinion that "I'm happy to cooperate with NATO, PRTs or whoever." Yet another was even more forthright: "we need to acknowledge the efforts of others. The military makes an effort to take into account the civilian voice. They are well resourced and not so rigid with their resources."

The ad hoc nature of PRTs and their experimental nature meant that, like the management of NGOs, they tended not to follow rigid command structures and the

PRTs lacked a common mission statement for most of their existence. However, in most cases military commanders made the final decision, and attached development assistance advisors were "frustrated because their advice was not followed ... [and] they learned to put things in military terms rather than development speak" because of this power imbalance. These differences caused friction not only within PRTs but spilling out into their external relationships. There was a feeling among many interviewees that NGOs were marginalized and not given funds to operate as they saw fit. Although it varied between each country contingent, within each PRT there was a significant amount of coordination before it extended to outside actors such as Afghans and NGOs.

The second element of organizational behavior was external relationships between NGOs and the military, focusing further on this notion of inter-organizational friction. This is closely related to issues of organizational differences, disagreement over the means of bringing about change and the use of force. Specifically, the practices and policies were examined, revealing that problems within these dynamics, such as policy dysfunction and "culture clash," led to friction within the relationship. This friction made smooth relations difficult and led to a wide variety of approaches adopted by NGOs as well as the military. This inter-organizational friction revealed itself in many situations in Afghanistan. Three related issues – how coordination meetings were held, complicated by the high degree of turn-over and implementation of reconstruction projects by the military – that contributed to friction in Afghanistan will be discussed further.

Inter-organizational "coordination" meetings provide an instance where friction in the relationship was clearly evident. In Afghanistan, there was a barrage of coordination meetings (see Box 6.2). Several interviewees expressed frustration with meetings where the military or PRTs were present. According to one reconstruction manager, the PRTs "spend at least ten minutes of every meeting explaining what they don't do ... then there isn't enough time to explain what they do do." Another NGO manager responsible for security saw it this way: "the civil–military relationship in Afghanistan no longer exists because of too many uninformative and useless meetings." Yet another manager expressed frustration that while some military units abided by rules governing issues like uniforms and respect for civilians, others did not, particularly those with murky affiliations (presumably with intelligence-gathering groups), known as "other governmental agencies." For meetings hosted by the military, a pattern would form where a solidarity NGO might attend once and not return to subsequent gatherings. Thus few NGOs attended meetings where the military might be present and some adopted an approach whereby meetings with military personnel had to be at a third-party location seen as neutral ground. Several examples were given during the time of field research. In the northern town of Kunduz, for example, the Coalition Force civil affairs unit was "uninvited" to area coordination meetings. This happened in other provinces as well. In the eastern city of Jalalabad, NGO members of "technical working groups," which focused on

---

Box 6.2   Mechanisms for civil–military coordination in Afghanistan

- The Civil–Military Working Group, co-chaired by UNAMA and ACBAR, with the participation of ISAF and a range of humanitarian actors, was established to "facilitate timely and sufficient communication between NGOs, international military forces and other stakeholders over military activities, security of operations and aid coordination with the objective of identifying and addressing issues of concern."
- The PRT Executive Steering Committee is a monthly meeting conducted with government ministers (led by Minster of Interior) ISAF, UNAMA, and senior Embassy representatives to coordinate major PRT strategic principles.
- The PRT/Civil–Military Working Group advises the PRT Steering Committee and includes representatives of UNAMA, Ministry of the Interior (MoI), ISAF, contributing troop nation military and aid representatives (including USAID and DFID), and national embassies. It meets on a weekly basis and is hosted by the MoI.
- The Joint Coordination Cell Meeting is a weekly meeting hosted by UNAMA where UN/UNAMA officers interact with the government, Combined Forces Command-Afghanistan and ISAF regarding all operational matters (including disaster management).
- The PRT Commander's Conference is a quarterly conference hosted by ISAF where UNAMA and NGOs are invited for a one-day session to raise concerns directly with Coalition PRT Commanders.
- Regional/Provincial/District Coordination meetings, under the government supported by UN/UNAMA/NGO Field offices.
- UN/UNAMA Field Office bilateral meetings with civilian and military organizations.
- UN/UNAMA/NGO Field office weekly security meetings.
- Bilateral engagement between local CIMIC/Civil Affairs teams and NGO/ International Organizations.

Source: Slightly modified from Civil–Military Working Group (2007b)

---

different sectoral programming issues, set two conditions for the military to attend. First, all NGO members of the group had to agree to the military's presence and second, the military had to be in uniform (and without weapons if the meeting was held inside an NGO compound). According to a convener of these meetings, the military did not regularly attend; the local PRT had attended only one meeting in the six months prior to the interview. As a result of this friction, little coordination was undertaken by the PRT, according to the provincial director of education

(Technical Working Group 2006). Others concurred: "they do lots of programs but don't inform anyone" responded one interviewee. This "go it alone" attitude among the PRTs was echoed by most of the NGO interviewees.

In another instance in 2006, the country-wide Child Protection Action Network (CPAN), a consortium of NGOs and government line-ministries involved in children's rights and wellbeing activities in Afghanistan, debated heavily on what relationship they should have with the military. While each organization had its individual approach, it was decided collectively that it was better to engage the military than to leave it out. After much deliberation, the NGO members felt they might be able to positively impact the actions of the military (as the military was going to carry out projects, whatever the protests and activities of other organizations). In this case, this meant following accepted standards with regard to child protection. The NGO members of CPAN agreed to allow military representatives to attend their coordination meetings as long as they did not carry weapons and they were discreet about their attendance. Similar situations occurred at the provincial level around the country, while in the capital it was common to have ISAF military representatives attend meetings in uniform (without firearms). In Kabul, for example, early in the period researched, the organization responsible for civil–military liaison within the Coalition Force (CJCMOTF) held its own meetings, which few NGOs attended (the few who did attend once did not return a second time), while ISAF Civil–Military Cooperation (CIMIC) attended UN weekly coordination meetings. Again, the reasoning was both calculated and pragmatic: it was felt that to engage and inform was better than to separate ("segregate") from the military. These examples show that some friction had a beneficial effect. It brought NGOs together to form a unified position and advocate for specific policies which were intended to result in better programming. As will be discussed later, this had consequences for humanitarian principles.

In Afghanistan, influencing coordination was made more difficult by the frequent turnover of personnel, managers and decision makers. The military normally had very short rotations; often as little as three months and at most a year. Some trained six months for three-month deployments. An aid official described the turnover as a "revolving door" of new internationals coming and going (whatever their organization). An NGO manager explained the situation this way: "there is too much turnover, there is a reluctance to help and information is one way or if they give information it is wishy-washy. It is too personality driven ... [and the way the military behaves is] like dogs peeing on a post." Two interviewees compared the military's approach to that of an "800-pound gorilla." In other words, they all sought credit for their activities without full consideration of the possible negative consequences. At the same time, the highly results-oriented personnel, who emphasized tangible results, were under pressure to produce tangible outputs. These projects included reconstruction of schools, district government centers and clinics. Some called such projects "lighthouses" because they were erected for their visibility rather than their need. Thus the military, and particularly the PRTs, was prone to lack of policy (in part as a result of turnover), which in turn caused friction in its relations with NGOs. The frustration of these issues led to policy dysfunction where no consistent approach was established, especially where problems with coordination, overlap and unnecessary waste of funds resulted (a case in point are the school and road projects discussed below).

A final and critical source of friction was the humanitarian and reconstruction projects implemented by the military. This issue will be discussed later with respect to the blending of security and development but deserves mention here. Of the humanitarians interviewed, most were perplexed and aggravated by these efforts. Perhaps no other issue drew the ire of relief workers interviewed as the perception that assistance projects were carried out so that the military could improve relations with Afghan communities. In describing the standard approach, several interviewees described their role as facilitators of community-led efforts. This involved working with local Afghans on prescribed standards (often referred to as "good practice"), and one interviewee added that "if a community builds a school, they will understand the value of it." Among those interviewed, this was contrasted sharply with the approach undertaken by the military. According to one interviewee, the PRTs followed a reconstruction process that "might have worked in 1960," suggesting a "charity" approach that was ill-suited to the realities of post-Taliban Afghanistan. Another NGO manager concluded that "it's easy [for beneficiaries] to just get a hand out." An NGO Country Director explained that "programming can be impacted in part because the military doesn't approach it in the same way [as NGOs do] … they don't look at it holistically." Further, integration was lost with the efforts of others, who were unlikely to take the considerations of an entire community into account, as one NGO manager explained: "military activities can undermine community-based approaches just as any organization following it might." Several of the NGO staff interviewed indicated a concern because the military did not follow recognized models such as the standards developed by the Sphere Project. These standards determine, for example, how far a latrine should be placed from a well, the size of shelters and the average number of liters of water a person should be provided per day. While aid advisors within the PRTs might have been aware of these models, interviewees suggested that they were side-lined by their military counterparts.

These examples also indicate that while the humanitarians' ability to influence the military was limited, it was nonetheless evident. One of the key ways NGOs did this was through advocacy and policy efforts. Several interviewees singled out specific national PRTs as more cooperative and adroit than others. One manager explained, "we like to think we can influence some PRTs," citing the British units in particular. To help gain a sort of indirect leverage, as was revealed by several instances during the research, NGOs often accepted grant funding to "give them a seat at the table," as one interviewee put it. As an "implementing partner," an NGO would gain control of increased resources, get access to donor and government staff and be able to influence decisions through reporting and persuasion. The NGOs interviewed felt that they were able to raise issues incrementally, when they would otherwise have been unable or disempowered. As one of the NGO representatives stationed at the United States military's Central Command (CENTCOM) explained, "it's good to have the dialogue [although] it's better if issues are ironed out at the field level but it helps to have another place to go." In Afghanistan, when it came to direct military necessity, as in the case of force protection measures (such as the problem with soldiers out of uniform), influencing the military to change their policy became especially difficult if not impossible. One aid official said that "force protection is just the way it is" and insisted that he could not do his job without it. Others interviewed, however, strongly disagreed. Another aid official lamented how a heavily armed military escort was needed to transport a single representative to monitor a project in the Panjshir Valley, arguably one of the safer and pro-Western areas of the country.

Such measures created a psychological and physical gap between the official international efforts (government and military) and NGOs as well as Afghans. Even the military's appearance could be seen as a detriment to achieving their non-military role. Referring to the body armor and weapons used by foreign militaries, an Afghan director asked, "how can you win hearts and minds when you look like that?" Despite their rhetoric to the contrary and the established military literature (US Army 2006, ISAF 2006a), the perception was that the military did projects to improve its image and enhance the protection of its soldiers. This statement was typical of the NGO staffers interviewed: the tactic of "using assistance [to bolster] force protection is a short-term measure with negative long-term consequences because it can foster disillusionment when a project fails and undermines the work of NGOs" who take a longer-term approach of the type discussed in this section. The Afghan Development Zones (ADZ) concept served as a prime example that divided humanitarians from the military. There the military expected kinetic operations to be followed by assistance and reconstruction to consolidate its military success. Following this approach, however, it would be difficult if not impossible to end the reconstruction process and turn tasks over to local counterparts (what was referred to by several interviewees as "working ourselves out of a job"). This led one researcher to describe force protection as "the military's Achilles heel" because it undid the painstaking collaborative work necessary for both stability and reconstruction. Despite this, the attempt at coordination, at reducing mistrust and pushing towards cooperation on certain issues continued. Nearly everyone interviewed felt that to engage was better than to disengage with the military. Even a representative from perhaps the most segregationist NGO interviewed said that while "it did not have a relationship with the military," it would "communicate necessary information" in life-threatening situations.

In sum, the research showed that inter-organizational friction is common in many relationships but it has not always been detrimental to the military–humanitarian relationship in Afghanistan and it suggests that this friction did not necessarily promote a close or distant relationship between humanitarians and the military. Rather, this friction was a part of decision making and policy formation. When there was friction, it was the result of individual (manager) choice, especially where organizational structures, including explicit policies, were weak or non-existent. Because of the way NGOs function, explicit policies are not always followed and thus may not be ultimately helpful, because they either "straightjacket" decision making or omit new eventualities. In other words, there was a strong feeling that policies were needed but that if they were too explicit or rigid, flexibility would be lost. NGO policies, if they existed, usually supported a segregated approach to relations with the military. In fact, no case was found of an explicitly integrated formal policy. A further finding suggests that most military projects do not follow established standards. In some cases civil–military operations follow what is commonly thought of as old-fashioned "charity," where goods and services are doled out and activities are not "development" in the contemporary understanding but are simply carried out for military purposes (such as improved force projection to reduce the number of attacks against foreign soldiers).

Humanitarian ethics: co-option and the politicization of NGOs

In this section, the co-option and politicization of humanitarianism by a military or government agenda is examined. The debate about humanitarian ethics is seen in the influence of politics and the possibility of co-option, with the implied assumption that humanitarian response was unwillingly or deceitfully integrated with the military. In other words, co-option brings with it the assumption of an asymmetric relationship in which one of the partners is a reluctant or duped participant. The evidence, however, showed that NGOs are not "being co-opted." Instead, in Afghanistan NGOs were generally part of the existing political process to bring about a liberal-democratic reconstruction of the country. Humanitarians, who placed a high value on pragmatism (the humanitarian impulse to focus on action was first mentioned in Chapter 1) and consequential ethical positions, accepted co-option willingly (although few would admit this explicitly) and tended toward an integrated position with the military. Principles are important but they are squeezed by the highly charged political environment in post-Taliban Afghanistan. This research revealed that the aid organizations researched showed an understanding that they were part of a wider political–military complex to reconstruct Afghanistan. In this way, the research showed that pragmatism was the overriding concern and that individual motivations appeared to be more important than particular NGO organizational culture or policy. To examine this issue further, three issues will be analyzed: policies, nationality and humanitarian space.

First, despite its prevalence in the literature, if the ethical debate was such an important concern among practitioners there would likely be stronger policies.

NGO staff were generally focused on and were sometimes overwhelmed by day-to-day concerns in the implementation of their activities. In other words, as practitioners they had little time for rarefied notions of principle, but were typically "swamped" with more immediate concerns. One experienced aid worker was blunt in asking "since when did principles make an impact on every day decisions?" Instead, most organizations ostensibly adhered to the Code of Conduct for the International Red Cross and Red Crescent Movement and NGOs in Disaster Relief or other collective measures such as widely available guidelines (including those described in Box 6.1). The policy statements issued by ACBAR (2002c, 2007) were examples of such guidance. As mentioned in the previous section, only two out of 20 NGOs interviewed had explicit policies to deal with external relations covering the military. However, a review of several organizational policies on relations with the military revealed that it was open to cooperation under certain circumstances, especially when there was no other mechanism for reaching disaster victims and if the military adhered to established standards and practices. These were what a senior NGO advisor termed "situations of exception," where there was an urgent catastrophe such as a life-threating natural event, for example an earthquake, or man-made emergency, especially genocide. Consider the most recent draft guidelines on military–humanitarian relations in Afghanistan, which stated:

> Any operation undertaken jointly by humanitarian actors with military forces may have a negative impact on the perception of the humanitarian actors' impartiality and neutrality as well as on their security. Hence, any joint civil–military activities should only take place as an urgent, last resort in order to save lives, in strictly [sic] adherence with humanitarian principles. (Civil–Military Working Group 2007a, p. 8)

Thus, flexibility was left for cooperation. Many were ready to take this a step further in practice. However, most take humanitarian ethics seriously even if there is difficulty in explaining and putting these principles into practice. If, for example, there is an urgent life-saving need, then strict adherence to principles can wait, such as in the case of the earthquake of 2002 near Nahrin in Baghlan Province, where both humanitarians and the military provided emergency assistance. One Afghan NGO manager explained a commonly held opinion:

> The relationship should exist but it needs to be clearly defined.... CSOs [Civil Society Organizations] should be open to military and at the same time keep their impartiality, neutrality and independence. It will do no good to blame each other. Try to work out a common goal of reaching out to the poor and bringing about development in the area.

This encapsulated the belief in a need to find accommodation with the military while "walking along a fence" to maintain a framework of humanitarian principles. This made it appear as if some organizations were not being consistent and may have "misrepresented themselves" (Slim 2004, p. 35). However challenging or contradictory that might have been, maintaining such standards proved especially contentious in the politically charged environment of post-invasion Afghanistan. For this reason, the approaches employed by different NGOs were not easily pegged to one specific position or another. Although organizations might lean toward either an integrated or segregated approach (as suggested in the last section), when looked at together the positions of NGOs changed, depending on the temporal and contextual context. While by no means universal, this prevailing flexibility runs contrary to the assumptions that humanitarians were inherently ethical or strictly pragmatic. When viewed broadly, more rigid and segregationist organizations, such as ICRC and MSF, were in a minority position, but then only for a particular time or specific context. If the case of the murder of five MSF staff members is considered again, even the reasons for MSF's departure were multifaceted and related more to security concerns and political posturing than simple humanitarian principle. With its often dissenting view, MSF was in a minority and fighting what was described as "something of a rear-guard action" (Frerks et al. 2006, p. 66). If they held as much influence as is often assumed, more NGOs would have left the country.

Second, the nationality of humanitarians themselves is often seen as a determining factor that results in undermining humanitarian principles, but the evidence to support this is scarce. Some have argued, for instance, that Americans were more likely or willing to accept a greater degree of politicization. HQ-based staff, particularly with European NGOs, were said to have rigid opinions, and these were shown as "indicating an unwillingness to work with a military force under any circumstances" (NGO Internal Report 2002, p. 4), whereas field staff were more likely to be pragmatic and flexible. Some agreed with the prevailing literature, as one NGO manager explained, that the "UK has a stronger poverty focus whereas the US groups follow it [the prevailing political–military agenda] more unquestionably." On closer inspection, however, the evidence shows that, rather than distinct European and American positions concerning politicization of aid through the military–humanitarian relationship, there is far more agreement. The American organizations, much like their European counterparts, preferred the military to have less involvement in political emergencies and provided direct assistance only after natural disasters. At the field level, humanitarians of American origin seem just as likely to highlight problems with the military–humanitarian relationship. A European relief worker might have seemingly pro-military views, as one noted: "there is no doubt that foreign troops have been a stabilizing force and a welcome presence." At the same time, an American might have a negative perspective, as when one American Country Director lamented about the PRTs: "disastrous would be too strong a word, but it has not been properly thought out …. American [PRTs] are generally the worst."

The overlapping views of different nationalities also had significant implications for policy. In the spring of 2002, for example, the ACBAR "Military Taskforce" drafted a statement and a smaller group consisting of CARE, Oxfam and Mercy

Corps was formed to create guidelines covering two topics: the first concerned the "blurring of distinctions between humanitarian and military" and the second was to articulate the "practical implications of NGO cooperation with the military" (NGO Forum 2002, pp. 1–2). Although two of these organizations were United States-based, the staff members of these organizations who dealt with policy were European. The various civil–military coordination efforts by European and North American governments as well as the UN provide other examples.

Another example was found in the United States. From 2001 to 2002, the American NGO coalition, InterAction, took a closer step in its relationship with the military. It involved contracting experienced humanitarians and temporarily stationing at the United States military's CENTCOM during the initial phases of involvement on the ground in Afghanistan (a practice repeated two years later during the Iraq invasion) (Jacoby 2005, pp. 223–4). According to those interviewed, there was less dialogue, information sharing and influence on military operations than was originally hoped for. The feeling was that it is better to engage and have involvement than to cut off ties completely. The same participant felt that it is better to "influence things to a small degree ... [because] at least some voice is heard." This was echoed by many other NGOs, including MSF. In all, our research shows that such views were not determined by nationality.

Afghans were asked about this divide and noted little difference between nationalities among humanitarians, even while substantial differences existed between national militaries. Afghan relief workers tended to voice a more critical opinion of the military than did their international counterparts. One Afghan NGO manager explained it using an analogy: "doctors treat patients, a teacher teaches children, engineers build things and soldiers keep security. If a doctor tries to teach, he'll make mistakes and waste a lot of resources. It is the same as soldiers being involved in development." The reasons for this generally stemmed from the blurring of the lines, causing insecurity and bolstering a general belief in established systems; in other words, the military's role was security while the NGOs' role was focused on humanitarian concerns. One Afghan NGO manager asked "can you expect the military to build peace? You can't. Soldiers can't do development [because] ... people won't trust them." Another Afghan with both humanitarian and military experience described the PRT concept as "a complete nonsense ... how can people know the difference when one man comes in [a] uniform fighting and another comes giving aid?" Two other Afghan interviewees quoted a well-known Afghan proverb, "you cannot carry two watermelons with one hand," to suggest that the military should stick with tasks it was designed for such as providing security and reconstructing the security sector.

Based on the interviews carried out in Afghanistan, the evidence therefore reveals a dynamic picture in which nationality does not play a predetermined role in either close or distant relations between humanitarians and the military. Instead, there seemed to be pressure on NGOs from both militaries and donors of the same national origin. With so many countries contributing military forces and other resources to Afghanistan, it is perhaps not surprising that pressure was felt by the humanitarian community. Most of those interviewed noted the important difference it made that the military forces present in Afghanistan were a belligerent actor and not formally constituted and approved for peacekeeping. Barbara Stapleton observed that just as United States NGOs felt challenged by the large American military presence, ISAF did the same for European NGOs: "with the rollout of NATO's phased expansion via the PRTs some European NGOs are coming under new pressures from the Europeans that fund them, to develop closer working relationships with PRTs than had previously been the case" (cited in NGO Internal Report 2004, p. 3). Reconstruction funds then followed where PRTs and other troops were based, helping to shore up political concerns among constituents in the originating country. This was confirmed by an Afghan NGO manager who said, "international NGOs want to work where their national armies are. Their governments are pushing for them to do this. Because they must go after funds, many of the INGOs are not independent." There appears to be no national divide when it comes to official aid; humanitarians from any country were typically in a position that could willingly take part of the official reconstruction effort in Afghanistan. In fact, there appeared to be a maturing of the relationship and, despite the friction, a workable tension was formed. An aid official said that the "debate [over how close a relationship NGOs and the military should have] has moved forward and become more nuanced" and described how it was no longer possible to decry partiality "if you are part of a large reconstruction effort." Thus, explained one NGO manager, "we're over the hump of the NGOs' problem with the military." Regarding PRTs, another said that "they are part of the landscape now" and it is up to NGOs to "figure out how to work with them." This degree of pragmatism indicates that the use of "us and them" language is not as prevalent as is often portrayed.

Finally, there was the issue of humanitarian space. As discussed in Chapter 1, humanitarian space indicates that humanitarians have room to maneuver, both physically and intellectually. It is where NGO staff can carry out activities without immediate danger either from physical threat or from confusion with the security and intelligence forces that may be participants in a conflict. This issue is discussed further in the next section but deserves mention here because it an important concept, because humanitarians cannot carry out their work in the absence of this space. In Afghanistan, NGO managers expressed a feeling that this was second only to the principle of "humanity." Whereas the principle of "neutrality" could be difficult to implement, humanitarian space was "fought for" and defined to suit the situation. In other words, this was "being practical." In Afghanistan, the PRTs were a pivotal issue with regard to humanitarian space. As one head of agency said, "we have very crowded humanitarian space," while another lamented that "humanitarian space has done nothing but shrink since 2001." For many NGOs, the "PRTs are seeking to do too much" (Waldman 2008) and thus encroaching on humanitarian space. Further, the PRTs could be a powerful political body, both as an influence on government and as a funding body. For example, the major donors in Afghanistan had representatives stationed with PRTs, while DFID provided funding directly to NGOs and the military. A funding scheme by the Japanese government under its "Grassroots Program" included PRTs as the process linking communities and NGOs with the embassy. As was mentioned above, some NGOs accepted grants in order to have a "seat at the table" and to try to influence actions through a piecemeal approach. One NGO staffer explained how they might accept funds from a PRT: "we would take funds under the conditions that it is not advertised and that they don't visit the projects." Of those NGOs interviewed, most explained how they would accept funds but then include a caveat that their acceptance was dependent on soldiers' not visiting projects. This indicates their willingness to work with the military if they can influence the process (as described above). In some of the more insecure areas of the country, this was the only way to access funds, but by doing so an organization's space was limited; thus NGOs accepted this degree of co-option and politicization as necessary conditions for accessing Afghans deemed to be in need of assistance.

In such a politically charged environment, it is challenging for humanitarians to apply specific principles, such as neutrality, and therefore what occurs may be movement along a spectrum of humanitarian principles. In many instances, there were those who were for a more ethical focus of humanitarianism, while most accepted the fact that their role was ill defined and uncertain in Afghanistan. Others saw the issue in strictly pragmatic terms, to gain access to donors, funding and new program areas. As was shown in Chapter 4, neutrality was not exercised in the 1980s in Afghanistan and few if any organizations tried to carry out programming on "both sides of the conflict" during the period 2001–2006, as prescribed by neutrality. What these findings reveal is that, rather than holding static ethical positions, most NGOs moved back and forth along the spectrum, depending on the context (described by Weiss 1997). In this way, NGOs find a way to maneuver around zero-sum choices (such as compromising principles or withdrawing from the country) and carry out their activities.

In sum, several preliminary conclusions can be drawn. Most humanitarians interviewed felt that ethical principles were important but believed that they had to be balanced with other, more practical considerations. Some organizations routinely espoused human rights agendas – either implicitly or in their promotional and advocacy statements. Others doubtlessly used principles as a mask for self-aggrandizement, making their rhetoric and pragmatism cover their true intentions, or at least make them difficult to discern. This suggests that the application of humanitarian principles was not static, but changed between organizations and varied among individuals. By being part of the aid architecture, NGOs were part of the West's political agenda, and nearly all of them willingly so. Under the Taliban, for example, this has led to clashes over gender and human rights. Interviewees generally took it as a given that most NGOs are and have been politicized. NGOs are organizations, affected by a number of concerns including survival and carrying out their mandate effectively. Humanitarian ethics were not rigid rules followed by humanitarians. The research revealed instead that they are flexible and dependent on situation and context. Rather than a landscape of two or more principles, a change in positions is a more appropriate description of the approach adopted by most NGOs. Few organizations, the research showed, made organizational decisions based solely on ethical judgments.

Security and development: the nature of conflict and insecurity

In this section, the complex relationship between security and development is examined. This basic cause of tension played out in the formation of policy (through the aid architecture) and in perceptions of the interplay between security and development. The complex characteristics of conflict in Afghanistan were often not well understood, leading to a mixed role of the military (in both security and humanitarian activities) and a mistaken belief in the utility of humanitarian action in reducing the incidence of violence and fostering stability. Thus, just as the distinction between civil society and the military has become blurred, the distinction between low- and high-intensity conflict has also become blurred (Mills, 2005). Further, just as old models of warfare confuse military leaders when they are confronted with new challenges (US Army 2006, Smith 2006), the conflict in Afghanistan, with its mixture of high- and low-intensity conflict, can also cause confusion and concern among humanitarians as they try to apply what might be older models of hostility to the military and humanitarian principles. The light-footprint concept adopted by the UN and national militaries only served to reinforce this. Thus the research revealed several strong tensions regarding the understanding of the relationship between humanitarians and the military and played out on the ground in Afghanistan. These tensions in turn affected decision making and the degree of politicization of NGOs in the country. Three key closely linked issues relating to security and development are presented here: strategy, NGO security and the reconstruction process.

First, perspectives on strategy and the approach to security and development were subject to change. On the one hand, the nature of the military mission and the large political commitment led to an attempt to bring policy coherence, such as the north–south shift in aid funding over time. One interviewee who noted that Afghanistan was "like two separate countries" added that it was "like Bosnia after the war." In that country, the Serbian enclave was initially recalcitrant and typically unwilling to cooperate with reconstruction efforts. Similarly in Afghanistan, initially after 2001 the Pashtun-dominated areas became a place with little assistance and even less security. Although some humanitarians carried out projects in these areas, they were largely ignored by reconstruction efforts, as compared to northern areas and urban areas, especially Kabul. Another issue which complicates understanding of the linkage between security and development is the perceived differences based on geographic, discursive and tangible manifestations found during the period under review. At times, the military took on an especially active role in providing assistance as areas became relatively more secure. In early 2002, one coalition Civil Affairs officer explained that:

> The humanitarian activities being undertaken by the civil affairs team are beginning to focus more on redevelopment projects as a result of the improved security situation. However, NGOs are encouraged to start projects in the area as the civil affairs team will not be able to fund all of these [reconstruction efforts]. (UNAMA 2002, p. 2)

On the other hand, as will be discussed further below, despite the encouragement to become more fully involved, the research suggests that humanitarian assistance had negligible impact on the outcome of the conflict, given the spending, effort and time involved. Assistance projects could contribute to reconstruction but the research showed that this occurred over long periods of time. According to one interviewee, it took more than a decade of "slow" community-based activity before he saw a positive change in relations between two groups in the central province of Urzugan:

> Through development, we can solve these problems, but it takes time, strategy and the right approach. We started in 1992 with a friendly card game [which brought people together]. The Pashtus had no qualified people and needed technical assistance. They had been fighting the Hazaras for centuries but they had qualified people but needed access to communications so a compromise was found through a project. The sign of a successful project is sharing local resources.

In this way, the impact of aid on security and the counter-insurgency activities of NATO in the country appeared to be less than was typically assumed by both humanitarians and the military.

The military was the main driver in a system of sticks and carrots. For those on the ground, the research showed that the practical question became which order to put these in: "reward and punishment" or "punishment and reward." According to several interviewees and observations taken during the research, there seemed to be some confusion between simple "winning hearts and minds" and reconstruction that had the potential to reduce the resort to violence by Afghans who had grievance against the government and international forces. Following the evidence presented earlier, humanitarian assistance was provided to support the central government, good local governance and with the aim to reduce violent conflict (in short, what several interviewees described as "good behavior") in order to cultivate among Afghan leaders at the provincial level and below. This was understood not just as an external notion, but as one that involved a collective civil and military as well as local and international "coherence". Regarding the work of PRTs, one commander explained what was meant by "good behavior" in the often volatile eastern province of Nangarhar:

> The idea of reinforcing success comes from the Governor of Nangarhar and not just the military. If districts have problems with security, cultivate poppy, or fight the government, then the Governor does not want us doing projects in that area. While some things will occur, the bulk of our projects should be in districts that complied with the government directions for security and poppy elimination. ANP [Afghan National Police] in Nangarhar are paid via electronic funds transfer so hopefully they all get paid on time if they make their way to the bank in town. We [PRTs] are not in the business of sticks, only carrots. Other coalition and Afghan forces provide the stick. It is not a simple formula and the time lag between nominating, funding, starting, and finishing projects can cause confusion and contradictions if the district's behavior changes.

As mentioned earlier, the idea that reconstruction equaled "gifts" was also strong and this was typical of how projects under the tactic of "winning hearts and minds" were viewed. The rationale for assistance was security; as one NGO manager explained, the military was "trying to give reconstruction in exchange for security." One expatriate NGO shared this sentiment by quoting an Afghan colleague: "'we accepted things from the Russians but that didn't mean we liked them.'" Instead, reconstruction assistance was a strategy to lower the incidence of violence. The nature of the conflict meant that armed opposition groups mixed political, ideological and criminal goals. In response, military action was tied together to include security and development goals while at the same time achieving a "light footprint," to maintain low causalities and to attempt to "win hearts and minds" of Afghans. NGOs were important to achieving the light footprint and it facilitated policy coherence. Soldiers simultaneously engaged in providing humanitarian assistance in one area, carrying out peacekeeping-type duties in another area and conducting combat operations in yet another. According to several interviews and observations of projects on the ground, the military emphasized the non-combat aspects of its role in Afghanistan, but conventionally minded militaries found this difficult to do. In late 2006, for instance, during the Canadian-led military campaign aimed at establishing government control in parts of Kandahar province, known as Operation Medusa, the decisive phases of combat used by NATO were not distinct. Heavy force was employed during Medusa and fighting continued for months after major operations had ceased. As a result, the "non-kinetic" last phase, which includes reconstruction and establishment of programs like the ADZ, "couldn't get off the ground" because of ongoing violence. According to one researcher, "there is a comprehensive planning and understanding of counter-insurgency but maybe during implementation the traditional mindset comes out." This "traditional mindset" emphasized high-intensity conflict with a stress on body count and ability to gain territory and carry out "kinetic" operations which focused on direct military strikes, as opposed to civil–military affairs and most aspects of counter-insurgency. The problem was the military's doctrine and training: "whether that gets translated into practice is another issue." In addition, during Operation Medusa there was "lack of experience, lack of capacity especially in CIMIC and a lack of links of cooperation with civilians."

The second element under analysis is NGO security. The research findings reveal that the relationship NGOs had with the military was not a significant concern relating to security and that only in certain contexts did the relationship actually endanger relief workers. The available data, both quantitative and qualitative, showed a gradual worsening of physical security throughout Afghanistan after the fall of the Taliban, but this was not a result of the link between security and development but because of the change in warfare itself. The main threats to humanitarians were the result of anonymous insecurity (Lee 1993) such as criminality and happenstance as a result of being near violent conflict, described as being "caught in the crossfire." The distinction between anonymous and presentational insecurity is key. If humanitarians were frequently targeted because of their relationships, a greater presentational danger would exist. Instead, the evidence discussed further below indicates that in Afghanistan anonymous danger has increased over time, leading to a less secure environment for NGOs based on their degree of visibility rather than on their proximity to military forces. Based on interviews with numerous NGOs in Kabul and elsewhere, the research showed that, despite the robust debate, few humanitarians believe that their association with the military, real or imagined, was a direct threat. Cases of presentational violence, such as disgruntled staff seeking revenge, occurred regardless of policy or position, and security management measures are needed. Some areas, particularly in the north of the country, were relatively stable and prospered following the end of Taliban rule. These areas experienced relatively low anonymous violence. The south and east, in contrast, did not appear to change following the fall of the Taliban and in those areas the level of anonymous violence was high. With a gradual change in the nature of the conflict and the way military operations were conducted, security objectives bled into the humanitarian concerns. More than half of those interviewed expressed concern about this development but felt that the rigidity of some aspects of humanitarian ethics (particularly neutrality) means that they are dated and difficult to apply in the politically charged environment found in Afghanistan.

The high-profile security incidents discussed in Chapter 5 each targeted large and well-known organizations (in those cases MSF, ICRC and CARE). When these incidents occurred, other NGOs were passed over or ignored by those undertaking violence. As the security incidents showed, when a small group or even a single humanitarian was attacked it could cause concern, especially in the local area. In May 2006 Kabul riots targeted highly visible NGOs, despite their proclaimed proximity to the military. In that incident, NGOs were attacked *en masse* in different parts of the city and this gave cause for concern throughout the humanitarian community, especially where high visibility was concerned. When security incidents are compared, a strong association with the level of violence and political instability became apparent. Often, the most high-profile –in terms of both their reputation and physical presence, which was increased with protection security measures – organizations were attacked. This shows that, rather than being protected by high visibility of identity (through reputation, outspokenness of humanitarian ethics such as neutrality and independence and a large and active staff) and physical presence (with, for example, flags, decals, travel routes and the like), these measures proved ineffective to protect against situational security. Fast (2014) notes similar concerns with protection and deterrence strategies which separate aid workers from other civilians and suggests a need for organizations achieve improved internal decision making that is more in line with their principles.

This indicates that high visibility led to organizations' being singled out because of their potential impact in terms on instilling and causing fear. This suggested that visibility is a more significant determining factor when it comes to insecurity than is an external relationship, including with the military. In other words, based on interviews and analysis of available information in Afghanistan, large, more visible NGOs that tried to have, and perceived themselves as having, a distant relationship the military suffered from more insecurity. Smaller, less visible organizations which may have had a closer relationship with the military were relatively more secure. These NGOs did not suffer the same attacks as the larger, more visible organizations, despite operating in the same locations and at the same time. This supports other research in suggesting that some assumptions, including the humanitarian ethic of neutrality, did not lead to improved security. Accordingly, as the AOG increased attacks following the departure of the heavy international presence, it "prioritized highly visible attacks" that included record NGO fatalities (INSO 2015; see more below).

Debate about the motivations behind insecurity was widespread. As one long-time Afghan NGO manager put it, "we'd been working under the most dangerous conditions for years without them [the military]" and questioned why now the military was needed. As insecurity increased, interest in the military–humanitarian relationship became more prevalent and coordination efforts more robust in 2005 and 2006. In turn, this renewed the debate. New staff arriving in Afghanistan would ask "why are we so heavily embedded here?" This led to doubts among those in country. Echoing the perspective of most interviewees, one NGO manager stated that "we have yet to see a proven direct link between perceived closeness with the military and our own insecurity … It has to do with increased insecurity in general." One incident in northern Afghanistan helped to illustrate this. "WFP [World Food Program] was attacked [with mortars] because the guards were going to be laid off … the [local] commander approved it so his guys would get their salaries. WFP tried to downsize but after the rockets worked the first time, there is no way to fire them now." In other words, this insecurity related to a severe type of management problem in a dangerous environment, but to be on the safe side distance is kept from the military for "strictly pragmatic reasons, in case if closely aligned with the military there is a greater security risk." Such situations led NGOs to conclude that "security depends on the direct relationship on history and trust." This approach is known as the "acceptance strategy," which is distinguished from deterrence, which presents an opposing threat and protection which relies on physical devices such as concertina wire (Martin 1999). Among those interviewed, it was perceived that, contrary to the opinion that close relations with the military caused insecurity, interacting with the military is less dangerous than having high visibility. During the Kabul riots, the NGOs that had arrived in the country as part of the post-11 September 2001 influx were at no greater risk than those that had a much longer presence. While any organization might be targeted, organizations with deep roots in Afghanistan and with well-established records of humanitarian ethics, especially independence and neutrality, suffered from attacks. With rising AOG activity every year since 2008, and the highest number of NGO fatalities on record in 2014, there was "still no dedicated shift towards the targeting of neutral NGOs" (INSO 2015, p. 8).

This deteriorating security situation triangulates with statistics available through the Aid Worker Security Database, a project of Humanitarian Outcomes. Figure 6.1 shows total security incidents against national and international aid staff, both UN and NGO. This clearly indicates that the danger to humanitarians has increased over time. This coincides with a dramatic increase in Coalition Forces deaths following a similar pattern. There was a perceived change in the relationship during that time. In other words, there was no leap toward either the integrated or segregated policies; instead, what changed was that the AOGs mobilized and criminality increased, resulting in an increase in anonymous danger. It is a common perception that insecurity has increased during the post-11 September 2001 period due

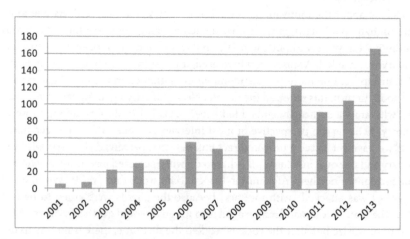

Figure 6.1 Total security incidents in Afghanistan

Source: Aid Worker Database, Humanitarian Outcomes (2014)

to United States-led military operations. In Afghanistan, however, humanitarians were more concerned than the general public about security (Asia Foundation 2006, PIPA 2006). This may be because they have jobs, but no doubt also relates to the perceived possibility of being directly targeted for attack, including bombing, kidnapping and murder.

The final element under analysis is the issue of development in Afghanistan, and its close linkage is symbolized in the military–humanitarian relationship. Because this issue is still being developed in the literature and among policy makers, it is the issue that "muddies the water" the most. Because security and development are so intimately linked, the two represent a kind of chicken-and-egg problem (Lischer 2007) where development cannot occur without security and security will not come without development. Nearly every actor interviewed voiced concern over this conundrum and strong voices could be heard for supporting both arguments. The simple and often-heard formula of more development results in less insecurity does not hold up, on closer scrutiny.

The idea that development brings security was a notion not only held by the military but also debated at length by political leaders, donors, policy staff and relief workers on the ground. Several interviewees supported this notion, that the lack of development led to insecurity. "The problem of joblessness is not good – people are thinking about bad things when they are not working." However, most interviewees were more critical and argued against the notion that an increase in reconstruction would equate to improved security. According to one staffer of a donor organization, regarding the security situation in the south, many say that "lack of development is the problem but that's not true ... the military thinks that security equals development" and vice versa. She went on to ask: "Would you accept an ice cream after being punched in the nose?" An Afghan NGO manager argued that "Development can't substitute for security ... you can't keep bad people busy." The interrelated problem of security and development (the chicken-and-egg problem) remained highly contested. This issue will be looked at further by examining international aid funding, vulnerability and insecurity in the country.

The funding for five top European donors (Denmark, Ireland, Holland, Sweden and the United Kingdom) during the early part of the war gives a good sense of the disbursement of resources generally. Funding was channeled into three provinces: Kabul, Nangarhar (to the east of Kabul, bordering Pakistan) and Mazar-i-Sharif (in the north). In addition, the northeast in general was favored over other parts of the country (Cutts 2005, p. 53). There were several reasons for this, including ease of access and, as some of those interviewed argued, that a reward was given to those areas for supporting the ousting of the Taliban. What is most relevant, however, is that this funding did not match or line up with the areas of greatest vulnerability. During the same period, areas of vulnerability, based on landmine/unexploded ordnance coverage, health, food security and accessibility, were spread throughout the country, while the northeast was generally the least vulnerable (with some exceptions such as the remote areas of Badakhshan). As discussed in Chapter 5, the southern and eastern parts of the country were also the most insecure. More funding, which equates to more reconstruction activity, did not translate into increased security. This triangulated with interviews and observations but the perception remained, particularly among the military, that it was critical to work on (and fund) both security and development-type activities. Following the pattern, there was a feeling that those areas that were less "cooperative" received less assistance. As one interviewee put it: "The north didn't need a 'winning the hearts and minds' campaign but it got it anyway because of politics."

In Afghanistan, it could be claimed that the "counter-insurgency and development strategies were the same." Some will note, for example, north–south or urban–rural differences in the country and then go on to make rather broad conclusions. This is supported by two examples: reconstruction of roads and buildings. The rehabilitation and construction of paved roads provides an interesting case with regard to the linkage between security and development. Roads are a key element of infrastructure for facilitating nearly every facet of the development enterprise. They are also critical for physical security. According to the effort to pave the road in the Panjshir valley, "Not only is the United States military's road project complementary to the USAID project, but the military and civilians worked together for negotiation of contentious issues such as water rights between elders and local leaders with the contractors" (USAID 2007, p. 1; see also Delesgues 2007).

In this way, USAID and the United States military can claim to carry out not only development but security through a type of peacebuilding in which different communal groups work on projects together. Thus in Afghanistan there was significant effort to repair and extend the network of roads. At the same time, however, good roads facilitate trafficking and other illicit activities (such as planting of roadside bombs) which have been linked to AOGs in Afghanistan. The first such effort was resurfacing the so-called "ring road" connecting Kabul with Kandahar in the south and Herat in the west. In the years since 2001, many other roads have been repaired, including roads that had never been paved before. Despite the effort, a perceived inequity developed where one area coveted the apparent or real benefits received by another. According to several interviewees, if one community had a key road paved, other communities nearby expected the same. In southern areas, insecurity continues, therefore the linkage between security and development does not appear to be strong. In this way, rather than more development funding leading to greater security, in certain areas assistance resulted in improved conditions for Afghans. As one UN official stated, reconstruction "can bring competition and jealousy when others see what they don't have." Indeed this was a familiar refrain in Afghanistan, with the idea that every village deserves what every town has and every town deserves what every city has, and so on.

A second example is the rehabilitation and construction of government buildings by the PRTs, such as provincial government centers and schools. The visibility of these ("lighthouse") projects and, some said, the apparent lack of Afghan input into these projects resulted in targeting by the insurgency. Formal education provides an interesting case for the link between security and development because of the role it plays in Afghanistan's reconstruction and because primary education is considered a right for all Afghan children. The estimated number of school buildings is a little more than 4,200 country-wide. In the period under review here, the number of schools attacked by AOGs increased from 12 in 2005 to 99 in 2006 (UNICEF 2006). According to some sources schools reconstructed under the NSP program, for example, were not attacked. Destruction of schools was also accompanied by threats and intimidation against teachers and students, resulting in the stoppage of education, particularly in the south and east of the country. In the southeastern province of Zabul, for example, approximately only 8 per cent of girls attended school and roughly half of the schools remained closed because of AOG attacks (HRW 2006). At one point, only one girls' school functioned in the province, and that because it was just 200 meters from a United States-run base in the provincial capital (Coghlan 2006).

Such projects were seen by the PRTs as symbols of their efforts and were part of the objective of supporting the Afghan government. Because they symbolized the government, were built with the support of "foreigners" and promoted ideas that were antithetical to those held by armed opposition groups, the provincial centers and schools were attacked first. One donor representative admitted that these structures "enticed the enemy" to attack and, at the same time, the building represented corrupt government officials, so it "just looked bad" to be seen to be supporting them. Reconstruction projects carried out with sufficient community input, such as those done under NSP, fared better. "Because they have been built by the people, not one NSP school has been burned down," remarked one Afghan familiar with the program. The conflict therefore linked the reconstruction of schools closely to both security and development.

In sum, in examining the issue of security and development, the research revealed two key findings. First, the link between the military–humanitarian relationship and NGO insecurity was not evident. There were cases where the closeness, in terms of physical proximity, could result in insecurity for NGOs (such as convoys, bases and operations) especially in fluid low-intensity conflict that did not have front lines, use of "terror" tactics and blurring of the line between combatant and non-combatant. Yet cases were rare in which NGOs were deliberately attacked. In some cases, the military helped to create secure conditions; however, when it was a direct belligerent there was a rapid increase in the likelihood of anonymous danger, which then impacted NGO security. In such cases, the security of humanitarians was compromised as a result of anonymous, not presentational, danger. While the security findings may suggest that a closer relationship with the military is possible or even desired, common sense dictates that there is not a good reason to make this relationship closer, because there would be few benefits. Despite the lack of a strong statistical or perceived connection between the insecurity of humanitarian workers and their relationship (to whatever degree) with the military, the perception among some humanitarians interviewed was still strong. Based on nearly 60 interviews, the particularly strong views held by some NGOs tend to be exceptions and do not necessarily indicate the majority view. The dominant perception, and perhaps the one that gets most to the truth of the matter, is a cautious pragmatism. It was also found that the role of development activities (of the type carried out by NGOs) was not strong in fostering stability. Thus an integrated policy of NGOs may not be needed.

Conclusion

In this chapter, the findings relating to the basic and underlying causes of tension within the military–humanitarian relationship and the underlying policy issue have been presented. These are decision making and external relationships related to structure and agency, the co-option and politicization of NGOs as an extension of ethical norms and the link between security and development. The discussion of the findings in this chapter has analyzed the key research question of the underlying policy issue: why should NGOs pursue an integrated or segregated policy toward the military? The answer depends on five specific findings.

First, the inter-organizational friction present in relations between humanitarians and the military does not necessarily contribute to negative relations. The main finding of this research relating to decision making and external relationships is that inter-organizational friction is common in many relationships, yet it is not always detrimental. In no case under consideration in this study was the friction debilitating enough to lead to a segregated approach. In support of the findings of other research (Janis 1989), friction is not necessarily a negative thing (but it is a normal part of decision making and policy formation). When there was friction, it originated with managerial decisions and choices, where organizational structures including explicit policies were weak or nonexistent.

Second, with both NGOs and the military, explicit policies are not always followed. For this reason, such policies may not be helpful because they are likely to leave out different contingencies and "straightjacket" decision making. In Afghanistan, existing policies usually supported a segregated approach to relations with the military and few organizations followed a "top down" approach. It was more common for individual managers to decide the way in which external relationships are handled. Only in a few cases were humanitarian relationships with the military determined by official policies and no case found was found of an explicitly integrated formal policy.

Third, only in certain situations does an integrated approach result in insecurity for NGOs. In some cases, the military may help to create secure conditions; however, when it was involved in conflict as a direct belligerent the likelihood was greater for a significant increase in anonymous danger, resulting in a reduced security environment for NGOs. There are other reasons to maintain a segregated approach, relating to the next points.

Fourth, humanitarian principles, especially in the field, are not particularly well established. Instead, humanitarians follow a flexible approach and are dependent on situation and context. Rather than operating in a landscape of two or more principles, NGOs adapt their principles to meet the contexts in which they operate. This results in a predominant view that is highly political and closely associated with the international political–military efforts in the country.

Finally, official development assistance seemed to lead to the co-option and politicization of humanitarian organizations, but most humanitarians understand that they are part of the stability and state-building process in the country. In fact, some NGOs accepted grants so as to influence donor governments and organizations, although their ability to influence was incremental and on a small scale.

These five findings are the most prominent issues in the military–humanitarian relations debate and help to instruct the decision whether NGOs have close or distant relations with the military. This reveals a mixed picture that cannot be easily understood as a simple dichotomy of "for" or "against" relations with the military. These five areas provide the basis for the application of wider considerations in the final chapter.

7

Conclusion

Introduction

The military–humanitarian relationship has received increased attention in recent years. The complex emergencies of the early 1990s led to the growth of humanitarian action, but this has occurred in a "policy vacuum" (Roberts 1996, p. 9) where many unproven assumptions remain. Equally, the events since 11 September 2001 have renewed the need for defining and clarifying the role of humanitarians and their relationship with the military. This, along with the realities found in Afghanistan, provides the rationale for deep analysis. The aim of this book has been to answer the underlying policy issue: why should aid organizations have a close or distant relationship with the military? To answer this question from a humanitarian perspective, this book has examined the relationship between NGOs and the military, using Afghanistan as a case study.

The first half of the book provided a grounding for the presentation of the research. In Chapter 1, the main topic was introduced, including five common assumptions. These are that the military–humanitarian relationship is "new," that differences between aid organizations and the military cause inter-organizational friction, that a close relationship with the military may lessen the security of NGOs, that principled positions are well established and that official aid leads to politicization and manipulation. In Chapter 2, the historical context was examined. It was demonstrated that, over time, three drivers – technology, strategy and ethics – were important in bringing humanitarians and the military together. Thus, rather than being "new," the relationship between humanitarians and the military can be traced to the origins of humanitarianism itself. Chapter 3 reviewed the disparate body of literature on security, international development and humanitarianism with a focus on the underlying policy issue – whether NGOs should have a close or distant relationship with the military. In so doing, it examined three controversies. These were the tension between organizational structure and individual agency, humanitarian ethics and the security–development debate. A research framework was developed which examined integrated ("for" or in support of) or segregated ("against" or opposed to) relations between humanitarians and the military.

In the second half of the book, a detailed case study of Afghanistan provided the basis for closer examination of the research, including the causes and manifestations that led to a difficult environment in which humanitarians worked. In Chapter 4, the historical backdrop of Afghanistan was discussed. In Chapter 5, an analysis of the period following the attacks of 11 September 2001 was presented, with specific focus on the military–humanitarian relationship. In Chapter 6, our research findings were laid out, including much of the primary evidence based on observation and key informant interviews. In this final chapter, the relevant findings of the research are reviewed and applied to a broader context of humanitarianism worldwide. An analysis of the research questions will be undertaken based on the assumptions first presented in Chapter 1. Within each area, the research findings will be placed in a wider context and their implications will be discussed. By unpacking these, the underlying policy issue will be addressed and discussed further with application to wider cases. The aim here is to get past simplistic analysis and explanations such as the idea that aid organizations and the military have intrinsically incompatible goals and organizational cultures. Instead a more nuanced and well-informed understanding of the implications is provided. In the process, a framework for understanding the contexts within which military–humanitarian relations occur is present.

The relationship between humanitarians and the military is not "new"

During the last 150 years or so, warfare developed in such a way that stimulated the need for humanitarianism. In this way, conflict has given rise to modern humanitarianism. This can be traced to the wars of the second half of the nineteenth century, when two distinct spheres – one civil and one military – emerged through experiences on the battlefield and the codification of international law. This distinction, formed by a line separating the two spheres, is a critical foundation for military–humanitarian relations. While these spheres were most distinct between the 1700s (during the rise of modern Western armies) and the end of the Second World War, this line has been blurred during other times. Contemporary conflict has eroded this distinction because the nature of war itself has evolved. In the process, the birth and growth of modern Western humanitarianism has put civilians in greater proximity to soldiers. Contrary to some literature widely held opinion on the topic, this relationship is not new. Three closely linked stimuli bringing about these changes in the military–humanitarian relationship were technology, strategy and humanitarian ethics. Technology stimulated changes in military strategy, which in turn stimulated the need for a more extensive codification of ethics.

In the realm of technology, three key areas had the most profound impact on humanitarianism in war: arms and military hardware, medical practice in war and the media. The development of arms and military hardware was the first stimulus that gave militaries increased levels of destructive capacity. Following the Battle of Solferino in 1859, the technological advancement of weapons contributed to an increased attention to the victims of those weapons, in what was termed the "Solferino Cycle" (Coupland 1999). From that point forward, advances in modern medicine were a springboard for humanitarianism in terms of service and, later, protection of human rights. Medical practice in times of war blurred, and at times eliminated, the distinctions between humanitarians and the military. Other technological advances, notably the development of mass media, further stimulated the impulse to assist the victims of war. During the twentieth century, mass media was used by elites to "manufacture consent" to carry out policies and to support "popular" causes. Regardless of the type or source, it provided a powerful impulse for humanitarian response in numerous instances – from Biafra to Somalia.

The second stimulus, military strategy, is important for the military–humanitarian relationship because it determined how militaries carried out their operations, which in turn influenced the work of humanitarians. The historically dominant military strategy was high-intensity conflict which pitted army against army. This type of war permitted a degree of humanitarian space because there was a generally clear distinction between civilians and those involved in combat and the principle of neutrality was widely accepted. During the Second World War, Western militaries developed civil affairs units to deal with the increasing interaction between civilians and the military. With decolonization and the Cold War as a backdrop, low-intensity conflict gained importance and became the more prevalent strategy. Civilians became more critical in determining the outcome of this type of war and humanitarian space began to shrink. Western militaries developed specific strategies that have led them to assume broadened roles, such as assisting civilians to reconstruct their communities. In the process, the line between humanitarians and the military eroded. With a larger number of humanitarian actors present in conflict-affected countries, there is less room for them to act freely without political or military interaction.

The final stimulus, humanitarian ethics and the codification of normative laws and values, is an integral determinant of the military–humanitarian relationship because it serves as a framework in which projects were implemented in the "field." Although early examples exist of the codification of the rules of war and IHL, for instance by Hugo Grotius, it was Henri Dunant's creation of the Red Cross following the Battle of Solferino that led to the formulation of what became known as classical humanitarianism. This was based on a deontological ethic which places primacy on *a priori* moral obligations that do not change in different contexts. To achieve this, neutrality and tacit cooperation with the military were undertaken as far as was necessary to carry out one's ethical duties. Following the experiences of the Second World War and the conflicts of the 1960s, and the Nigerian civil war in particular, the limits of classical humanitarianism became evident. This led to the formation of neo-humanitarianism. This approach adopted a consequentialist ethic in order to maximize the potential benefits of an action even in the face of negative outcomes. Neo-humanitarianism emphasized the readiness to speak out against perceived atrocities and the right to interfere (*le droit d'ingérence*). In extreme cases, neo-humanitarians were willing to call for military protection. Viewed historically, those undertaking these approaches have maintained a close, albeit different, relationship with the military and have formed a key element for understanding the underlying policy question of how close or distant a relationship humanitarians should have with the military.

Considered broadly, the implication of this finding is that different conditions (primarily political but also relating to the three stimuli) contributed to integrated or segregated relations. While this finding reinforces a common understanding of the importance of history in analyzing different phenomena, it confirms the conclusion of others that context is also important (Lewis et al. 2003). This context is not static and has evolved over time, but understanding what came before can help to inform the present. Positions that rest on the false assumption that the relationship is "new" place its analysis on a shaky foundation. By understanding that the relationship has deep roots and that it is truly as old as humanitarianism itself, NGO managers involved in decision making on the relationship with the military can make informed choices rather than simply react to situations. With this understanding, organizational policy and practice can be tailored to specific contexts.

Inter-organizational friction in the relationship is not always negative

Inter-organizational friction is an important issue in military–humanitarian relations. The underlying reasons for inter-organizational friction have been: the blurring of the line between the humanitarian and military spheres; reduced humanitarian space; and policy coherence. The basic causes behind these underlying reasons included several factors such as policy dysfunction and a culture clash between organizations. This friction resulted in resistance and sometimes hostility between humanitarians and the military. Increasingly segregated policy positions adopted by aid organizations often led to an increased amount of inter-organizational friction. While there was variation among organizations in Afghanistan, those few that had policies and an ethos of independence typically had segregated policies that positioned them against close relations with the military. There is a rich body of work on this theme in psychology and group dynamics (Forsyth 2006) and international development (Archer 2003, George 2005, Wheeler and Harmer 2006). Further, the military had a tendency in Afghanistan to behave as an unwieldy organization (an "800-pound gorilla" as it was described) when it came to interacting with others through its heavy-handed presence and ability to exercise its own prerogative. This frustration on the part of NGOs against the military's power and ability to make unilateral decisions contributed to friction (a number of examples described earlier in the case study how this occurred). Yet, not all interactions were characterized by negative friction and there have been times, even in Afghanistan, where relations have been positive and beneficial.

In both the Afghan case study and beyond, inter-organizational friction is highly dependent on context. To better elucidate this concept, a framework is offered here. This provides a way for better understanding positions that manifest themselves in different contexts and which then shape the nature of the relationship. In this way, this framework facilitates understanding by the military and the development of informed policy by aid organizations. It is based in part on the model developed by Stepan (1988) which seeks to differentiate the contexts in which civil society and military forces find themselves. A key element of Stepan's model is "military prerogative," which he defines as:

> those areas where, whether challenged or not, the military as an institution assumes they have an acquired right or privilege, formal or informal, to exercise effective control over its internal government, to play a role within extramilitary areas within the state apparatus, or even to structure relationships between the state and political or civil society. (1988, p. 93)

Stepan's model is useful for illustrating how two diverse spheres – one civilian and one military – relate to each other.

The framework offered here (Figure 7.1) presents three positions evident in military–humanitarian relations: disaster response; transitional situations in which peace operations occur; and warfare. This is arrived at by plotting different types of humanitarian emergencies (or, more simply, "disasters") with estimated levels of military prerogative. Along the horizontal axis, different types of disasters are plotted, ranging from natural events (such as earthquakes and tsunami) to violent

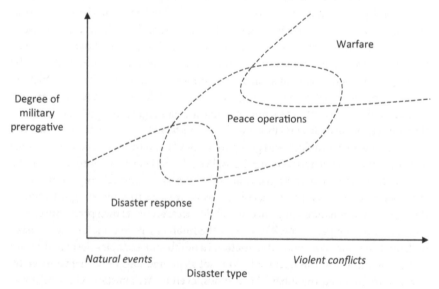

Figure 7.1 Military–humanitarian relations framework

conflict (including wars of differing intensities). In theory, these are distinct areas but in practice there is rarely a definitive line between types of disaster. For instance, food insecurity, market failure and political violence can combine in what are called complex emergencies. There is an argument that all are caused by people through the creation of extreme forms of vulnerability and are closely associated with exclusion, deprivation and suffering. This also mirrors the typical degree of security in a particular country, which can be measured in numerous ways (e.g. battlefield deaths, incidents of violent crime and attacks on aid workers).

Along the vertical axis, the degree of military prerogative following Stepan's usage can be plotted. In the lower left quadrant, the military takes a supporting or even benign role in what can be termed "military support to humanitarian assistance" but the imposition of military power increases along the axis, leading to outright military rule or a junta higher on the axis. The upper left quadrant would be untenable for democratic societies and the bottom right quadrant is typically unsustainable in any form of government (which leads to state collapse/statelessness). When considered theoretically, three broad categories can be identified and are discussed next. These three sets of positions are similarly discussed in the literature (Lilly 2002, Klingebiel and Roehder 2004, InterAction 2005, Frerks et al. 2006) and are echoed in Weiss's (1999) typology. However, these are usually described as fixed positions and not the dynamic change suggested in the contingency approach mentioned in Chapter 3. Instead, most aid organizations moved back and forth along the spectrum, depending on the temporal and situational context. Context is a key determinant of relationships between organizations. Thus, this framework follows a spectrum recognizing that these relationships change over time and are relative. It also offers a remedy to the one-size-fits-all problem of having an unreflexive and rigid policy by understanding the context and potential amount of military prerogative.

In the first category, in the figure's lower left-hand quadrant, identified in Figure 7.1 as disaster response, there is the least amount of contestation and military prerogative. Examples include the domestic and international responses to severe natural hazards such as the 2004 Indian Ocean tsunami, the 2005 Kashmiri earthquake and the 2010 earthquake in Haiti as well as the 2002 Nahrin earthquake in Afghanistan. While it varied from country to country, military prerogative was generally low after the tsunami and the earthquake despite the fact that much of the assistance went to areas formerly under security restriction. In this category, inter-organizational friction is at its lowest and an integrated approach to military–humanitarian relations is most likely to be followed or is at least acceptable to a majority of the humanitarian actors. During these relief operations, for example, aid organizations openly critical of the military were known to have actively cooperated including unloading supplies from military helicopters, sharing information and coordinating activities. In short, most humanitarians find it acceptable to be strategically engaged with the military when conditions of low military prerogative and natural hazards occur, such as tsunami and earthquakes. In such cases, where insecurity is generally low and political influence is (at least temporarily) pushed lower on the agenda, the humanitarian principle of humanity trumps security concerns, over time blurring the line between humanitarian and military spheres and the co-option of humanitarians into political and military agendas.

In the middle category are activities which are considered to have been undertaken to bring about settlement to violent conflict, identified in Figure 7.1 as peace operations. Examples include the 16 UN peacekeeping missions currently in operation, such as the UN's Mission in Liberia and UN's Mission in the Republic of South Sudan, as well as peace enforcement and peacemaking efforts where increasing levels of force are used (Boulden 2001, Findlay 2002). A key feature of this category is the areas of overlap, which are particularly contentious and lead to a number of problems including blurring of the line between humanitarian and military spheres and the co-option of humanitarians into political and military agendas. There, NGOs often interact with combined civil–military structures and are called on to perform a variety of tasks, such as peacebuilding activities and the demobilization and reintegration of former combatants. Under such scenarios, humanitarians tend to be divided on which position to take, both integrated and segregated positions are evident and inter-organizational friction often results.

In the final category is the upper right quadrant of the figure (identified as "warfare" in Figure 7.1), where war fighting, violent conflict and kinetic military operations take place. In this category, the military forms a significant element of the government and experiences increased interaction in the civil sphere through a heavy involvement in reconstruction. Military prerogative is at its highest. With a faint or absent line between the different levels of conflict, this prerogative comes about as the result of military occupation and during interim or transitional governments. Here, inter-organizational friction is also at its highest. In Iraq, for example, where the situation is especially dangerous for humanitarians, debate is most robust and positions taken by aid organizations toward the military are most likely to be segregated.

In areas of overlap between categories, contestation and anonymous insecurity increases. The prime example is Afghanistan from 2002 to 2014 (during 2001, with the exceptions of aerial food drops, military activity was devoted to forcibly removing the Taliban regime and seeking those associated with the use of terrorism). The challenge in Afghanistan has been that a mixed military mission (peace or stability operations under ISAF and counter-terrorism under the Coalition Force) and humanitarian assistance have been undertaken at the same time, all under the complex aid architecture combining security with political and developmental goals. Thus there is a high degree of military prerogative in the country but the government remains in sovereign power. Similarly, the disaster affecting the country is highly violent – although not to the same degree as, for example, in Iraq, based on the death count, incidents of insecurity and observation of the precautions used by

Box 7.1 The Salang Threshold

The Salang Tunnel is located high in the Hindu Kush mountains. At an altitude of 3,400 meters, and nearly 2.6 kilometers long, it provides a vital strategic logistical connection in central Afghanistan. Traveling there during conflict and in winter is a dangerous prospect. It has been fought over since the 1980s and has witnessed multiple natural catastrophes including avalanches and internal fires (the worst occurring in 1982, when 176 people died). Aid workers and the military alike have had to make the decision when to follow the route, when to postpone travel or when to use alternative means such as air transport. In much the same way, humanitarians face a "Salang-like" threshold where they must make difficult, sometimes dangerous life-or-death, choices. As situations shift between peace operations and warfare, humanitarians must navigate the practical, policy and moral challenges of operating in areas of high insecurity where the military undertakes multiple roles. Depending on their position, they can elect to work with the military or apart from the military or to withdraw altogether.

humanitarians operating in both countries. Looking broadly, the policy coherence and "integrated missions" of the UN, which combine humanitarian and military functions and responsibilities under a unified structure, have likewise generated considerable controversy. Because situations evolve with high degrees of violence, military prerogative and armed forces taking on multiple roles, humanitarians face a multitude of dangerous choices. We describe this as the "Salang Threshold" (Box 7.1).

When the specific examples discussed here are plotted along the same horizontal and vertical axes as in Figure 7.1, their relative positions are as shown in Figure 7.2. As contexts change toward the third category, aid organizations cross a principled threshold where they often feel compelled to speak out about issues of humanitarian principles. At the same time, as is noted in the framework, the military holds considerable prerogative which can lead to highly contentious situations. In Afghanistan, the different manifestations of tension between humanitarians and the military led to debate, the development of collective policies and an increasingly segregated approach. In Iraq, many of the same debates occurred but at an earlier point in the evolution of that conflict and organizations were faced with the choice of cooperating with the military occupation or leaving the country altogether.

With this understanding of the military–humanitarian relationship, finding a balance between organizational structures and individual agency is crucial for NGO management. This is made more difficult by the dangerous and politically complex situations in which humanitarians often work. Rather than following hierarchical structures and rigid established policies, this research has shown that few organizations follow a top-down approach. Individuals are more likely to determine the

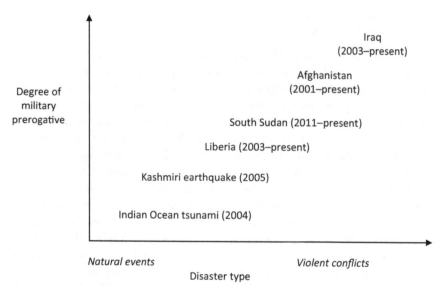

Figure 7.2 Recent world events

manner in which external relationships are handled. In cases of high stress, of which Afghanistan certainly qualifies, this can lead to policy dysfunction (supporting the work of Janis 1989, Walkup 1997) and other problems such as poor decisions about programming and partnerships. When beneficiaries are involved, a pattern develops known as the "Samaritan's Dilemma" whereby humanitarians are compelled to provide assistance regardless of the actions of the recipients. This was evident in the Afghanistan case and supports the findings of others (Buchanan 1977, Lagerlof 2004, Gibson et al. 2005). In much the same way, aid workers' choices can be limited or similarly forced, especially in contexts with high degrees of military prerogative and violence. Partnerships in particular can have unintended outcomes, such as the perception of co-option by a dominant group over another. Indeed, some donors require partnership alongside security forces in order to access their funds. In Afghanistan, this was seen in the design of the aid architecture where NGOs were meant to be part of a system and in partnership with government and security elements, including the military. This facilitated the light-footprint concept and made policy coherence possible. Without this policy coherence, it was argued, organizations would be uncoordinated and would work at cross purposes, wasting resources. In other examples, this was done through the UN integrated mission concept, which combined the military and civilian aspects of peace operations under one command. In this way, the notion of coherence has been institutionalized and has become standard practice in many post-conflict reconstruction efforts worldwide.

Even with the framework discussed here, the implication is that some friction can be productive and may help NGOs to preserve principles. As other research has shown (Assael 1969), some friction can have beneficial effects in that it can bring more equitable relationships where new agendas can be forwarded. As described in the case of the program networking (CPAN) and the NGO representative at CENTCOM, in Afghanistan it led to improved programming. At the same time, however, too much friction can be detrimental by minimizing dialogue, restricting coordination and de-legitimizing other organizations. It is important that decision makers understand and take into account the context in which they are operating. Closely related to this, it appears that organizations should be prepared to accept imperfection. The "quality" approaches prescribed in popular business models are not necessarily appropriate for the work undertaken in the challenging environments where complex emergencies occur. Of the many approaches, the "70% solution" (Freedman 2000, see also Janis 1989), where implementation goes forward without every element in place, is but one. Further, this research demonstrates that NGO management practices deserve more attention because this is a neglected area and many questions remain.

The relationship does not necessarily make aid organizations less secure

In practice, the quest for security is the most contentious issue connected to the military–humanitarian relationship. Humanitarian action is inherently dangerous and it is not surprising that threats increase in tandem with the amount of violent conflict. There are at least three issues related to security which contradict the common assumption that proximity to military forces per se is automatically dangerous for humanitarians. First, the nature of conflict itself is important. High-intensity conflict has largely subsided, and, with it, battle-related deaths (Lacina et al. 2006, Pinker 2011), but the proliferation of intra-state conflicts ("small wars") continues. Recent conflicts, notably the Syrian civil war, have been marked by a disregard for international law, rejecting traditional distinctions between combatants and civilians, which blurs the distinction between civil and military. This tendency has produced a very dangerous environment in which humanitarians work.

Second, and leading from the first issue, the strategies employed by militaries to adapt to the nature of war can put them in closer proximity to aid organizations, in terms of both physical presence and the policy arena. As shown above, a key rationale that is often given for military relations with humanitarians and, in fact, for intervention itself is the necessity of providing security to relief workers. In many contexts since the end of the Cold War, the military has sought to expand safe access for humanitarians. In some places the military was relatively successful, but those cases are relatively few. In Afghanistan, the military presented multiple images – as counter-terrorist, "peacekeeper" and promoter of reconstruction – which made the situation complex and difficult to manage. The evidence shows that while the military rarely puts relief workers in direct danger, it may be part of, or create, insecure environments with a high degree of anonymous violence. By having militaries with similar or shared backgrounds (such as dominant cultural and religious elements) in addition to similar goals (such as the establishment of a semi-liberal state), humanitarians are inherently at risk due to the blurred line which closes the proximity of "identity" as seen by local residents and insurgents alike (Kilcullen 2009). More broadly, even with such similarities, there are contextual concerns involved based on Stepan's model. In different scenarios, where there is a greater distance from conflict, the more likely it is that humanitarians may find it acceptable to have a closer relationship with the military.

Finally, the evidence has shown that NGO visibility may be a more important determinant of insecurity or risk than proximity to the military. In Afghanistan, aid workers did not see consistently a link between their security and their relationship with the military. In the incidents discussed in the second half of this book, highly visible organizations with a widely known and perceived distance from the military were attacked, while less visible organizations which may have had a close relationship were less likely to suffer from targeted attack. To understand this, the level of analysis is important. Although on an international scale it could be perceived that all organizations in Afghanistan from 2001 to 2014 were "working" with the military, a more localized analysis reveals that there were important differences between organizations. As outlined earlier, this visibility can be thought of in terms of identity (including general recognition, decals and flags, reputation and degree of outspokenness) and presence (such as location of offices, travel routes and size of staff). Viewed more broadly, high visibility and an integrated approach toward the military may be beneficial. For example, peacekeeping operations where there are a high degree of presentational violence and military forces have a high degree of legitimacy. The framework developed in the previous section helps to distinguish between such contexts.

While the overall number of incidents of insecurity has increased, insecurity is largely targeted at locals without a link or reference to the military. The main threats are the result of anonymous insecurity, such as criminality and happenstance as a result of being near violent conflict (described as being "caught in the crossfire"). The distinction between anonymous and presentational insecurity is key. While the Taliban has frequently made clear that its targeting policy has been influenced by its targets' degree of alignment with the invaders, the evidence from Afghanistan shows that anonymous danger has increased over time, leading to a less secure environment for aid workers based on their degree of visibility (and not simply their perceived proximity to military forces). Despite the considerable debate on the subject, few humanitarians believed that their association with the military, real or imagined, was a direct threat. Cases of presentational violence, such as disgruntled staff seeking revenge, occurred regardless of policy or position.

The implication of this is that the visibility and proximity of aid organizations to the military should be re-examined. With a poor recognition of the context and a lack of understanding that humanitarians do not have fixed principles under which they operate, dysfunctional decisions made by NGO managers can contribute to the security vulnerability of humanitarians. In the security incidents discussed in Chapters 5 and 6, policies that professed neutrality and positions independent of the military could be trumped by visibility, making humanitarians subject to increasing rates of presentational violence.

The Afghan case is plagued by gaps and inconsistencies during the period examined (only in 2007 did ANSO begin systematic data collection and analysis of insecurity in Afghanistan). While this finding does not necessarily validate or support the managerial–positivist position (first described in Chapter 3) which aligns with the integrated position, the critical position remains within a minority of aid groups. The critical position appears to dominate current humanitarian practice, yet there are clearly efforts under way that support the managerialist–positivist position. In other words, the military–humanitarian relationship is determined by individuals (agency) and the power of organizations, and institutions (structure) are not strong or particularly well developed among relief-oriented NGOs. This supports the conclusions of Farrington et al. (1993) that people work despite boundaries set by the organizations they work for.

The need for more research has been noted by others (Sheik et al. 2000, Barnett 2004, Fast 2007) and the need for improved NGO practice is evident. Members of the cadre of NGO security managers are still untrained and unfamiliar with humanitarian security approaches: instead they bring skills from previous employment in the military or law enforcement fields. The setting of criteria for effective security management such as InterAction's Minimum Operating Security Standards is helpful, as is the professionalization of humanitarian security management, and these began to be implemented in Afghanistan during the period looked at here. Also important is the need for continued resources, especially to address the higher incidence of attacks on local staff. At the same time, more data are needed, specifically the systematic collection and analysis of information on events of insecurity, and several groups are working on this, including the International NGO Safety Organization, Humanitarian Outcomes' Aid Workers Security Database and the International NGO Safety and Security Association.

Without clear and universal guidance, the many negative outcomes in the military–humanitarian relationship included inter-organizational friction, inefficiency, competition and duplication of effort. While problems may arise out of cultural differences (Lewis et al. 2003), a lack of such guidance does not necessarily lead to poorer project performance. In short, there seemed to be a constant relearning of the lessons learned. The question has been how to make inter-organizational relations less arbitrary and more predictable. Yet there has been a reliance on individual agency and less emphasis on structures in determining relations between humanitarians and the military. Few organizations have explicit policies or internal guidelines specifically governing their relationship with the military. Instead, there has been the development of a collective of guidelines, which should be at the organizational and institutional levels and thus tailored to specific context. This offers a way of dealing with the "800-pound gorilla."

Humanitarian principles are important, but have been moderated by Afghanistan's political realities

As earlier discussed, the consequentialist and deontologist positions of the classical and neo-humanitarian approaches roughly correspond to the integrated and segregated positions related to military–humanitarian relations. As Weiss (1999) points out, though, it is important to note that while different ethical positions may be taken up by humanitarians, organizations tend to move back and forth along a spectrum of opinion depending on time and context. The four positions are presented along a spectrum in relation to humanitarian principles available to humanitarians in delivery of their programs. To review these, at one end of the spectrum are the "classicists," commonly represented by the ICRC, who hold most closely to an apolitical humanitarianism with the principles of neutrality and impartiality being of significant importance. The ICRC rarely changes its policies with respect to its principles and relationships with other organizations and so they are more rigid compared with those of other aid organizations.

Next, the "minimalists" and "maximalists" seek to grapple with the notion of politicized humanitarianism, but each in their own way: "minimalists" aim to "do no harm" and "maximalists" have a "more ambitious agenda of employing humanitarian action as part of a comprehensive strategy to transform conflict" (Weiss 1999, p. 3). Earlier, this book outlined how it was a reaction to the ICRC's principled position stressing neutrality in Biafra in the late 1960s that led to the founding of the more outspoken MSF and other organizations (Bortolotti 2004). These organizations saw it as not just a responsibility but a right to interfere (*le droit d'ingérence*) when concerns of human rights were raised.

At the far end of the spectrum are "solidarists," who have allied themselves closely in what they have seen as particular humanitarian causes. The group of NGOs that began work helping Afghans during the Soviet intervention of the 1980s is a prime example. In support of the "third position," the tensions found within the different approaches to humanitarian programming and described in Weiss's typology form the basis of the debates about humanitarian ethics in the literature (Pugh 1998). Organizational identity is fluid, adaptive and changes to meet new situations, which is what aid groups did in Afghanistan. This finding runs against much existing literature (but not all, such as Gioia et al. 2000), which often portrays them as fixed positions.

As the Afghan case study shows, the ethical position of humanitarians changed over time and in line with the political and military context. With the fall of the Taliban, policy coherence served as the basis for the aid architecture. As a result, aid organizations debated and adopted different positions within the minimalist and maximalist approaches. Thus, principles exercised substantial influence when "big powers are preoccupied with other matters and in those places where 'principles' happen to coincide with the economic interests of the host organization" (Stockton 2004b, p. 10). When viewed broadly, it appears evident that the "economic interests" of host organizations have expanded significantly over the last decade. According to Kouchner, in some cases this has been "applied well," while in others (such as Iraq) it has been applied "horribly" (2007, p. 66). The changes were not just to the principles but also to temporal and situational context, influenced by other factors such as inter-organizational friction, the nature of programming and factors such as insecurity.

Humanitarian principles are not fixed and are dependent on contexts and situations. Similarly, the military–humanitarian relationship is best characterized as flexible rather than fixed. Given the complexity of the situations they face, many senior NGO managers said that the "humanitarian imperative … could trump other humanitarian principles but only after careful analysis of the circumstances of each case" (NGO Internal Report 2004, p. 1, see also Martone 2002). Indeed, Afghanistan experienced this several times and instead of claiming fixed duties based on perceived political situations, humanitarians modified their principles accordingly. As complex systems, they are "metamorphic and continually change and mutate" (Duffield 2001, p. 254). As a result, the most decisive standard developed thus far is the Code of Conduct of the Red Cross and NGOs. The Code states that the "humanitarian imperative" is above all others; given the inherent tensions, neutrality is not mentioned. Instead, point two of the Code states: "Aid is given regardless of the race, creed or nationality of the recipients and without adverse distinction of any kind. Aid priorities are calculated on the basis of need alone" (Code of Conduct 1994, p. 2). Roberts notes that "the Code's avoidance of all difficult issues, including security, renders it of limited value, and its endorsement by over 140 governments only confirms the impression that they do not always take humanitarian issues seriously" (1996, p. 84). Indeed, neutrality and impartiality in certain cases can be at odds and impossible to achieve at the same time. Even as the most widely used set of principles available, the Code's interpretation and application can be problematic. Most organizations continue to say they are impartial and neutral even when they clearly are not. This gap between rhetoric and practice is where the understanding of the flexible approach adopted by humanitarians is helpful. Thus the humanitarians continue to struggle with finding a path forward. Examples abound, including the attempt by NGOs and other actors to formulate acceptable guidelines for interaction in Afghanistan.

The implication of these different perspectives on humanitarian ethics is that the role and function of aid organizations are under continual discussion and evolution. In Afghanistan, the basic question of the role of NGOs was under scrutiny in that country from the start. Coordination meetings and discussions in Kabul soon after the fall of the Taliban, in which the role of NGOs was questioned, ACBAR's public information campaign to clarify the role (ACBAR 2007) and much research

(Donini 2004, O'Brien 2004, Stockton 2004a) provide concrete examples that this issue has not been resolved. Through ACBAR, the NGO community struggled with the decision on the idea of "re-branding" but it was found to be too difficult and there was an effort to prevent the hijacking of the term "humanitarian" by military and commercial actors. This was part of the "soul searching" by humanitarians about who they are, what they do and how they are perceived (O'Brien 2004, p. 187, see also Frerks et al. 2006).

Predicted more than a decade ago as part of this evolution, there has been a continued hybridization, an increased amount of partnering and involvement in networks. This evolution led Frumkin and Andre-Clark (2000, p. 141) to suggest that NGOs "need to develop a strategy that emphasizes the unique value-driven dimension of their programs." The concern, however, has been that aid organizations have become little more than service providers by government contract and that the military has become "too much" of a partner. With ethical norms discussed as a central theme of this research, a natural concern is what path NGOs might take. In other words, have NGOs become catalysts for change or a cat's paw ("useful idiots," to borrow Lenin's term) of wider interests?

Aid agencies were mostly willingly incorporated into official reconstruction efforts

The final key sub-question examined was the link between security and development. Within this controversy, three sub-areas were examined, each with its own set of criticisms. The first concerned the inclusion of a wider human rights agenda in humanitarianism and the role of policy positions such as humanitarian intervention. The second related to what was termed policy coherence for development. Increasingly, policy makers have combined the previously separate fields of diplomacy, security and development, causing consternation among some commentators (Duffield 2001, Thomas 2001). Third, the notion of security, and human security in particular, was analyzed. Like the wider coherence debate, the human security literature broadens the concepts of security and development to the point where each is poorly understood and even more poorly implemented. In the process, the linkage between security and development, through policy coherence, has brought the humanitarian and military spheres especially close. Where once these spheres were seen as "complete opposites" (Roberts 1996, p. 9), since the end of the Cold War the two have become confused. This has contributed to an increased blurring of the distinction between humanitarians and the military which, some have argued, has contributed to an increasingly less secure environment for humanitarians.

In contrast to much of the literature (see, for example, Donini et al. 2004) we found that instead of "being co-opted," most aid organizations willingly took part in the political and military reconstruction process meted out by the large donor countries (NGOs were in fact a tool that facilitated the "light footprint" approach). Differences in the ways in which this incorporation took place were driven by nationality, involvement in different sectors (such as single- or multi-mandate), size, geographic focus and affiliation. Simply comparing United States and European NGOs is thus misleading and it is a mistake to assume that a European view has been most influential during the formation of policy on military–humanitarian relations. On the one hand, the literature and much of the public relations material generated by aid organizations indicates that many humanitarians of all nationalities wish to represent the voices of the deprived and vulnerable. On the other hand, their views are often confused by the thick complexity of identities, resource allocation issues and multiple constituencies. One example was the different lumping together of organizations under the rubric of aid groups. While often having the rhetoric of neutrality, the organizations adopted a pragmatic and at times integrated relationship with the military. Our findings support Slim's (2004, p. 35) contention that NGOs sometimes "misrepresent themselves," not only in the larger role they play but also in overtly pushing a Western liberal agenda (Duffield 2001, Stockton 2004b).

The larger question is whether incorporating aid organizations into security endeavors (and the militarys' taking on humanitarian tasks) ultimately has the outcome of making periods of violent conflict shorter and bringing stability to vulnerable countries. The influence of development assistance in peace and counter-insurgency operations taking place in Afghanistan was less than is typically believed (ACBAR 2006, Senlis Council 2006, Parker 2007). In Afghanistan, a number of outcomes were possible which were not dependent on a particular security or development intervention. Generally, there was some confusion between simple winning of hearts and minds, which is largely designed to protect military forces, and development that in theory reduces the resort to violence by the aggrieved. Because of the way policy coherence was approached in Afghanistan, increases in funding have not easily translated into improvements in security. This is consistent with the findings of other researchers (Barakat 2002, Suhrke 2006), who argue that the important factor in reconstruction and stability in Afghanistan was not simply the amount spent but the local state capacity to implement all aspects of effective reconstruction.

Ultimately, there is an understanding that modern conflict cannot be won through military means alone, yet in practice the emphasis is still strongly on the military in terms of funding, public relations, policy formation and doctrine. There is a high degree of criticism of the military lodged by humanitarians and those involved in reconstruction and development. In Afghanistan, there was a strong feeling that the military should have redirected its focus toward tasks to which it is best suited, instead of working on assistance projects. This is supported by the findings of other research, including that carried out by the Danish International Development Agency, which notes that "military considerations should not be permitted to determine humanitarian and development actions. Excessive use of military power can easily prove counterproductive in relation to peace enforcement" (2005, p. 48).

Conclusion

Based on current trends and the backdrop of the two decades since 1995, the military–humanitarian relationship will remain a consistent issue in the implementation of security and development activities. There continue to be misunderstanding, confusion and robust debate on the most fundamental issues about the relationship. This includes how relations should be managed, humanitarian ethics and the policy linkages between security and development. From a humanitarian perspective, the basic question of how close a relationship an aid organization should maintain with the military remains unsuccessfully addressed and many common assumptions are based on false premises. This book has argued that humanitarians need a way of dealing with the impact of the tensions arising from their relationship with the military that gets past simplistic notions of incompatible goals and organizational cultures. Five areas were examined. These were historical context, inter-organizational friction, insecurity, principled positions, and the co-option and politicization of humanitarians. The research findings and their implications were discussed within each of these areas. The evidence has shown that organizations alter their policy approach and make other management decisions for pragmatic reasons such as funding, programming and insecurity, not primarily for principled ones. This has led to humanitarians adopting different ethical positions based on contexts heavily influenced by individual aid worker choice.

As for the key question of the underlying policy issue of whether humanitarians should adopt an integrated approach "for" close relations with the military, or a segregated approach "against," this research has demonstrated that humanitarians have not generally had a rigid "either/or" position. In reality, most aid organizations follow neither a strict integrated nor a segregated policy, but move along a spectrum, depending on time and context. This can be explained by an emphasis on individual agency, specific context and pragmatic concerns such as security, access and programming. This approach may be preferred over a more structured and formalized system. Regarding structure and agency, the findings suggest that there is an ongoing move toward the managerial–positivist approach. In other words, there is an ongoing effort to formalize the relationship between humanitarians and the military by means of policies and standardized means of coordination. For humanitarian ethics, the evidence supports the consequentialist position, while elements found within the deontological tradition such as independence, impartiality and neutrality are still powerful. Finally, for the link between security and development, there is a growing movement toward policy coherence for development. The relationship between security and development was not uniform across Afghanistan, showing that there is not a straightforward relationship between the two (described as a chicken-and-egg problem). As a result, there were pockets of development and security in certain areas but not in others.

In many ways, these conclusions raise as many questions as they answer. To what degree does the hybridization of NGOs indicate a fashion and what are its ramifications? What indelible qualities do genuine NGOs have and how can these be systematized so that other organizations do not disingenuously adopt the label? What is an NGO's "essential core" (Donini et al. 2004, p. 198)? Is there an effective way of separating these organizations such as non-governmental humanitarian agencies, NGO contractors and commercial firms? Ultimately, do people on the ground know or care about these differences? Finally, if the link between security and development is going to be made "coherent," will this achieve the ultimate goal of making humanitarian and post-conflict reconstruction efforts more efficient and effective (than they might be if they were separate)? What are the links going forward? In other words, do Afghanistan and Iraq represent anomalies or are these examples of a new standard? Finally, what role can genuine NGOs have in this process?

A final thought

In 2015 and beyond, new chapters to the Afghan story are being written. After decades of chaos and violence, it is now a threadbare cliché to say that the country is at a crossroads or some sort of turning point. What is known is that Afghanistan remains a country with an uncertain future. In September 2014, despite promises of attack, Afghans braved the polls several times to finally elect President Ashraf Ghani and, with ISAF's responsibilities now turned over, the 340,000 personnel of the Afghan military oversee security in the country. At the same time, Operation Resolute Support – which will keep thousands of NATO troops in the country – allows anti-government forces to continue the narrative that the country remains under the yoke of foreign military influence. As a result, common Afghans remain deeply pessimistic about the future. The latest Gallup poll (October 2014) shows two consistent years of declining confidence in the future. Of the 1,000 Afghan interviewed, 61 per cent felt that they are "suffering" and 86 per cent said they are dissatisfied with the efforts to deal with the country's poor. This has been further exacerbated by a "sharp increase in civilian deaths and injuries in 2014 [which] resulted from escalating ground engagements between Anti-Government Elements and Afghan national security forces particularly in civilian-populated areas" (UNAMA 2014, p. 14). Along this evolving set of circumstances, the military–humanitarian complex continues its unsettled and confounding trajectory where the dangers of aid work in the country are more heightened than perhaps at any other point in its history. It is our hope that this book will help to bring about both a better understanding of this relationship and, more importantly, a better future for Afghans.

Bibliography

Aall, P., 2000. NGOs, Conflict Management and Peacekeeping. *International Peacekeeping.* 7(1), pp. 121–41.

Aall, P., Miltenberger, D., and Weiss, T.G. (eds.), 2000. *Guide to IGOs, NGOs and the Military in Peace and Relief Operations*, Washington, D.C.: The US Institute of Peace Press.

Abbot, M., 2006. "Dangerous Intervention: An Analysis of Humanitarian Fatalities in Assistance Contexts." PhD Dissertation. Ohio State University.

Abbott, D., 1998. Dilemmas of Researching Poverty. In: Thomas, A., Chataway, J., and Wuyts, M. (eds.), 1998. *Finding out Fast: Investigative Skills for Policy and Development*. London: Open University/Sage, pp. 201–20.

Abdullah, A., 2005. "Statement by H.E. Dr A. Abdullah Minister of Foreign Affairs of Afghanistan at Afghanistan Development Forum – 2005." Available at: http://www.afghanistan-mfa.net/pressrelease/STKBApril42005.html.

Abrahms, M., 2006. Al Qaeda's Scorecard: A Progress Report on Al Qaeda's Objectives. *Studies in Conflict and Terrorism*, 29(5), pp. 509–29.

ACBAR, 2002a. "Minutes from the NGO Coordination Meeting," Sunday, 5 May, Kabul.

—— 2002b. "Minutes from the NGOs Public Image Working Group," Sunday, 3 October, Kabul.

—— 2002c. "ACBAR General Assembly Meeting," remarks by Nigel Fischer at Sitarah Hotel, 15 September, Kabul.

—— 2003. "Minutes from NGO Coordination Meeting," Sunday, 5 January, Kabul.

—— 2006. "Aid Effectiveness in Afghanistan: At a Crossroads," ACBAR Briefing Paper, November. Kabul.

—— 2007. "A Handbook for Understanding NGOs," (pamphlet). Kabul.

—— 2010a. "Code of Conduct for NGOs engaged in Humanitarian Action, Reconstruction, and Development," Kabul.

—— 2010b. "Highlighting the Impartiality of NGOs in Afghanistan: NGOs are not a 'Soft Power'," Kabul.

ACVFA, 2005. "Public Meeting Minutes on USAID's Office of Military Affairs," 19 October, Washington, DC: ACVFA.

ADB, 2009. *Overview of Civil Society Organizations: Afghanistan*. Manila: Asian Development Bank.

Afghan Compact, 2006. *The Afghan Compact: Building on Success: The London Conference on Afghanistan*. London: 31 January–1 February.

Afghan President Office, 2005. *Afghanistan's Millennium Development Goals Report*. Kabul.

Afghan Statistical Yearbook, 2003. Kabul: Afghanistan Central Statistics Office.

Afghan Statistical Yearbook, 2014. Kabul: Afghanistan Central Statistics Office. Available at: http://www.tradingeconomics.com/afghanistan/gdp-growth-annual.

AFP (Agence France Presse), 2006. "Afghan Aid 'Wastage' Under the Spotlight at London Conference," 28 January. Available at: http://www.nawaayeafghanistan.net/article. php3?id_article =137.

Aga Khan, S., 1990. "Operation Salam: To Build a Future: Humanitarian and Economic Assistance to Afghanistan," *UN Chronicle*, June.

Agrawal, A., 2001. Common Property Institutions and Sustainable Governance of Resources. *World Development*, 29, pp. 1648–72.

Ahmad, E., and Barsamian, D., 2001. *Terrorism: Theirs and Ours*. London: Seven Stories Press.

Aid/Watch, 2012. "Submission to Inquiry into Australia's overseas development programs in Afghanistan," Erskineville: Aid/Watch.

Allan, T., and Styan, D., 2000. A Right to Interfere? Bernard Kouchner and the New Humanitarianism. *Journal of International Development*. 12, pp. 825–42.

Amos, V.A., 2013. Back to the Drawing Board: The Challenges of Humanitarian Action. *Harvard International Review*, 35/2, Fall, http://hir.harvard.edu/amos-back-to-the-drawing-board/.

Anderson, M., 1999. *Do No Harm: How Aid Can Support Peace – Or War*. Boulder, CO: Lynn Rienner.

Anderson, M., and Woodrow, P., 1998. *Rising from the Ashes: Development Strategies in Times of Disaster*. Boulder, CO: Lynne Rienner.

Ankersen, C., 2004. *Coordination, Cooperation, or Something Else: A Framework for Assessing Power Relations in the Discourse of Civil–Military Cooperation in Peace Support Operations*. London: London School of Economics.

ANSO, 2012. "Quarterly Data Report: Q4," Kabul.

ANSO/CARE (Afghan NGO Security Office/CARE), 2005. "NGO Insecurity in Afghanistan," May. Kabul: ARIC.

Archer, S., 2003. Civilian and Military Cooperation in Complex Humanitarian Operations. *Military Review*, March–April, pp. 32–41.

AREU (Afghan Research and Evaluation Unit), 2004. "Draft Charter of NGO Civil–military Working Group." Kabul.

Armstrong, K., 2001. *Holy War: The Crusades and their Impact on Today's World*. 2nd ed. Wilmington, NC: Anchor Press.

Arreguin-Toft, I., 2001. How the Weak Win Wars: A Theory of Asymmetric Conflict. *International Security*. 26(1), pp. 93–126.

Asia Foundation, 2006. *Afghanistan in 2006: A Survey of the Afghan People*. San Francisco: Asia Foundation.

Assael, H., 1969. Constructive Role of Interorganizational Conflict. *Administrative Science Quarterly*, December, pp. 573–82.

Ayoob, M., 1991. The Security Problematic of the Third World. *World Politics*. 42(2), pp. 257–83.

—— 1995. *The Third World Security Predicament: State Making, Regional Conflicts and the International System*. Boulder: Lynne Rienner.

—— 2002. Humanitarian Intervention and State Sovereignty. *International Journal of Human Rights*. 6(1), pp. 81–102.

Azarbaijani-Moghaddam, S., 2004. Afghan Women on the Margins of the Twenty-first

Century. In: Donini, A., Niland, N., and Wermester, K. (eds.), *Nation-Building Unraveled? Aid, Peace and Justice in Afghanistan*. Bloomfield: Kumarian, pp. 95–113.

BAAG (British Agencies Afghanistan Group), 2006. Press Release: "Make or Break for Afghanistan: Donor Governments Must Renew and Increase Long-term Commitment if Recovery Process is to Succeed," London: BAAG. 27 January.

—— 2007. "March Monthly Report," London: BAAG.

Baitenmann, H., 1990. NGOs and the Afghan War: The Politicisation of Humanitarian Aid. *Third World Quarterly*. 12(1), January, pp. 62–85.

Balabanova, E., 2005. "Media–Foreign Policy Interaction in the Age of 'New Military Humanitarianism': Britain and Bulgaria Compared," PhD Thesis. University of Manchester.

Barakat, S., 2002. Setting the Scene for Afghanistan's Reconstruction: The Challenges and Critical Dilemmas. *Third World Quarterly*. 23(5), pp. 801–16.

Barnett, K., 2004. *Security Report for Humanitarian Organizations: Directorate-General for Humanitarian Aid*. Brussels: European Commission Humanitarian Office.

Barnett, M., 2005. Humanitarianism Transformed. *Perspectives on Politics*. 3(4), December, pp. 723–40.

Barnett, M., and Finnemore, M., 1999. The Politics, Power, and Pathologies of International Organizations. *International Organization*. 53(4), Autumn, pp. 699–732.

Barnett, T., 2005. *Blueprint for Action*. New York: Berkley Books.

Barry, J., and Jefferys, A., 2002. "A Bridge too Far: Aid Agencies and the Military in Humanitarian Response," Humanitarian Practice Network (HPN) Report No. 37, London: Overseas Development Institute (ODI).

Beaumont, R., 1995. Small Wars: Definitions and Dimensions. *Annuals of American Academy of Political and Social Science*. 541, September, pp. 20–35.

Beauregard, A., 1998. Civil Military Relations: Lessons from Somalia, the Former Yugoslavia and Rwanda. *Ploughshares Monitor*, December. Available at: http://www.ploughshares.ca/content/MONITOR/mond98g.html.

Bebbington, A., Hickey, S., and Mitlin, D. (eds.), 2007. *Can NGOs Make a Difference? The Challenge of Development Alternatives*. London: Zed Press.

Beckwith, S., 2012. "The Militarisation of Aid in Afghanistan: Implications for Humanitarian Actors and the Way Ahead," Social Science Research Network. Available at: http://papers.ssrn.com/sol3/papers.cfm?abstract_id=2167857.

Beljan, R., 2013. Afghanistan: Lessons Learned from an ISAF Perspective. *Small Wars Journal*, May 30, http://smallwarsjournal.com/jrnl/art/afghanistan-lessons-learned-from-an-isaf-perspective.

Bellamy, A., 2002. The Great Beyond: Rethinking Military Responses to New Wars and Complex Emergencies. *Defence Studies*. 2(1), Spring, pp. 25–50.

Benthall, J., 1993. *Disasters, Relief and the Media*. London: I.B. Tauris.

Berntsen, G., and Pezzullo, R., 2006. *Jawbreaker: The Attack on Bin Laden and Al-Qaeda: A Personal Account by the CIA's Key Field Commander*. New York: Three River Press.

Best, G., 1994. *War and Law since 1945*. Oxford: Oxford University Press.

Beswick, D., and Jackson, P., 2014. *Conflict, Security and Development: An Introduction*. New York: Routledge.

Bhatia, M., 2007. The Future of the Mujahideen: Legitimacy, Legacy and Demobilization in Post-Bonn Afghanistan. *International Peacekeeping*. 14(1), February, pp. 90–107.

Bhatia, M., Lanigan, K., and Wilkinson, P., 2004. "Minimal Investments, Minimal Results:

The Failure of Security Policy in Afghanistan," AREU Briefing Paper. June. Kabul: AREU.

Black, J., 2002a. *European Warfare 1815–2000*. New York: Palgrave.

—— 2002b. *European Warfare: 1494–1660*. London: Routledge.

—— 2006. Civilians in Warfare: 1500–1789. *History Today*. May, pp. 10–17.

Black, M., 1992. *A Cause for Our Times*. Oxford: Oxford University Press.

Blaikie, N., 2000. *Designing Social Research*. Cambridge: Polity Press.

Blaisdell, F.W., 1988. Medical Advances During the Civil War. *Archives of Surgery*. 123(9), pp. 1045–50.

Boesen, I., 1988. What Happens to Honour in Exile? Continuity and Change among Afghan Refugees. In: Huldt, B., and Jansson, E. (eds.), 1988. *The Tragedy of Afghanistan: The Social, Cultural and Political Impact of the Soviet Invasion*. London: Croom Helm, pp. 219–39.

Boli, J., and Thomas, G. (eds.), 1999. *Constructing World Culture: International Nongovernmental Organizations since 1875*. Stanford: Stanford University Press.

Bollet, A.J., 2002. *Civil War Medicine: Challenges and Triumphs*. Tucson, AZ: Galen.

Bolletino, V., 2006. *Designing Security*. Program on Humanitarian Policy and Conflict Research. Cambridge, MA: Harvard University Press.

Bolling, L., 1982. *Private Foreign Aid: US Philanthropy for Relief and Development*. Boulder, CO: Westview.

Boot, M., 2002. *Savage Wars of Peace*. New York: Basic Books.

Booth, K., 1995. Human Wrongs and International Relations. *International Affairs*. 71(1), pp. 103–26.

Borchgrevink, K., 2007. *Religious Actors and Civil Society Post-2001 Afghanistan*. Oslo: International Peace Research Institute.

Borovik, A., 2001. *The Hidden War: A Russian Journalist's Account of the Soviet War in Afghanistan*. Berkeley: Grove Press.

Bortolotti, D., 2004. *Hope in Hell*. New York: Firefly Books.

Borton, J., 1998. "The State of the International Humanitarian System," Briefing Paper. London: ODI.

Boulden, J., 2001. *Peace Enforcement: The United Nations Experience in Congo, Somalia, and Bosnia*. Westport/London: Praeger/Greenwood.

Boutrone, J., 2006. "Missed opportunities: the role of the international community in the return of the Rwandan refugees from Eastern Zaire July 1994–December 1996." Available at: http://web.mit.edu/cis/www/migration/pubs/rrwp/1_missedop.pdf.

Brauman, R., 1996. *L'Action Humanitaire*. Paris: Dominos Flammarion.

—— 2013. "Médecins Sans Frontières and the ICRC: matters of principle. International Review of the Red Cross," www.icrc.org/eng/assets/files/review/2013/irrc-888-brauman.pdf.

Brinkerhoff, J., 2002. Government-Nonprofit Partnership: A Defining Framework. *Public Administration and Development*. 22, pp. 19–30.

Bristol, N., 2006. Military Incursions into Aid Work Anger Humanitarian Groups. *The Lancet*, 367(9508), February 4, pp. 384–6.

Brodie, B., 1976. Technological Change, Strategic Doctrine and Political Outcomes. In: Knorr, K. (ed.), *Historical Dimensions of National Security Problems*. Lawrence: University of Kansas Press, pp. 263–306.

Bryans, M., Jones, B., and Stein, J., 1999. *Mean Times: Humanitarian Action in Complex Political Emergencies: Report of the NGOs in Complex Emergencies Project*. Coming to Terms, 1(3). Toronto: University of Toronto.

Buchanan, J., 1977. The Samaritan's Dilemma. In: Buchanan, J. (ed.), *Freedom in Constitutional Contract*. College Station: Texas A&M University Press, pp. 169–80.

Burkle, F., 2005. Anatomy of an Ambush: Security Risk Facing International Humanitarian Assistance. *Disasters*. 29(1), pp. 26–37.

Bush, G., 2002. The National Security Strategy of the United States of America. Washington, D.C.: White House.

Buur, L., Jensen, S., and Stepputat, F. (eds.), 2007. *The Security Development Nexus: Expressions of Sovereignty and Securitization in Southern Africa*. Cape Town: South Africa: IDRC and HSRC Press.

Buzan, B., Weaver, O., and De Wilde, J., 1997. *Security: A New Framework for Analysis*. Boulder, CO: Lynne Rienner.

Byman, D., 2001. Uncertain Partners: NGOs and the Military. *Survival*. 43(2), Summer, pp. 97–114.

—— 2005. *Deadly Connections: States that Sponsor Terrorism*. Cambridge: Cambridge University Press.

Calas, F., and Salignon, P., 2004. From "Militant Monks" to Crusaders. In: Weissman, F. (ed.), *In the Shadow of "Just Wars."* London: Hurst and MSF, pp. 66–85.

Callwell, C., 1976. *Small Wars: Their Principles and Practice*. 3rd ed. Wakefield: E.P. Publishing.

Cardoso, F., 1979. *Dependency and Development in Latin America*. Berkeley: University of California Press.

Cassidy, R., 2004. Back to the Street without Joy: Counterinsurgency Lessons from Vietnam and Other Small Wars. *Parameters*. 32(4), Summer, pp. 73–83.

Centeno, M., 2003. Limited War and Limited States. In: Davis, D., and Pereira, A. *Irregular Armed Forces and their Role in Politics and State Formation*. Cambridge: Cambridge University Press, pp. 82–95.

Centlivres, P., and Centlivres-Demont, M., 1988. The Afghan Refugee in Pakistan: An Ambiguous Identity. *Journal of Refugee Studies*. 1(2), pp. 141–52.

Cervenka, Z., 1971. *The Nigerian War: 1967–1970*. Frankfurt: Verlag.

Chabbott, C., 1999. Development INGOs. In: Boli, J., and Thomas, G. (eds.), *Constructing World Culture: International Nongovernmental Organizations Since 1875*. Stanford: Stanford University Press, pp. 222–48.

Chaliand, G., 1982. *Guerrilla Strategies: An Historical Anthology from the Long March to Afghanistan*. Berkley: University of California Press.

Chambers, J.D., and Madgwick, P.J., 1968. *Conflict and Community: Europe since 1750*. London: George Philip Limited.

Chandler, David C. (2001) The Road to Military Humanitarianism: How the Human Rights NGOs Shaped a New Humanitarian Agenda. *Human Rights Quarterly*. 23(3), pp. 678-700.

Chapman, T., 1998. *The Congress of Vienna: Origins, Processes and Results*. London: Routledge.

Chayes, S., 2006. *The Punishment of Virtue: Inside Afghanistan after the Taliban*. New York: Penguin.

CHC (Center for Humanitarian Cooperation), 2003. "The Provincial Reconstruction Team (PRT) in Afghanistan and its role in reconstruction." 31 May. New York: CHC.

Chemlali, H., and Sadat, S., 2013. *US Military and Civilian Surge in Afghanistan: An Immanent Critique of the Obama Administrations' 2nd Surge Policy*. Roskilde: Roskilde University.

Chesterman, S., 2001. *Just War or Just Peace? Humanitarian Intervention and International Law*. Oxford: Oxford University Press.

Childress, J., 1978. Just-War Theories: The Bases, Interrelations, Priorities, and Functions of Their Criteria. *Theological Studies*. 39, pp. 427–45.

Chomsky, N., 1999. *The New Military Humanism*. London: Pluto Press.

Chomsky, N., and Herman, E., 2002. *Manufacturing Consent: The Political Economy of the Mass Media*. New York: Pantheon.

Chopra, J., and Weiss, T., 1992. Sovereignty Is No Longer Sacrosanct: Codifying Humanitarian Intervention. *Ethics and International Affairs*. 6, pp. 95–117.

Christopher, P., 1999. *The Ethics of War and Peace*. Upper Saddle River, NJ: Prentice Hall.

Churchill, W., 1941. *My Early Life, Chapter XI*. London: MacMillan.

Cilliers, J., 2006. The New Interfaces between Security and Development. In: Klingebiel, S. (ed.). *New Interfaces Between Security and Development: Changing Concepts and Approaches*. Bonn: German Development Institute, pp. 93–105.

Cioffi-Revilla, C., 1991. The Long-Range Analysis of War. *Journal of Interdisciplinary History*. XXI(4), Spring, 1991, pp. 603–29.

Civil–military Working Group, 2007a. "Guidelines for the International and Coordination of Humanitarian and Development Actors and Military Forces in Afghanistan." Kabul: Draft, June.

—— 2007b. "Mechanisms for Civil–Military Coordination in Afghanistan." Unpublished document, Kabul.

Clammer, J., 2005. Culture, Development and Social Theory: On Cultural Studies and the Place of Culture in Development. *The Asia Pacific Journal of Anthropology*. 6(2), August, pp. 100–19.

Clark, K., 2004. The Struggle for Hearts and Minds: The Military, Aid and the Media. In: Donini, A., Niland, N., and Wermester, K. (eds.), *Nation-Building Unraveled? Aid, Peace and Justice in Afghanistan*. Bloomfield: Kumarian, pp. 83–94.

Code of Conduct, 1994. "Code of Conduct for the International Red Cross and the Red Crescent Movement and NGOs in Disaster Relief." https://www.icrc.org/eng/assets/files/publications/icrc-002-1067.pdf.

Coghlan, T., 2006. "Taliban Beheadings and Beatings to Keep Afghanistan's Schools Closed." *Independent*. 11 July. http://www.independent.co.uk/news/world/asia/taliban-use-beheadings-and-beatings-to-keep-afghanistans-schools-closed-407452.html.

Coker, C., 2004. *The Future of War: The Re-Enchantment of War in the Twenty-First Century*. Oxford: Blackwell.

Colby, W., 1970. "Vietnam: Policy and Prospects, 1970. Civil Operations and Rural Development Support Program." Tuesday, February 17. Washington, D.C: United States Senate.

Coll, S., 2005. *Ghost Wars: The Secret History of the CIA, Afghanistan and Bin Laden from the Soviet Invasion to September 10, 2001*. London: Penguin.

Collier, P., Hoeffler, A., Elliot, L., Hegre, H., Reynal-Querol, M., and Sambanis, N., 2003. *Breaking the Conflict Trap: Civil War and Development Policy*. World Bank Policy Research Report. Washington, DC: World Bank.

Collins, J., 2004. Afghanistan: Winning a Three Block War. *The Journal of Conflict Studies*. 24(20), Winter, pp. 61–75.

Cooley, J., 2000. *Unholy Wars: Afghanistan, America and International Terrorism*. London: Pluto Press.

Cope, Z., 1958. *Florence Nightingale and the Doctors*. London: Museum Press Limited.

Cordesman, A., and Chair, A., 2006. *Winning in Afghanistan: How to Face the Rising Threat*. Washington, DC: Center for Strategic and International Studies (CSIS).

Cornish, S., 2007. No Room for Humanitarianism in 3D Policies: Have Forcible Humanitarian Interventions and Integrated Approaches Lost their Way? *Journal of Military and Strategic Studies.* 10(1), pp. 1–48.

Cosgrave, J., and Andersen, R., 2004. *Aid Flows to Afghanistan. A Study of Aid Flows from Denmark, the UK, the Netherlands, Sweden, and Ireland to Afghanistan from January 2001 to June 2004 Inclusive.* Ohain, Belgium: Channel Research Limited/Danida.

Counterpart, 2011. *Afghanistan Civil Society Assessment,* Kabul: Counterpart International.

Coupland, R., 1999. The Effects of Weapons and the Solferino Cycle. *British Medical Journal.* 319, October, pp. 864–5.

Crawford, N., 1998. Postmodern Ethical Conditions and a Critical Response. *Ethics and International Affairs.* 12(1), March, pp. 121–40.

Creswell, J., 2003. *Research Design: Qualitative, Quantitative and Mixed Methods Approaches* (2nd ed.). Thousand Oaks, CA: Sage.

Crile, G., 2003. *Charlie Wilson's War.* New York: Grover Press.

Cross, T., 2003a. Military Values and Traditions. In: Cahill, K. (ed.), *Traditions, Values and Humanitarian Action.* New York: Fordham University Press, pp. 85–112.

—— 2003b. Military/NGO Interaction. In: Cahill, K. (ed.), 2003. *Emergency Relief Operations.* New York: Fordham University Press, pp. 191–224

Crowe, J., 2014. International Humanitarian Law and the Challenge of Combatant Status. *International Law Annual.* Vol. 2, pp. 17–22.

Cullather, N., 2002. Damming Afghanistan: Modernization in a Buffer State. *The Journal of American History.* 89(2), September, pp. 512–37.

Currion, P., 2011. *Strength in Numbers: A Review of NGO Coordination in the Field,* Geneva: ICVA.

Curti, M., 1963. *American Philanthropy Abroad: A History.* New Brunswick: Rutgers University Press.

Cutts, M., 1998. Politics and Humanitarianism. *Refugee Survey Quarterly.* 17(1), pp. 1–15.

—— 2005. *Humanitarian and Reconstruction Assistance to Afghanistan: 2001–2005.* Copenhagen: Ministry of Foreign Affairs.

Danish International Development Agency, 2005. *Humanitarian and Reconstruction Assistance to Afghanistan 2001–05.* Copenhagen, October 2005.

Dannreuther, R., 2014. *International Security: The Contemporary Agenda* (2nd ed.). New York: John Wiley and Sons.

Darcy, J., and Hofmann, C., 2003. *According to Need? Needs Assessment and Decision-Making in the Humanitarian Sector.* HPG Report 15. London: ODI.

Date, T., 2011. "Comparative Study of Three PRTs (Germany, Hungary and the Netherlands) in Afghanistan," NATO Civil–military Centre of Excellence, Enschede, Netherlands. www.cimic-coe.org/download/t_date_cimic_messenger_draft.pdf.

Davis, W., and Shariat, A., 2004. *Fighting Masoud's War.* Melbourne: Lothian Books.

De St. Jorre, J., 1972. *The Nigerian Civil War.* London: Hodder and Stoughton.

De Waal, A., 1995. *Humanitarianism Unbound.* London: Africa Report.

—— 1997. *Famine Crimes: Politics and the Disaster Relief Industry in Africa.* Oxford: James Currey.

De Zeeuw, J., 2001. *Building Peace in War-Torn Societies: From Concept to Strategy.* The Hague: Netherlands Institute of International Relations Conflict Research Unit.

Delesgues, L., 2007. *Integrity in Reconstruction, Afghan Roads Reconstruction: Deconstruction of a Lucrative Assistance.* London: TIRI/Integrity Watch Afghanistan.

Denzin, N., and Lincoln, Y. (eds.), 2003. *Strategies of Qualitative Inquiry*. London: Sage.

DIA, 1983. *The Economic Impact of Soviet Involvement in Afghanistan*. Washington, DC: DIA.

Dick, W., 2003. Anglo-American vs. Franco-German Emergency Medical Services System. *Prehospital and Disaster Medicine*. 18(1), January–March, pp. 29–35.

Dil, S., 1977. The Cabal in Kabul: Great-Power Interaction in Afghanistan. *The American Political Science Review*. 71(2), June, pp. 468–76.

DiPrizio, R., 2002. *Armed Humanitarians: US Interventions from Northern Iraq to Kosovo*. Baltimore: Johns Hopkins University Press.

Dixon, N., 1979. *On the Psychology of Military Incompetence*. London: Futura.

Dobbins, J., 2007. "Ending Afghanistan's Civil War: Testimony Presented before the Senate Foreign Relations Committee." 8 March. Santa Monica: RAND.

DOD (US Department of Defense), 1993. *Civil Affairs Operations, Field Manual 41–10*. Washington, DC.

—— 2001. *Joint Publication 3–07.6: Joint Tactics, Techniques, and Procedures for Foreign Humanitarian Assistance*. Washington, DC.

—— 2005. *Directive for Military Support for Stability, Security, Transition and Reconstruction: Number 3000.5*. Washington, DC.

—— 2012. *Report on Progress Towards Security and Stability in Afghanistan*, Washington, DC.

Donini, A., 2004. Principles, Politics and Pragmatism in the International Response to the Afghan Crisis. In: Donini, A., Niland, N., and Wermester, K. (eds.), *Nation-Building Unraveled? Aid, Peace and Justice in Afghanistan*. Bloomfield: Kumarian, pp. 117–42.

Donini, A., Minear, L., and Walker, P., 2004. The Future of Humanitarian Action: Mapping the Implications of Iraq and Other Recent Crises. *Disasters*. 28(2), pp. 190–204.

DOS (US Department of State), 2004. Country Reports on Human Rights Practices: Bureau of Democracy, Human Rights and Labor.

Doyle, A., 1982. *A Study in Scarlet*. Harmondsworth: Penguin. (First printed in 1887.)

Drori, G., and Keiko, I., 2006. The Global Institutionalization of Health as a Social Concern. *International Sociology*. 21(2), March, pp. 199–219.

Duffield, M., 2001. *Global Governance and the New Wars: The Merging of Development and Security*. London: Zed Books.

Duffy, C., 1987. *The Military Experience in the Age of Reason*. London: Routledge and Paul Kegan.

Dunant, H., 1986. *A Memory of Solferino*. Geneva: ICRC. (First published 1862).

Duncan, B., 2003. *The Struggle to Develop a Just War Tradition in the West*. Melbourne: Yarra Theological Union. Available at: http://www.socialjustice.catholic.org.au/Content/pdf/the_struggle_to_develop_a_just_war_tradition_in_the_west.pdf.

Dunleavy, P., 1986. *Studying for a Degree in the Humanities and Social Sciences*. London: Macmillan.

Dupree, L., 1980. *Afghanistan*. Princeton, NJ: Princeton University Press.

—— 1988. Cultural Changes among the Mujahideen and Muhajerin. In: Huldt, B., and Jansson, E. (eds.), *The Tragedy of Afghanistan: The Social, Cultural and Political Impact of the Soviet Invasion*. London: Croom Helm, pp. 20–37.

Dupuy, T., 1984. *The Evolution of Weapons and Warfare*. Fairfax, VA: De Capo Press.

Duyvesteyn, I., 2005. The Concept of Conventional War and Armed Conflict in Collapsed States. In: Duyvesteyn, I., and Angstrom, J. (eds.), *Rethinking the Nature of War*. London: Frank Cass, pp. 65–87.

Duyvesteyn, I., and Angstrom, J., 2005. *Rethinking the Nature of War*. London: Frank Cass.

Edwards, D., 1986. *Heroes of the Age: Moral Fault Lines on the Afghan Frontier.* Berkeley: University of California Press.

Edwards, M., and Hulme, D., 1995. NGO Performance and Accountability in the Post-Cold War World. *Journal of International Development.* 7(6), pp. 849–56.

Eiselein, G., 1996. *Literature and Humanitarian Reform in the Civil War Era.* Bloomington: Indiana University Press.

Elphinstone, M., 1842. *An Account of the Kingdom of Caubul.* London: Richard Bentley (Volumes 1 and 2).

Eltis, D., 1989. Towns and Defence in Later Medieval Germany. *Nottingham Medieval Studies.* 33, pp. 91–103.

Es'haq, M., 1988. The Afghan Resistance: Achievements and Problems. In: Huldt, B., and Jansson, E. (eds.), *The Tragedy of Afghanistan: The Social, Cultural and Political Impact of the Soviet Invasion.* London: Croom Helm, pp. 155–63.

Euben R., and Zaman, M., 2009. *Princeton Readings in Islamist Thought: Texts and Contexts from al-Banna to Bin Laden.* Princeton NJ: Princeton University Press.

Evans, G., and Newnham, J., 1998. *Dictionary of International Relations.* London: Penguin.

Evans, G., and Sahnoun, M., 2002. Responsibility to Protect. *Foreign Affairs.* November/ December, 81(6), pp. 99–121.

Ewans, M., 2001. *Afghanistan: A New History.* Richmond: Curzon.

Fandl, K., 2006. Recalibrating the War on Terror by Enhancing Development Practices in the Middle East. *Duke Journal of Comparative and International Law.* 16(2), Spring, pp. 299–329.

Farer, T., 2003. Humanitarian Intervention Before and After September 11 2001: Legality and Legitimacy. In: Holzgrefe, J., and Keohane, R. (eds.), *Humanitarian Intervention: Ethical, Legal, and Political Dilemmas.* Cambridge: Cambridge University Press, pp. 52–90.

Farrington, J., Bebbington, A., Wellard, K., and Lewis, D. (1993). *Reluctant Partners? Non-Government Organizations, the State and Sustainable Agricultural Development.* London: Routledge.

Fast, L., 2007. Characteristics, Context and Risk: NGO Insecurity in Conflict Zones. *Disasters.* 31(2), pp. 130–54.

—— 2014. *Aid in Danger: The Perils and Promise of Humanitarianism.* Philadelphia: University of Pennsylvania Press.

FCO, 2010. "Communiqué of Afghanistan: The London Conference," London: FCO.

Fearon, J., and Laitin, D., 2003. "Postmodern Imperialism." Stanford University, 29 April. Available at: www.international.ucla.edu/cms/files/PostModernImperialism. doc.

Feaver, P., and Kohn, R., 2001. *Soldiers and Civilians: The Civil–military Gap and American National Security.* Cambridge, MA: MIT Press.

Ferguson, J., and Gupta, A., 2002. Spatializing States: Towards an Ethnography of Neoliberal Governmentality. *American Ethnologist.* 29(4), pp. 981–1002.

Ferguson, N., 2006. *The War of the World: Twentieth-Century Conflict and the Descent of the West.* New York: Penguin.

Ferre, J.L., 1995. *L'Action Humanitaire.* Toulouse: Editions Milan.

Ferris, J., 2006. Invading Afghanistan, 1938–2006: Politics and Pacification. *Journal of Military and Strategic Studies.* 9(1), Fall, pp. 1–32.

Findlay, T., 2002. *The Use of Force in UN Peace Operations.* Stockholm: SIPRI.

Finer, S., 1962. *The Man on Horseback: The Role of the Military in Politics.* London: Pall Mall.

Finnemore, M., 2000. *Paradoxes of Humanitarianism Intervention*. Washington, DC: George Washington University.

Fischerkeller, M., 2011. The Premature Debate on CERP Effectiveness. *PRISM*. 2(4), pp. 139–50.

Fishel, J., and Manwaring, M., 2006. *Uncomfortable Wars Revisited*. Norman: University of Oklahoma Press.

Fisher, C., 2006. The Illusion of Progress: CORDS and the Crisis of Modernization in South Vietnam, 1965–1968. *Pacific Historical Review*. 75(1), pp. 25–51.

Fishstein, P., and Wilder, A., 2011. *Winning Hearts and Minds: Examining the Relationship between Aid and Security in Afghanistan*. Medford, MA: Tufts University.

Flavin, W., 2004. *Civil Military Operations: Afghanistan*. Carlyle Barracks, PA: US Army Peacekeeping Institute.

Flipse, S., 2002. The Latest Casualty of War: Catholic Relief Services, Humanitarianism, and the War in Vietnam, 1967–1968. *Peace and Change*. 27(2), pp. 245–70.

Forey, A., 1992. *The Military Orders: From the Twelfth to the Early Fourteenth Centuries*. London: Macmillan.

Forsyth, D., 2006. *Group Dynamics* (4th ed.). Belmont: Thomson Wadsworth.

Fowler, A., 1998. *Striking a Balance: A Guide to Enhancing the Effectiveness of Non-Governmental Organizations in International Development*. London: Earthscan.

Fox, F., 1999. "The Politicization of Humanitarian Aid." Discussion Paper for Caritas Europa. November. London: CAFOD.

—— 2001. New Humanitarianism: Does It Provide a Moral Banner for the 21st Century? *Disasters*. 25(4), pp. 275–89.

Foxley, T., 2007. *The Taleban's "Hearts and Minds" Campaign: How Well is the Afghan Insurgency Communicating and What is it Saying?* London: SIPRI Project.

Franck, R., 2004. Innovation and the Technology of Conflict during the Napoleonic Revolution in Military Affairs. *Conflict Management and Peace Science*. 21, pp. 69–84.

Frandsen, G., 2002. *A Guide to NGOs*. Washington, DC: Center for Disaster and Humanitarian Assistance Medicine.

Frechette, L., 1999. UN Press Release DSG/SM/70: "Deputy Secretary-General Addresses Panel on Human Security Marking Twentieth Anniversary of Vienna International Center." 12 October.

Freedman, D., 2000. *Corps Business*. New York: Harper Business.

Freire, P., 1972. *Pedagogy of the Oppressed*. Harmondsworth: Penguin.

French, N., 2006. *Our Seven Wars in Afghanistan: Progress Under the SWORD Model*. In: Livingstone, A., and Arnusch, A. (eds.), *Measure of Effectiveness: Peace Operations and Beyond*. The Pearson Papers, Vol. 10, Issue 1, pp. 1–28.

French, S., 2003. *The Code of the Warrior: Exploring Warrior Values Past and Present*. Lanham, MD: Rowman and Littlefield.

Frerks, G. et al., 2006. *Principles and Pragmatism: Civil–military Action in Afghanistan and Liberia*. Utrecht: Cordaid.

Frost, M., 2004. "Ethics and War: Beyond Just War Theory," paper presented to Fifth Pan-European International Relations Conference, The Hague, September 2004.

Frumkin, P., and Andre-Clark, A., 2000. When Missions, Markets, and Politics Collide: Values and Strategy in the Nonprofit Human Services. *Nonprofit and Voluntary Sector Quarterly*. 29, pp. 141–63.

Fukuyama, F. (ed.) 2006. *Nation-building: Beyond Afghanistan and Iraq*. Baltimore, MD: Johns Hopkins University Press.

Furneaux, R., 1944. *The First War Correspondent: William Howard Russell of the Times*. London: Cassell.

Gabriel, R., 2007. *Muhammad: Islam's First Great General*. Norman OK: Oklahoma University Press.

Gabriel, R., and Metz, K., 1992. *A History of Military Medicine: Vols 1 and 2*. New York: Greenwood Press.

Gagrin, M., 1986. *Early Greek Law*. Berkeley: University of California Press.

Gall, S., 1983. *Behind Russian Lines: An Afghan Journal*. London: Sidgwick and Jackson.

Garb, M., 2005. Civil–military Gap Issues and Dilemmas: A Short Review. In: Carforio, G., and Kuemmel, G. (eds.), *Military Missions and their Implications Reconsidered: The Aftermath of September 11th Contributions to Conflict Management*. Peace Economies and Development, Vol. 2, pp. 83–92.

Garrigues, J., 2007. *Why Sometimes More is More: Military Assistance to Afghanistan*. FRIDE Commentary. Madrid: FRIDE.

Garwood, R., 2006. "The Blurring of the Lines; Is it Dangerous for the Affected Population and us and does it Deprive them of Assistance?" Unpublished research paper, 9 November.

Gautier, L., 1965. *Chivalry*. London: Phoenix House.

George, J., 2005. The Politics of Peace: The Challenge of Civil–military Cooperation in Somalia. *Public Administration and Management*. 10(2), pp. 153–90.

Germain, R., and Kenny, M. (eds.), 2005. *The Idea of Global Civil Society: Politics and Ethics in a Globalizing Era*. London: Routledge.

Gibbs, D., 2006. Reassessing Soviet Motives for Invading Afghanistan: A Declassified History. *Critical Asian Studies*. 38(2), pp. 239–63.

Gibson, C., Andersson, K., Ostrom, E., and Shivakumar, S., 2005. *The Samaritan's Dilemma: The Political Economy of Development Aid*. Oxford: Oxford University Press.

Giddens, A., 1984. *The Constitution of Society: Outline of the Theory of Structuration*. Cambridge: Polity.

Gillet, M., 1987. *The Army Medical Department 1818–1865*. Washington, DC: Library of Congress.

Gioia, D., Schultz, M., and Corley, K., 2000. Organizational Identity, Image, and Adaptive Instability. *Academy of Management Review*. 25(1), pp. 63–81.

Girardet, E., 1985. *Afghanistan: The Soviet War*. London: Croom Helm.

GOA (Government of Afghanistan), 2001. "Agreement on Provisional Agreements in Afghanistan Pending the Re-Establishment of Permanent Government Institutions." Kabul.

—— 2007. "Afghan Development Framework Frequently Asked Questions." Available at: http://www.adf.gov.af/index.asp? page=faqs.

Gompert, D., and Gordon, J., 2008. *War by Other Means: Building Complete and Balanced Capabilities for Counterinsurgency*. Santa Monica: RAND.

Goodhand, J., 2001. *Conflict Assessments: A Synthesis Report: Kyrgyzstan, Moldova, Nepal and Sri Lanka*. London: DFID and King's College.

—— 2002. Aiding Violence or Building Peace? The Role of International Aid in Afghanistan. *Third World Quarterly*. 23(5), pp. 837–59.

—— 2004. "Aiding Violence or Building Peace? NGOs, Conflict and Peacebuilding in Afghanistan and Sri Lanka: 1997–2000." PhD thesis. Manchester: University of Manchester.

Goodhand, J., and Atmar, H., 2002. *Aid, Conflict and Peacebuilding in Afghanistan*. London: International Alert.

Goodhand, J., and Hulme, D., 1997. *NGOs and Peacebuilding in Complex Political Emergencies: An Introduction*. Manchester: Intrac/University of Manchester.

Goodson, L., 2001. *Afghanistan's Endless War: State Failure, Regional Politics, and the Rise of the Taliban*. Seattle: University of Washington.

Gorman, R., 2000. *Historical Dictionary of Refugee and Disaster Relief Organizations* (2nd ed.). Lanham, MD: Scarecrow Press.

Gottfried, R., 1986. *Doctors and Medicine in Medieval England: 1340–1530*. Princeton, NJ: Princeton University Press.

Grau, L., 2004. The Soviet-Afghan War: A Superpower Mired in the Mountains. *Journal of Slavic Military Studies*. 17, pp. 129–51.

Gray, C., 2005. *Studying Organizations*. London: Sage.

Grayling, A.C., 2006. *Among the Dead Cities*. London: Bloomsbury Publishing.

Gregorian, V., 1969. *Emergence of Modern Afghanistan: Politics of Reform and Modernization 1840–1946*. Stanford: Stanford University Press.

Grenville, J., 1994. *A History of the World in the Twentieth Century*. Cambridge, MA: Belknap Press.

Grimsley, M., and Rogers, C., 2002. *Civilians in the Path of War*. Lincoln: University of Nebraska Press.

Guelzo, A., 1997. Abraham Lincoln and the Doctrine of Necessity. *Journal of the Abraham Lincoln Association*. 18 (1), Winter, pp. 57–81.

Guillaume, D., 2000. Taliban Asks: What Does It Take to Join the UN Club? *Christian Science Monitor*. September 26, 92(214), p. 7.

Gurr, T., 2000. *People versus States: Minorities at Risk in the New Century*. Washington, DC: US Institute of Peace Press.

Guttieri, K., 2005. Humanitarian Space in Insecure Environments: A Shifting Paradigm. *Strategic Insights*. IV(11), November, pp. 1–7.

Haas, P., 1992. Introduction: Epistemic Communities and International Policy Coordination. *International Organization*. 46(1), Winter, pp. 1–35.

Hacker, B., 2005. The Machines of War: Western Military Technology 1850–2000. *History and Technology*. 21(3), September 2005, pp. 255–300.

Haftendorn, H., 1991. The Security Puzzle: Theory Building and Discipline-Building in International Security. *International Studies Quarterly*. 35(1), March, pp. 3–17.

Hahlweg, W., 1986. Clausewitz and Guerrilla Warfare. In: Handel, M. (ed.), *Clausewitz and Modern Strategy*. London: Frank Cass, pp. 126–33.

Haidari, M., 2007. "Afghan Officials Concerned about Effectiveness of Foreign Aid." April 10. Available at: http://www.shfwire.com/afghan-officials-concerned-about-effectiveness-foreign-aid.

Haller, J., 1992. *Farmcarts to Fords: A History of the Military Ambulance, 1790–1925*. Carbondale: Southern Illinois University Press.

Hallett, B., 1998. *The Lost Art of Declaring War*. Chicago: University of Illinois Press.

Halliday, F., 2002. *Two Hours That Shook the World: September 11, 2001: Causes and Consequences*. London: Saqi Books.

Hancock, G., 1991. *Lords of Poverty*. London: Mandarin Paperbacks.

Hanning, H., 1970. *Defence and Development*. London: Royal United Service Institution.

Hanson, V., 2000. *The Western Way of War: Infantry Battle in Classical Greece*. Berkley: University of California Press.

Hardin, G., 1968. The Tragedy of the Commons. *Science*. 162(1), pp. 243–48.

Harrell-Bond, B., 2002. Can Humanitarian Work with Refugees be Humane? *Human Rights Quarterly*. 24, pp. 51–85.

Hatch Dupree, N., 1970. *An Historical Guide to Afghanistan.* Tokyo: Jagra.

—— 1988. The Role of the VOLAGS. In: Huldt, B., and Jansson, E. (eds.), *The Tragedy of Afghanistan: The Social, Cultural and Political Impact of the Soviet Invasion.* London: Croom Helm, pp. 248–62.

—— 2002. Cultural Heritage and National Identity in Afghanistan. *Third World Quarterly.* 23(5), pp. 977–89.

Hayter, T., 1971. *Aid as Imperialism.* Harmondsworth: Penguin.

Heilburnn, O., 1969. When the Counter-Insurgents Cannot Win. *RUSI Journal.* 114, March, pp. 55–8.

Heinze, E., 2006. Maximizing Human Security: A Utilitarian Argument for Humanitarian Intervention. *Journal of Human Rights.* 5(3), July–September, pp. 283–302.

Hekmatyar, G., 1999. *Secret Plans Open Faces: From the Withdrawal of Russians to the Fall of the Coalition Government.* She Zaman Taizi (trans.), S. Fida Yunas (ed.), Peshawar: University of Peshawar.

Henghuber, H., 2004. "The Humanitarian Space In Peril: How Do Recent Political Developments Challenge the Work of International Relief NGOs?" Master's thesis. Medford, MA: Tufts University.

Hensel, H., 2007. *The Law of Armed Conflict: Constraints on the Contemporary Use of Military Force.* London: Ashgate.

Herring, E., 2007. Military Security. In: Collins, A. (ed.). *Contemporary Security Studies.* Oxford: Oxford University Press, pp. 129–45.

Hewad, 2004. "I Will Place Flowers on the Graves of Foreign Workers of NGOs of Golden Times." *e-Ariana.* Available at: http://e-ariana.com/ariana/eariana.nsf/allDocs/CA628423B6D4ADF387256F6600397EEE?OpenDocument.

Hills, A., 2003. Dissolving Boundaries? The Development Marketplace and Military Security. *Contemporary Security Policy.* 24(3), December, pp. 48–66.

Hindley, G., 2003. *The Crusades.* London: Robinson.

Hobsbawm, E., 1994. *The Age of Extremes: A History of the World, 1914–1991.* New York: Vintage.

Hoffman, B., 1998. *Inside Terrorism.* New York: Columbia University Press.

—— 2004. "Insurgency and Counterinsurgency in Iraq." Occasional Paper 127. Santa Monica: RAND.

Holzgrefe, J., and Keohane, R. (eds.), 2003. *Humanitarian Intervention: Ethical, Legal, and Political Dilemmas.* Cambridge: Cambridge University Press.

Hopkirk, P., 1991. *The Great Game: The Struggle for Empire in Central Asia.* Oxford: Oxford University Press.

HPCR (Harvard Program on Humanitarian Policy and Conflict Research), 2002. *Central Asia Policy Brief.* March 13, 4(1).

HRW (Human Rights Watch), 2006. Lessons in Terror: Attacks on Education in Afghanistan. *Human Rights Watch Report.* 18(6(C)), July.

Hudson, A., 2000. Making the Connection: Legitimacy Claims, Legitimacy Chains and Northern NGOs' International Advocacy. In: Lewis, D., and Wallace, T. (eds.), *New Roles and Relevance: Development NGOs and the Challenge of Change.* Bloomfield: Kumerian, pp. 89–99.

Hudson, M., 1999. *Managing Without Profit.* London: Penguin UK.

Huldt, B., and Jansson, E. (eds.), 1988. *The Tragedy of Afghanistan: The Social, Cultural and Political Impact of the Soviet Invasion.* London: Croom Helm.

Hulme, D., and Goodhand, J., 2000. "NGOs and Peacebuilding in Complex Political

Emergencies: Final Report to DFID." Working Paper #12. Manchester: University of Manchester.

Human Development Report (2005) http://hdr.undp.org/sites/default/files/ reports/266/ hdr05_complete.pdf.

Human Security Commission, 2003. *Human Security Now*. New York: Human Security Commission.

Human Security Report, 2005. *Human Security Report: War and Peace in the 21st Century*. Vancouver: Simon Fraser University/Human Security Research Press.

——— 2013. *Human Security Report: The Decline in Global Violence: Evidence, Explanation, and Contestation*. Vancouver: Simon Fraser University/Human Security Research Press.

Humanitarian Outcomes, 2013. "Aid Worker Security Report: The New Normal, Coping with the kidnapping threat." London.

Humayoon, H., 2007. *The Iraqization of Insurgency in Afghanistan*. Kabul: Centre for Conflict and Peace Studies.

Huntington, S., 1957. *The Soldier and the State*. Cambridge, MA: Belknap Press.

Hutchinson, J., 1989. Rethinking the Origins of the Red Cross. *Bulletin of the History of Medicine*. Winter, 63(4).

——— 1992. The Nagler Case: A Revealing Moment in Red Cross History. *Canadian Bulletin of Medical History*, 9, pp. 177–90.

——— 1996. *Champions of Charity: War and the Rise of the Red Cross*, Boulder, CO: Westview Press.

Ibrahim, A., 2004. Conceptualization of Guerrilla Warfare. *Small Wars and Insurgencies*. 15(3), Winter, pp. 112–24.

ICG (International Crisis Group), 2003. *Afghanistan: The Problem of Pashtun Alienation*. Asia Report No. 62. 5 August. Brussels.

——— 2005. *Afghan Elections: Endgame or New Beginning?* Asia Report No. 101, 21 July, Brussels.

——— 2006. *Countering Afghanistan's Insurgency: No Quick Fixes*. Asia Report No. 123, 2 November. Brussels.

ICISS (International Commission on Intervention and State Sovereignty), 2001. *The Responsibility to Protect*. Ottawa.

ICOS, 2010. *Afghanistan Transition: Missing Variables*, London.

——— 2011. *Afghanistan Transition: Dangers of a Summer Drawdown*. London.

ICVA, 2003. *Afghanistan: A Call for Security*. Kabul.

Ignatieff, M., 1998. *The Warrior's Honor: Ethnic War and the Modern Conscience*. New York: Owl Books.

——— 2004. "The Lesser Evil: Hard Choices in a War on Terror." 23 January. Available at: http://www.carnegiecouncil.org.

Ikenberry, G., 1996. The Myth of Post-Cold War Chaos. *Foreign Affairs*. 75(3), May–June, pp. 79–91.

INSO, 2015. *INSO Afghanistan – Quarterly Data Report* (1 January–31 December 2014). January 2015. Kabul: International NGO Safety Organization.

InterAction, 2005. *InterAction Forum Meeting Report: HPPC Panel on Post-September 11 2001 Relations with the Military*, 3 June. Washington, DC.

IRIN, 2009. "Afghanistan: USAID rejects NGO concerns over aid militarization." Available at: http://www.irinnews.org/report/87288/afghanistan-usaid-rejects-ngo-concerns-over-aid-militarization.

Iriye, A., 1999. A Century of NGOs, *Diplomatic History*. 23(3), Summer, pp. 421–35.

ISAF (International Security Assistance Force), 2006a. *Provincial Reconstruction Team Handbook* (2nd ed.). Kabul.

—— 2006b. "Afghan Development Zone Concept Brief." 11 August, Kabul: Unpublished.

Isby, D., 1989. *War in a Distant Country: Afghanistan, Invasion and Resistance*. London: Arms and Armor.

Jackson, A., and Haysom, S., 2013. "The Search for Common Ground: Civil–military Relations in Afghanistan, 2002–13." ODI/HPG Working Paper, April.

Jackson, A., and Giustozzi, A., 2012. *Talking to the Other Side: Humanitarian Engagement with the Taliban in Afghanistan*. London: Humanitarian Policy Group.

Jackson, R., 1995. The Political Theory of International Society. In: Booth, K., and Smith, S. (eds.), *International Relations Theory Today*. Cambridge: Polity Press, pp. 110–28.

Jackson, S., and Walker, P., 1999. Depolarising the "Broadened" and "Back-to-Basics" Relief Models. *Disasters*. 23(2), pp. 93–114.

Jacobsen, K., and Landau, L., 2003. The Dual Imperative in Refugee Research: Some Methodological and Ethical Considerations in Social Science Research on Forced Migration. *Disasters*. 27(3), pp. 185–206.

Jacoby, T., 2005. Cultural Determinism, Western Hegemony and the Efficacy of Defective States. *Review of African Political Economy*. Nos.104/5, pp. 215–33.

Jacoby, T., and James, E., 2009. "Emerging Patterns in the Reconstruction of Conflict-Affected Countries." *Disasters*. Special Issue: The Politicization of Reconstructing Conflict-Affected Countries. Vol. 34 (S1).

Jakobsen, P.V., 2010. "Right Strategy, Wrong Place: Why NATO's Comprehensive Approach Will Fail in Afghanistan." UNISCI Discussion Papers, 22. Available at: http://pendientedemigracion.ucm.es/info/unisci/revistas/UNISCI%20DP%2022%20-%20JAKOBSEN.pdf.

Jalal, M., 2013. *Aid Effectiveness at Sub-National Level: A Study of Provincial Development Committees (PDCs): Provincial Coordination, Planning and Monitoring*. Kabul: Integrity Watch Afghanistan.

Jalali, A., 2007. The Legacy of War and the Challenge of Peacebuilding. In: Rotberg, R. (ed.). *Building a New Afghanistan*. Cambridge, MA: World Peace Foundation, pp. 32–44.

Jalalzai, M., 1999. *Taliban and the Great Game in Afghanistan*. Lahore: Vanguard.

James, E., 2003. Two Steps Back: Relearning the Military–humanitarian Lessons Learned in Afghanistan and Iraq. *Journal of Humanitarian Assistance*. November. Available at: http://sites.tufts.edu/jha/archives/70.

—— 2008. *Managing Humanitarian Relief: An Operational Guide for NGOs*. Rugby: Practical Action.

Janis, I., 1989. *Crucial Decisions: Leadership in Policymaking and Crisis Management*. New York: Free Press.

Janowitz, M., 1971. *The Professional Solider: A Social and Political Portrait*. New York: The Free Press.

Johnson, C., and Leslie, J., 2002. Afghans Have Their Memories: A Reflection on the Recent Experience Assistance in Afghanistan. *Third World Quarterly*. 23(5), pp. 861–74.

—— 2004. *Afghanistan: The Mirage of Peace*. London: Zed Books.

Johnson, G., Ramachandran, V., and Walz, J., 2011. *The Commanders Emergency Response Program in Afghanistan and Refining US Military Capabilities in Stability and In-Conflict Development*. West Point, New York: U.S. Military Academy.

Jones, S., 2009. *In the Graveyard of Empires: America's War in Afghanistan*. New York: W.W. Norton and Company.

Jones, S., Wilson, J., Rathmell, A., and Riley, K., 2005. *Establishing Law and Order after Conflict*. Santa Monica: RAND.

Kaldor, M., 1999. *New and Old Wars: Organized Violence in a Global Era*. Stanford: Stanford University Press.

Kalyvas, S., 2001. "New" and "Old" Civil Wars: A Valid Distinction? *World Politics*. 54(1), October, pp. 99–118.

Kant, I., 1957. *Perpetual Peace*. Indianapolis: Bobbs-Merrill. (First published 1795).

Kaplan, R., 1991. *Soldiers of God*. New York: Vintage.

—— 1994. The Coming Anarchy. *Atlantic Monthly*. 273(2), February.

Karzai, H., 2007. Strengthening Security in Afghanistan: Coping with the Taliban. In: Rotberg, R. (ed.). *Building a New Afghanistan*. Cambridge, MA: World Peace Foundation, pp. 45–61.

Katz, M., 1986. *In the Shadow of the Poorhouse: A Social History of Welfare in America*. New York: Basic Books.

Keck, M., and Sikkink, K., 1998. *Activists beyond Borders*. Ithaca, NY: Cornell University Press.

Keegan, P., 1976. *The Face of Battle*. London: Barrie & Jenkins.

—— 1993. *A History of Warfare*. New York: Vintage.

Keeley, L., 1996. *War Before Civilization*. Oxford: Oxford University Press.

Keen, D., 2000. War and Peace: What's the Difference? *International Peacekeeping*. 7(4), Winter, pp. 1–22.

Keen, W., 1905. *Surgical Reminiscences of the Civil War*. Available at: http://www.civilwarsur geons.org/articles/surgical%20 reminiscences.htm.

Kennedy, D., 2004. *The Dark Sides of Virtue: Reassessing International Humanitarianism*. Princeton, NJ: Princeton University Press.

Kennedy, P., 1988. *The Rise and Fall of the Great Powers*. London: Unwin Hyman.

Kent, G., 2003. "Humanitarian Agencies, Media and the War against Bosnia: 'Neutrality' and Framing Moral Equalisation in a Genocidal War of Expansion." Available at: http://sites. tufts.edu/jha/files/2011/04/a141.pdf.

Keohane, R., and Ostrom, E. (eds.), 1995. *Local Commons and Global Interdependence: Heterogeneity and Cooperation in Two Domains*. London: Sage.

Kerr, P., 1997. *The Crimean War*. London: Boxtree.

Keylor, W., 1992. *The Twentieth Century World: An International History* (2nd ed.). New York: Macmillan.

Kilcullen, D., 2006. Counterinsurgency Redux. *Survival*. 48(4), Winter, pp. 111–30.

—— 2009. *The Accidental Guerrilla: Fighting Small Wars in the Midst of a Big One*. Oxford: Oxford University Press.

Kirk, D., 1996. Demographic Transition Theory. *Population Studies*. 50, pp. 361–87.

Kitson, F., 1971. *Low Intensity Operations: Subversion, Insurgency and Peacekeeping*. London: Faber and Faber.

Klingebeil, S., 2006. "Introduction: New Interfaces between Security and Development." In: *New Interfaces between Security and Development: Changing Concepts and Approaches*. Bonn: German Development Institute, pp. 1–11.

Klingebiel, S., and Roehder, K., 2004. "The Development–Military Relationship: the Start of a New Alliance?" GDI Briefing Paper. Bonn: German Development Institute.

Knorr, K., 1976. *Historical Dimensions of National Security Problems*. Lawrence: University Press of Kansas.

Koch, H.W., 1981. *The Rise of Modern Warfare*. London: Crescent.

Kolhatkars, S., and Ingalls, S., 2006. *Bleeding Afghanistan: Washington, Warlords, and the Propaganda of Silence*. New York: Seven Stories Press.

Kouchner, B., 2007. A Humanitarian-in-Chief: Interview with Bernard Kouchner. *Newsweek*. CL(10), 3 September.

Kovats-Bernat, J., 2002. Negotiating Dangerous Fields: Pragmatic Strategies for Fieldwork amid Violence and Terror. *American Anthropologist*. 104(1), pp. 1–15.

Kraft, H., 2003. Human Rights, Security and Development in Southeast Asia: An Overview. In: Dewitt, D., and Hernandez, C. (eds.), 2003. *Development and Security in Southeast Asia. Volume 3: Globalization*. Aldershot: Ashgate, pp. 106–24.

Krähenbühl, P., 2011. *The Militarization of Aid and its Perils*, Geneva: ICRC.

Krauss, E., and Lacey, M., 2002. Utilitarian vs. Humanitarian: The Battle over the Law of War. *Parameters*. Summer, pp. 73–85.

Kreczko, A., 2003. The Afghan Experiment: The Afghan Support Group, Principled Common Programming and the Strategic Framework. *Disasters*. 27(3), pp. 239–58.

Kristovič, A., and Tomić, V., 2011. *Compendium on Major Non-Military Actors in Afghanistan*. Enschede, Netherlands: Civil–military Co-operation Centre of Excellence.

Krulak, C., 1997. The Three Block War: Fighting in Urban Areas. *Vital Speeches of the Day*. 15 December, 64(5), pp. 139–42.

Kushkaki, S., 1988. An Assessment of the New Mujaheddin Alliance. In: Huldt, B., and Jansson, E. (eds.), 1988. *The Tragedy of Afghanistan: The Social, Cultural and Political Impact of the Soviet Invasion*. London: Croom Helm, pp. 164–72.

Lacina, B., and Gleditsch, N., 2005. Monitoring Trends in Global Combat: A New Dataset of Battle Deaths. *European Journal of Population*. 21, pp. 145–66.

Lacina, B., Gleditsch, N., and Russett, B., 2006. The Declining Risk of Death in Battle. *International Studies Quarterly*. 50, pp. 673–80.

Lagerlof, J., 2004. Efficiency-Enhancing Signalling in the Samaritan's Dilemma. *The Economic Journal*. 114, January, pp. 55–68.

Larsdotter, K., 2005. New Wars, Old Warfare? Comparing US Tactics in Vietnam and Afghanistan. In: Duyvesteyn, I., and Angstrom, J. (eds.), *Rethinking the Nature of War*. London: Frank Cass, pp. 135–58.

Lauritzen, E.K., Olesen, G., and Strand, A., 2006. *The Role Assignment of External Armed Forces in Societal Reconstruction*. Oslo: Research for Development and Justice.

Lawrence, P., 1997. *Modernity and War: The Creed of Absolute Violence*. London: Macmillan.

Lawry, L. (ed.), 2009. *Guide to Nongovernmental Organizations for the Military: A Primer for the Military about Private, Voluntary, and Nongovernmental Organizations Operating in Humanitarian Emergencies Globally*. Center for Disaster and Humanitarian Assistance Medicine.

Laws, S., 2003. *Research for Development: A Practical Guide*. London: Sage.

Leader, N., 1998. Proliferating Principles; Or How to Sup with the Devil without Getting Eaten. *Disasters*. 22(4), pp. 288–308.

Lee, R., 1993. *Doing Research on Sensitive Topics*. London: Sage.

—— 2003. The Demographic Transition: Three Centuries of Fundamental Change. *Journal of Economic Perspectives*. 17(4), pp. 167–90.

Lewis, D., 2001. *The Management of Non-Governmental Development Organizations*. London: Routledge.

—— 2002. The Rise of Non-Governmental Organisations. In: Kirkpatrick, C., Clarke, R., and Polidano, C. (eds.), *Handbook on Development Policy and Management*. Cheltenham: Edward Elgar, pp. 373–88.

Lewis, D., Bebbington, A., Batterbury, S., Shah, A., Olson, E., Siddiqi, M.S., and Duvall, S. (2003). Practice, Power and Meaning: Frameworks for Studying Organizational Culture in Multi-agency Rural Development Projects. *Journal of International Development*. 15, pp. 541–57.

Liddell Hart, B.H., 1967. *Strategy: The Indirect Approach*. London: Faber.

—— 1970. *History of the Second World War*. London: Cassell.

Lieber, F., 1863. "Lieber Code." Available at: http://lawofwar.org/general_order_100.htm.

Lieberman, S., 1980. Afghanistan: Population and Development in the "Land of Insolence." *Population and Development Review*. 6(2), June, pp. 271–98.

Lieser, J., 2002. *Minimum Standards Regarding Staff Security in Humanitarian Aid*. Bonn: Venro.

Lijphart, A., 1977. Political Theories and the Explanation of Ethnic Conflict in the Western World. In: Esman, M. (ed.). *Ethnic Conflict in the Western World*. Ithaca, NY: Cornell University Press, pp. 55–62.

Lilly, D., 2002. *The Peacebuilding Dimension of Civil–military Relations in Complex Emergencies: A Briefing Paper*. London: International Alert.

Lin, J., 1995. "Humanitarianism and Military Force: Humanitarian Intervention and International Society." DPhil thesis. Oxford: Oxford University.

Linborg, N., 2003. "Aid Groups Raise Concerns on Use of Coalition Reconstruction Teams in Afghanistan." March 4, Mercy Corps International.

Lind, W., 2004. Understanding Fourth Generation War. *Military Review*. September–October, pp. 12–16

Lipson, M., 2003. "Interorganizational Networks in Peacekeeping and Humanitarian Relief: An Institutional Theory Perspective." Unpublished, presented to the APSA, Philadelphia, PA, 28–31 August.

Lischer, S., 2003. Collateral Damage: Humanitarian Assistance as a Cause of Conflict. *International Security*. 28(1), pp. 79–109.

—— 2007. Military Intervention and the Humanitarian "Force Multiplier." *Global Governance*. 13, pp. 99–118.

Lister, S., 2000. Power in Partnership? An Analysis of an NGO's Relationship with its Partners. *Journal of International Development*. 12, pp. 227–39.

Lockhart, C., 2005. "From Aid Effectiveness to Development Effectiveness: Strategy and Policy Coherence in Fragile States." Background Paper Prepared for the Senior Level Forum on Development Effectiveness in Fragile States.

Luce, D., and Sommer, J., 1969. *Vietnam: The Unheard Voices*. Ithaca, NY: Cornell University Press.

Luckham, R., Ahmed, I., Mugah, R., and White, S., 2001. "Conflict and Poverty in Sub-Saharan Africa: An Assessment of the Issues and Evidence." IDS Working Paper 128. Brighton: Institute of Development Studies.

Lyons, G., and Mastanduno, M., 1995. *Beyond Westphalia? State Sovereignty and International Intervention*. Baltimore: Johns Hopkins University.

McGlynn, S., 1994. The Myths of Medieval Warfare. *History Today*. January 44(1), pp. 28–35.

Macmunn, G., 1977. *Afghanistan*. London: Bell and Sons.

McPherson, J., 1990. *Battle Cry of Freedom: The Civil War Era*. Harmondsworth: Penguin.

Macpherson, M., 2005. *Roberts Ridge*. London: Bantam Press.

MacQueen, G., McCuthceon, R., and Sanat, B., 1997. The Use of Health Initiatives as Peace Initiatives. *Peace & Change.* 22(2), April, pp. 175–97

Macrae, J., 1998. The Death of Humanitarianism: An Anatomy of an Attack. *Disasters.* 22(4), pp. 309–17.

—— 2002. "The New Humanitarianisms: A Review of Trends in Global Humanitarian Action." HPG Paper 11. London: ODI.

Macrae, J., and Leader, N., 2000. "Shifting Sands: The Search for 'Coherence' Between Political and Humanitarian Responses to Complex Emergencies." HPG Paper 8. London: ODI.

Macrae, J., and Zwi, A., with M. Duffield and H. Slim (1994), *War and Hunger: Rethinking International Responses to Complex Emergencies.* Zed Books: London.

Magnus, R. (ed.), 1985. *Afghan Alternatives: Issues, Options, and Policies.* New Brunswick: Transaction Books.

Maley, W., 1998. *Fundamentalism Reborn? Afghanistan and the Taliban.* Washington Square: New York University Press.

Maloney, S., 2007. Conceptualizing the War in Afghanistan: Perceptions from the Front, 2001–2006. *Small Wars and Insurgencies.* 18(1), March, pp. 27–44.

Mandelbaum, M., 2002. *The Ideas that Conquered the World: Peace, Democracy, and Free Markets in the Twenty-First Century.* New York: Public Affairs.

Maney, P., 2003. *Operations Enduring Freedom: Lessons Learned In Afghanistan.* National Defense Industrial Association, SO/LIC Symposium. 11 February.

Mann, M., 1988. *States, War and Capitalism.* Oxford: Blackwell.

—— 1993. *The Sources of Social Power: Volume 2, The Rise of Classes and Nation States 1760–1914.* Cambridge: Cambridge University Press.

Mansfield, D., and Pain, A., 2006. *Opium Poppy Eradication: How to Raise Risk when there is Nothing to Lose?* Kabul: AREU.

March, J., and Olsen, J., 1989. *Rediscovering Institutions: The Organizational Basis of Politics.* New York: Free Press.

Maren, M., 1997. *The Road to Hell – The Ravaging Effects of Foreign Aid and International Charity.* New York: Free Press.

Margolis, E., 2000. *War at the Top of the World: The Struggle for Afghanistan, Kashmir, and Tibet.* New York: Routledge.

Marsden, P., 2000. *The Taliban: War, Religion and the New Order in Afghanistan.* London: Zed Books.

Martin, R., 1999. NGO Field Security. *Forced Migration Review.* 4 (April), pp. 4–7.

Martone, G., 2002. Relentless Humanitarianism. *Global Governance.* 8 (April), pp. 149–54.

Mascini, P., 2006. Can the Violent *Jihad* Do without Sympathizers? *Studies in Conflict and Terrorism.* 29, pp. 343–57.

Maxwell, M., 1990. *Morality Among Nations: An Evolutionary View.* New York: SUNY Press.

Meyer, J., 2003. "Globalization, National Culture, and the Future of World Polity." Wei Lun Lecture. Hong Kong: The Chinese University of Hong Kong.

Michel, A., 1972. The Impact of Modern Irrigation Technology in the Indus and Helmand Basins of Southwest Asia. In: Farvar, M., and Milton, J. (eds.), *The Careless Technology: Ecology and International Development.* New York: Natural History Press, pp. 257–75.

Mientka, M., 2002. Army Medics Aid Afghanistan. *US Medicine.* October.

Miller, E., and Yetiv, S., 2001. The New World Order in Theory and Practice: The Bush Administration's Worldview in Transition. *Presidential Studies Quarterly.* 31(1), March, pp. 56–68.

Miller, S., 1995. "Dr. Simon's Prescription." *Chicago Reader*. 4 August. Available at: http://www.chicagoreader.com/features/stories/archive/robertsimon/.

Mills, G., 2005. *The Security Intersection: The Paradox of Power in an Age of Terror*. Johannesburg: Wits University Press.

Mills, K., 2005. Neo-Humanitarianism: The Role of International Humanitarian Norms and Organizations in Contemporary Conflict. *Global Governance*. 11, pp. 161–83.

Minear, L., 1996. The Humanitarian and Military Interface: Reflections on the Rwanda Experience. *Hunger Notes*. Summer.

—— 1997. "Humanitarian Action and Peacekeeping Operations." Conference Background Paper UNITAR/IPS/NIRA, Singapore, 24–26 February.

Minear, L., Scott, C., and Weiss, T., 1996. *The News Media, Civil War and Humanitarian Action*. Boulder, CO: Lynne Rienner.

Ministry of Education, 1956. *Education in Afghanistan during the last Half-Century*. Munich: Royal Afghan Ministry of Education.

MOD (UK Ministry of Defence), 2004. *Joint Warfare Publication 3-50: The Military Contribution to Peace Support Operations* (2nd ed.). Swindon: Ministry of Defence.

MoFA, 2011. *Istanbul Process on Regional Security and Cooperation for a Secure and Stable Afghanistan*. Ankara.

Monshipouri, M., 2003. NGOs and Peacebuilding in Afghanistan. *International Peacekeeping*. 10(1), Spring, pp. 138–55.

Monshipouri, M. (2014) NGOs and Peace Building in Afghanistan. In: Carey, H. and Richmond, O. (eds.), *Mitigating conflict: the role of NGOs*. Abingdon: Routledge, pp. 135–54.

Moore, R., 2003. *The Hunt for Bin Laden*. New York: Presidio Press.

Moorehead, C., 1998. *Dunant's Dream: War, Switzerland and the History of the Red Cross*. New York: Harper Collins Publishers.

Moorehead, R., 2004. Technology and the American Civil War. *Military Review*. May–June, pp. 61–3.

Morgan, M., 2005. An Evolving View of Warfare: War and Peace and the American Military Profession. *Small Wars and Insurgencies*. 16(2), pp. 147–69.

Morris, S., 2000. Defining the Nonprofit Sector: Some Lessons from History. *Voluntas: International Jorunal of Voluntary and Nonprofit Organizations*. 11(1), pp. 25–43.

Morris, T., 2003. Civil–military relations in Afghanistan. *Forced Migration Review*. 13, June, pp. 14–15.

MSF, 1995. "Deadlock in the Rwandan Refugee Crisis: Repatriation Virtually at a Standstill." Available at: http://www.doctorswithoutborders.org/news-stories/special-report/deadlock-rwandan-refugee-crisis-repatriation-virtually-standstill.

—— 2004. "Six Days Surrounding MSF's Decision to Withdraw from Afghanistan." 1 August. Available at: http://www.msf.org/article/six-days-surrounding-msfs-decision-withdraw-afghanistan.

—— 2005. Editorial. 2 June. Available at: http://www.msf.org/msfinternationalinvoke.cfm?-component=article&objectid=50EC5CB4-E0180C72091599C1C60C8D03&method=full_html.

—— MSF, 2010. "Breaking the Cycle: Calls for Action in the Rwandese Refugee Camps in Tanzania and Zaire." November. Available at: http://www.doctorswithoutborders.org/publications/article.cfm?id=1465.

Nash, D., 1994. Civil Affairs in the Gulf War: Administration of an Occupied Town. *Special Warfare*. October, pp. 18–27.

NATO, 2006. *Riga Summit Declaration*. Brussels.

—— 2008. *Bucharest Summit Declaration*. Brussels.

—— 2010a. *Lisbon Summit Declaration*. Brussels.

—— 2010b. *Prague Summit: Provincial Reconstruction Teams, What's Next?* Brussels.

—— 2012. *Chicago Summit Declaration*. Brussels.

—— 2013. *Transition to Afghan Lead*. Inteqal, Kabul.

New York Times, 2007. "PRT Officers Comments on the Taliban." 7 April.

NGO Forum, 2002. "The Need for a Clear Distinction between Humanitarian Programme and Military Activities in Afghanistan." March, Kabul: ACBAR.

NGO Internal Report, 2002. "Issues and Views Regarding the Relationship between Humanitarian Organizations and Military Forces Party to a Conflict During and Following the Conflict: The Humanitarian Imperative." Unpublished report.

—— 2004. "NGO Security and Relations with the Military in High Threat Situations." Unpublished report.

NHRP, 2010. "Call for Strengthened Humanitarian Coordination in Afghanistan." The NGOs and Kabul: Humanitarian Reform Project.

Nijssen, S., 2012. *Civil Society in Transitional Contexts: A Brief Review of Post-Conflict Countries and Afghanistan*. Civil–military Fusion Centre: Kabul

Nixon, H., 2007. *Aiding the State? International Assistance and the Statebuilding Paradox in Afghanistan*. Kabul: AREU.

NRC et al., 2009. "Letter to the Special Envoy: Key proposals of NGOs operating in Afghanistan." Kabul.

—— 2012. *A Partnership at Risk?: The UN–NGO relationship in light of UN integration*. Oslo.

Nyrop, R., and Seekins, D. (eds.), 1986. *Afghanistan Country Study*. Washington, DC: American University Press.

O'Brien, P., 2004. Old Woods, New Paths, and Diverging Choices for NGOs. In: Donini, A., Niland, N., Wermester, K., 2004. *Nation-Building Unraveled? Aid, Peace and Justice in Afghanistan*. Bloomfield, CT: Kumarian, pp. 187–203.

OECD (Organization for Economic Cooperation and Development), 2002. "Action for a Shared Development Agenda." Ministerial Statement. Paris: OECD.

Oliker, O., Kauzlarich, R., Dobbins, J., Basseuner, K., Sampler, D., McGinn, J., Dziedzic, M., Grissom, A., Pirnie, B., Bensahel, N., and Guven, A., 2004. *Aid During Conflict: Interaction Between Military and Civilian Assistance Providers in Afghanistan: September 2001–June 2002*. Santa Monica: RAND.

Olsen, G., Carstensen, N., and Hoyen, K., 2003. Humanitarian Crises: What Determines the Level of Emergency Assistance? Media Coverage, Donor Interests and the Aid Business. *Disasters*. 27(2), pp. 109–26.

Olson, L., and Gregorian, H., 2007. *Side by Side or Together? Working for Security, Development and Peace in Afghanistan and Liberia*. Workshop report "Coordinated Approaches to Security, Development and Peacemaking: Lessons Learned from Afghanistan and Liberia," Centre for Military and Strategic Studies, University of Calgary and Institute of World Affairs, March 30–31, Washington, DC.

Omrani, B., and Leeming, M., 2005. *Afghanistan*. New York: Odyssey.

Ostrom, E., Dietz, T., Dolsak, N., Stern, P., Stonich, S., and Weber, E., 2002. *The Drama of the Commons*. Washington, DC: National Academy Press.

Ostrom, E., Gibson, C., Shivakumar, S., and Andersson, K., 2002. "Aid, Incentives, and

Sustainability: An Institutional Analysis of Development Cooperation." Main Report. *SIDA Studies in Evaluation*, No. 02/01. Stockholm: SIDA.

Oxfam, 2001. "Humanitarian Situation in Afghanistan and on its Borders." Briefing Paper 6, 27 September. Oxford.

—— 2006. "Serve the Essentials: What Governments and Donors Must do to Improve South Asia's Essential Services." Oxford.

—— 2010. "Quick Impact, Quick Collapse." Kabul.

—— 2011. "Whose Aid is it Anyway? Politicizing Aid in Conflict and Crises." Oxfam Briefing Paper, 145, Oxford.

Parekh, B., 1997. Rethinking Humanitarian Intervention. *International Political Science Review*. 18(1), pp. 49–69.

Paris, R., 2001. Human Security: Paradigm Shift or Hot Air? *International Security*. 26(2), pp. 87–102.

Parker, S., 2007. *Programming Development Funds to Support a Counterinsurgency: A Case Study of Nangahar, Afghanistan in 2006*. Case Studies in National Security Transformation, Number 10. Washington, DC: National Defence University.

Parmelee, M., 1915. The Rise of Modern Humanitarianism. *The American Journal of Sociology*. 21(3), pp. 345–59.

Passant, V., 2009. "The Great Lakes Refugee Crisis and the Dilemma of Contemporary Humanitarianism." Available at: http://www.polis.leeds.ac.uk/assets/files/students/student-journal/ma-winter-09/victoria-passant-winter-09.pdf.

Patterson, R., and Robinson, J., 2011. "The Commander as Investor: Changing CERP Practices." *PRISM*. 2 (2), pp. 115–26.

Pearn, J., 1994. The Earliest Days of First Aid. *British Medical Journal*. 309, pp. 1718–20.

Pedersen, D., 2003. As Irrational As Bert and Bin Laden: The Production of Categories, Commodities, and Commensurability in the Era of Globalization. *Public Culture*. 15(2), pp. 238–59.

Peters, G., 1999. *Institutional Theory in Political Science: The "New Institutionalism."* London: Continuum.

Pfanner, T., 2004. Military Uniforms and the Law of War. *International Review of the Red Cross*. 86(853), March, pp. 93–124.

Pfeffer, J., 1997. *New Directions for Organization Theory: Problems and Prospects*. Oxford: Oxford University Press.

Phelan, J., and Wood, G., 2005. *Bleeding Boundaries: Civil–military Relations and the Cartography of Neutrality*. Woking: Ockenden International.

Phillips, R., 1984. *War and Justice*. Norman OK: University of Oklahoma Press.

Picciotto, R., 2005. The Evaluation of Policy Coherence for Development. *Evaluation*. 11(3), pp. 311–30.

—— 2006. "What is Human Security?" Paper Delivered to the Seventh Annual Global Development Conference, Global Development Network, 19–21 January, St Petersburg, Russia.

Pick, D., 1993. *War Machine: The Rationalization of Slaughter in the Modern Age*. New Haven, CT: Yale University Press.

Piiparinen, T., 2007. A Clash of Mindsets? An Insider's Account of Provincial Reconstruction Teams. *International Peacekeeping*. 14 (1), January, pp. 143–57.

Pinker, S., 2011. *The Better Angels of Our Nature: Why Violence Has Declined*. New York: Viking Press.

PIPA (Program on International Policy Attitudes), 2006. "Afghan Approval of the Karzai Government and Western Forces, Though Still Strong, Is Declining." 14 December.

Pollick, S., 2000. Civil–military Cooperation: A New Tool for Peacekeepers. *Canadian Military Journal.* Autumn, pp. 52–67.

Poole, L., 2011. *Afghanistan: Tracking major resource flows 2002–2010,* Somerset: Global Humanitarian Assistance.

Postma, W., 1994. NGO Partnership and Institutional Development: Making it Real, Making it Intentional. *Canadian Journal of African Studies.* 28, pp. 543–53.

Poulton, R., 2001. The Kalashnikov in Afghanistan, Tajikistan and the other "Stans." *Asian Affairs.* 32(3), November, pp. 295–99.

Powell, C., 2001. "Remarks to the National Foreign Policy Conference for Leaders of Nongovernmental Organizations." 26 October.

Powell, W., and DiMaggio, P. (eds.), 1991. *The New Institutionalism in Organizational Analysis.* Chicago: Chicago University Press.

PRT (Provincial Reconstruction Team), 2004. *Trip Report: Memorandum for record to A/S Christina Rocca, AMB William Taylor.* Kabul: US State Department.

——— 2006. *PRT Handbook.* Kabul: ISAF.

Pugh, M., 1998. Military Intervention and Humanitarian Action: Trends and Issues. *Disasters.* 22(4), pp. 339–51.

——— 2000. Civil–Military Relations in the Kosovo Crisis: An Emerging Hegemony? *Security Dialogue.* 31(2), pp. 229–42.

Pyemont, G., 1855. On Military Medical Practice in the East. *The Lancet.* 1855, pp. 647–8.

Ramsbotham, O., 1998. Islam, Christianity, and Forcible Humanitarian Intervention. *Ethics and International Affairs.* 12(1), pp. 81–102.

Ramsbotham, O., and Woodhouse, T., 1999. *Encyclopedia of International Peacekeeping Operations.* Santa Barbara: ABC-CLIO.

Rana, R., 2004. Contemporary Challenges in the Civil–military Relationship: Complementarity or Incompatibility. *International Review of the Red Cross.* 86(855), September, p. 568.

Rashid, A., 2001. *Taliban: Islam, Oil and the New Great Game in Central Asia.* London: I.B. Tauris.

Rastegar, F., 1991. "Education and Revolutionary Political Mobilization: Schooling Versus Uprootedness as Determinants of Islamic Political Activism among Afghan Refugee Students in Pakistan." PhD dissertation. Los Angeles: University of California.

Reality of Aid, 2006. *Political Overview.* Quzon City, Philippines: Realty of Aid Project.

Reid, D., 1911. *Memories of the Crimean War: January 1855 to June 1856.* London: St Catherine Press.

Rich, J., and Shipley, G., 1995. *War and Society in the Greek World.* London: Routledge.

Richards, D., 1990. *Savage Frontier.* London: Macmillan.

Richie, J., 1999. *Weapons: Designing the Tools of War.* Bristol, CN: Oliver Press.

Rieff, D., 2002. *A Bed for the Night: Humanitarianism in Crisis.* New York: Simon and Shuster.

Rigby, A., 2001. Humanitarian Assistance and Conflict Management: The View from the Non-Governmental Sector. *International Affairs.* 77(4), pp. 957–66.

Riley, P., 1983. *Kant's Political Philosophy.* Totowa, NJ: Rowman and Littlefield.

Riley-Smith, J., 1999. *Hospitallers: The History of the Order of St. John.* London: Hambledon Press.

Riphenburg, C., 2006. Afghanistan: Out of the Globalisation Mainstream? *Third World Quarterly.* 27(3), pp. 507–24.

Rist, G., 2014. *The History of Development: From Western Origins to Global Faith*. London: Zed Books.

Roberts, A., 1993. Humanitarian War: Military Intervention and Human Rights. *International Affairs*. 69(3), pp. 429–49.

—— 1996. "Humanitarian Action in War." Adelphi Paper #305. Oxford: Oxford University Press.

Roberts, A., 2009. Afghanistan and International Security. *International Law Studies*. 85, 3–43.

Roberts, J., 2003. *The Origins of the Conflict in Afghanistan*. Westport: Praeger Publishing.

Robinson, P., 2005. The CNN Effect Revisited. *Critical Studies in Media Communication*. 22(4), October, pp. 344–9.

Rollins, J., 2001. Civil–military Cooperation (CIMIC) in Crisis Response Operations: The Implications for NATO. *International Peacekeeping*. 8(1), Spring, pp. 122–29.

Rosenman, S., 1952. *Working with Roosevelt*. New York: Harper.

Roy, O., 1990. *Islam and Resistance in Afghanistan*. Cambridge: Cambridge University Press.

Rozario, K., 2003. Delicious Horrors: Mass Culture, The Red Cross, and the Appeal of Modern American Humanitarianism. *American Quarterly*. 55(3), September, pp. 417–44.

Rubin, B., 1995. *The Search for Peace in Afghanistan: From Buffer State to Failed State*. New Haven, CT: Yale University Press.

—— 2007. Congressional testimony, February. Available at: www.senate.gov/~ armed_services/statemnt/2007/March/Rubin%2003–01–07.pdf.

Rubin, B., and Armstrong, A., 2003. Regional Issues in the Reconstruction of Afghanistan. *World Policy Journal*. 20(1), Spring, pp. 31–40.

Rubin, B., Hamidzada, H., and Stoddard, A., 2003. *Through the Fog of Peacebuilding: Evaluating the Reconstruction of Afghanistan*. New York: Center for International Cooperation.

Rubin, M., 2002. Who is Responsible for the Taliban? *Middle East Review of International Affairs*. 6(1), March, pp. 1–16.

Ryan, J., 1998. *Media and Society: The Production of Culture in the Mass Media*. Boston: Allyn and Bacon.

Ryan, M., 2007. *Battlefield Afghanistan*. London: Spellmount.

Ryerson, C., 2012. The Pacification of Soldering, and the Militarization of Development: Contradictions Inherent in Provincial Reconstruction in Afghanistan. *Globalizations*. 9(1), pp. 53–71.

Saikal, A., 2004. *Modern Afghanistan: A History of Struggle and Survival*. London: IB Tauris.

—— 2006. Afghanistan's Transition: ISAF's Stabilisation Role? *Third World Quarterly*. 27(3), pp. 525–34.

Salazar, R., 2000. *The Treatment of War Wounds in Graeco-Roman Antiquity*. Boston: Brill.

Save the Children, 2004. *Provincial Reconstruction Teams and Military–humanitarian Relations in Afghanistan*. London: Save the Children.

—— 2007. *State of the World's Mothers Report*. Westport: Save the Children.

Scales, J., 2005. "Studying the Art of War." *Washington Times*, 17 February.

Schein, E., 1992. *Organizational Culture and Leadership* (2nd ed.). San Francisco: Jossey-Bass.

Scheltinga, T. et al., 2005. Cultural Conflict within Civil–military Cooperation: A Case Study in Bosnia. *Low Intensity Conflict and Law Enforcement*. 13(1), Spring, pp. 54–69.

Schulz, J., and Schulz, L., 1999. The Darkest of Ages: Afghan Women under the Taliban. *Peace and Conflict: Journal of Peace Psychology*. 5(3), pp. 237–54.

Sedra, M., 2002. *Challenging the Warlord Culture: Security Sector Reform in Post-Taliban Afghanistan*. Bonn: Bonn International Center for Conversion.

Seiple, C., 1996. *The US Military/NGO Relationship in Humanitarian Intervention*. Carlisle Barracks, PA: US Army War College.

Sellstrom, T., and Wohlgemuth, L., 1996. *Synthesis Report: The International Response to Conflict and Genocide: Lessons from the Rwandan Experience*. Uppsala: Joint Evaluation of Emergency Assistance to Rwanda.

Semple, M. et al., 2012. *Taliban Perspectives on Reconciliation*, London: RUSI.

Sen, A., 1999. *Development as Freedom*. Oxford: Oxford University Press.

Sen, A., and Williams, B. (eds.), 1982. *Utilitarianism and Beyond*. Cambridge: Cambridge University Press.

Senlis Council, 2006. *Afghanistan Five Years Later: The Return of the Taliban*. London.

Sharp, T., Luz, G., and Gaydos, G., 1999. Military Support of Relief: A Cautionary Review. In: Leaning, J., Briggs, S., and Chen, L. (eds.), *Humanitarian Crises*. Cambridge: Harvard University Press, pp. 273–92.

Sharp, T., Winghtman, J., Davis, M., Sherman, S., and Burkle, F., 2001. Military Assistance in Complex Emergencies: What Have We Learned Since the Kurdish Relief Effort? *Prehospital and Disaster Medicine*. 16(4), October–December, pp. 197–208.

Sheik, M., Gutierriez, M., Bolton, P., Speigel, P., Thieren, M., and Burnham, G., 2000. Deaths Among Humanitarian Workers. *British Medical Journal*. 15 July, 321, pp. 166–8.

Sheikh, M.K., and Greenwood, M.T.J. (eds.), 2013. *Taliban Talks: Past, Present and Prospects for the US, Afghanistan and Pakistan*. Copenhagen: Danish Institute for International Studies.

Shepherd, R., 2007. USAID and Defense Officials Urge Better Cooperation Between NGOs and the Military. *Monday Developments*. 25(5), May.

Showalter, D., 2002. Europe's Way of War 1815–64. In: Black, J. (ed.), *European Warfare 1815–2000*. New York: Palgrave, pp. 27–50.

Siddiqui, H., 2006. "Expert Advice on Afghanistan." *Toronto Star*. 14 September.

Siegel, A., 2002. Civil–military Marriage Counseling: Can this Union be Saved? *Special Warfare*. December, pp. 28–34.

Singer, C., 1928. *A Short History of Medicine*. Oxford: Clarendon Press.

Sirrs, J., 2001. Lifting the Veil on Afghanistan, *National Interest*. 65, pp. 43–8.

Skaine, R., 2002. *The Women of Afghanistan under the Taliban*. Jefferson, NC: McFarland.

Slim, H., 1996. The Stretcher and the Drum: Civil–military Relations in Peace Support Operations. *International Peacekeeping*. 3(2), pp. 123–40.

—— 1997a. "Positioning Humanitarianism in War: Principles of Neutrality, Impartiality and Solidarity." Aspects of Peacekeeping Conference, 22–24 January 1997. Oxford: Oxford Brookes University.

—— 1997b. Relief Agencies and Moral Standing in War: Principles of Humanity, Neutrality, Impartiality and Solidarity. *Development in Practice*. 7(4), pp. 342–52.

—— 2000. Fidelity and Variation: Discerning the Development and Evolution of the Humanitarian Idea. *The Fletcher Forum of World Affairs*. 24(1), pp. 5–22.

—— 2001a. "Military Intervention to Protect Human Rights: The Humanitarian Agency Perspective. Background." Paper for the International Council on Human Rights' Meeting on *Humanitarian Intervention: Responses and Dilemmas for Human Rights Organisations*, Geneva, 31 March–1 April. International Council on Human Rights Policy. Oxford: Oxford Brookes University.

—— 2001b. Violence and Humanitarianism: Moral Paradox and the Protection of Civilians. *Security Dialogue*. 32(3), September, pp. 325–39.

—— 2002. Making Moral Low Ground: Rights as the Struggle for Justice and the Abolition of Development. *Praxis: The Fletcher Journal of Development Studies.* XVII, pp. 1–5.

—— 2004. With or Against? Humanitarian Agencies and Coalition Counter-Insurgency. *Refugee Survey Quarterly.* 23(4), pp. 34–47.

Smail, R., 1956. *Crusading Warfare, 1097–1193.* Cambridge: Cambridge University Press.

Smart, J., 1973. *Utilitarianism, For and Against.* Cambridge: Cambridge University Press.

Smith, A., 2002. *Machine Gun: The Story of the Men and the Weapon that Changed the Face of War.* London: Piatkus.

Smith, J., Rochester, C., and Hedly, R., 1995. *An Introduction to the Voluntary Sector.* London: Routledge.

Smith, M., 2003. Guerrillas in the Mist: Reassessing Strategy and Low Intensity Warfare. *Review of International Studies.* 29(1), pp. 19–37.

—— 2005. Strategy in an Age of "Low Intensity" Warfare: Why Clausewitz is Still More Relevant than His Critics. In: Duyvesteyn, I., and Angstrom, J. (eds.), *Rethinking the Nature of War.* London: Frank Cass, pp. 28–64.

Smith, R., 2006. *The Utility of Force: The Art of War in the Modern World.* London: Penguin.

Smythe, T., 2003. *The Gilded Age Press, 1865–1900.* Westport, CT: Praeger.

Soussan, J., 2008. "MSF and Protection: Pending or Closed." CRASH, Paris. Available at: www.msf-crash.org/drive/fc62-cahier-protection-va.pdf.

Stake, R., 2003. Case Studies. In: Danzin, N., and Lincoln, Y. (eds.), *Strategies of Qualitative Inquiry.* London: Sage, pp. 119–50.

Stapleton, B., 2005. *NATO: New Tasks and Responsibilities.* Brussels: NATO-WIIS Conference, 11 July.

Starr, F., 2006. Sovereignty and Legitimacy in Afghan Nation-Building. In: Fukuyama, F. (ed.), *Nation-Building: Beyond Afghanistan and Iraq.* Baltimore: John Hopkins University Press, pp. 114–28.

Steinberger, M., 2001. "So, Are Civilizations at War? Interview with Samuel P. Huntington." *Observer,* 21 October.

Stepan, A., 1988. *Rethinking Military Politics: Brazil and the Southern Cone.* Princeton, NJ: Princeton University Press.

Stephens, J., and Ottaway D., 2005. "A Rebuilding Plan Full of Cracks." *Washington Post.* 20 November, p. A01.

Stern, J., 2004. *Terror in the Name of God.* London: Harper Perennial.

Stockton, N., 2004a. Afghanistan, War, Aid, and International Order. In: Donini, A., Niland, N., Wermester, K. (eds.), *Nation-Building Unraveled? Aid, Peace and Justice in Afghanistan.* Bloomfield, CT: Kumarian, pp. 9–36.

—— 2004b. *Operating in an Age of Uncertainty: New Challenges in Humanitarian and Development Work.* May, InterAction Forum, Washington, DC.

Stoddard, A., 2003. Humanitarian NGOs: Challenges and Trends. In: Macrae, J., and Harmer, A. (eds.), *Humanitarian Action and the "Global War on Terror:" A Review of Trends and Issues.* HPG Report No. 14. London: ODI, pp. 25–36.

Stoddard, A., Harmer, A., and Haver, K., 2006. *Providing Aid in Insecure Environments: Trends in Policy and Operations.* HPG Report No. 23, September. London: ODI.

Strand, A., 2002. *Aid Coordination in Afghanistan.* Bergen: Norwegian Ministry of Foreign Affairs.

Strickland, M., 1996. *War and Chivalry: The Conduct and Perception of War in England and Normandy. 1066–1217.* Cambridge: Cambridge University Press.

Suhrke, A., 2006. "When More is Less: Aiding Statebuilding in Afghanistan." Occasional Paper No. 26, September. Paper Madrid: FRIDE.

Sulehria, F., 2013. "Militarisation of aid." *The News*. Islamabad, 26 November, http://www.thenews.com.pk/Todays-News-9-216397-Militarisation-of-aid.

Taber, R., 1965. *The War of the Flea: A Study of Guerrilla Warfare Theory and Practice*. New York: Lyle Stuart.

Taithe, B., 1999. *Defeated Flesh: Welfare, Warfare and the Making of Modern France*. Manchester: Manchester University Press.

—— 2004. Reinventing (French) Universalism: Religion, Humanitarianism and the "French doctors." *Modern and Contemporary France*. 12(2), pp. 147–58.

Tanner, S., 2003. *Afghanistan: A Military History from Alexander the Great to the Fall of the Taliban*. New York: Perseus Books.

Taylor, A., 2004. *Civil–Military Coordination: Perspective from Afghanistan*. Cambridge, MA: Carr Center for Human Rights Policy, Harvard University.

Taylor, A.J.P., 1957. *The Struggle for Mastery in Europe, 1848–1918*. Oxford: Clarendon Press.

Technical Working Group, 2006. "Report of the Technical Working Group on Education." Unpublished report, 18 July. Jalalabad: ACBAR.

Teson, F., 2003. The Liberal Case for Humanitarian Intervention. In: Holzgrefe, J., and Keohane, R. (eds.), 2003. *Humanitarian Intervention: Ethical, Legal, and Political Dilemmas*. Cambridge: Cambridge University Press, pp. 52–90.

Thomas, C., 2001. Global Governance, Development and Human Security: Exploring the Links. *Third World Quarterly*. 22(2), pp. 159–75.

Thomas, L., and Spataro, S., 1998. *Peacekeeping and Policing in Somalia*. Washington, DC: National Defense University Press.

Tomlin, R., 2000. "Reversing the Downward Spiral: Exploring Cultural Dissonance between the Military and NGOs on Humanitarian Operations." MA dissertation. Cranfield: Cranfield University and the Royal Military College of Science.

Torabi, Y., 2007. *Assessing the NSP: The Role of Accountability in Reconstruction*. London: TIRI.

Tornquist, O., 1999. *Politics and Development: A Critical Introduction*. London: Sage.

Torrente, N., 2004. Humanitarianism Sacrificed: Integration's False Promise. *Ethics and International Affairs*. 18(2), pp. 3–12.

TRADOC 2014. *The US Army Operating Concept*. Pamphlet 521-3-1, 31 October, www.tradoc.army.mil/tpubs/pams/tp525-3-1.pdf.

Trunkey, D., 2000. History and Development of Trauma Care in the United States. *Clinical Orthopaedics and Related Research*. 374, pp. 36–46.

Tsing, A., 2004. *Friction: an Ethnography of Global Connection*. Princeton, NJ: Princeton University Press.

Turcan, M., 2011. Seeing the Other Side of the COIN: A Critique of the Current Counterinsurgency (COIN) Strategies in Afghanistan. *Small Wars Journal*. pp. 1–27. http://smallwarsjournal.com/jrnl/art/seeing-the-other-side-of-the-coin-a-critique-of-the-current-counterinsurgency-coin-strategi.

UN, 1998. "Strategic Framework for Afghanistan." Available at: www.undg.org/documents/1071-Afghanistan_-_Strategic_Framework_-_Afghanistan_-_Strategic_F.pdf.

—— 2013. *The Situation in Afghanistan and its Implications for International Peace and Security*. New York: General Assembly Security Council.

UNAMA, 2002. "Minutes of the UNAMA chaired Emergency Task Force meeting, 28 June 2002." Kabul.

—— 2014. *Afghanistan Midyear Report: Protection of Civilians in Armed Conflict*. Kabul: (and UNOHCHR), July.

UNDP, 1994. *Human Development Report, 1994*. Oxford: Oxford University Press.

—— 2004. *Afghanistan National Human Development Report – Security with a Human Face: Challenges and Responsibilities*. New York.

—— 2006. *Afghan New Beginnings Programme*. Available at: www.undpanbp.org.

—— 2013. *Human Development Report 2013: The Rise of the South – Human Progress in a Diverse World*. New York.

—— 2006. *Human Development Report, 2006*. Oxford: Oxford University Press.

UNGA, 1997. "The Situation in Afghanistan and its Implications for International Peace and Security." A/51/838, S/1997/240. Available at: http://www.hri.ca/fortherecord 1997/documentation/security/s-1997–240.htm.

UNHCR, 1995. *Handbook for the Military on Humanitarian Operations*. Geneva.

—— 2006. *State of the World's Refugees*. Geneva.

UNICEF, 2006. "UNICEF Alarmed as Attacks on Afghan Schools Rise." Press Release. 7 August. Kabul. Available at: http://www.unicef.org/media/ media_35196.html.

US Army, 1990. *FM 100–20 Military Operations in Low Intensity Conflict*. Washington, DC. Available at: http://www.globalsecurity.org.

—— 2006. *Counterinsurgency*. FM 3-24. Washington, DC.

US Marines, 1940. *Small Wars Manual*. Washington, DC: US Government Printing Office.

USAID, 2007. "Panjshir Valley Road Transformed." Available at: http://afghanistan. usaid. gov/en/Article.65.aspx.

Van Brabant, K., 2000. *Operational Security Management in Violent Environments*. London: ODI.

—— 2001. *Mainstreaming the Organizational Management of Safety and Security*. London: ODI.

Van Brabant, K., and Killick, T., 1999. *The Limits and Scope for the Use of Development Assistance Incentives and Disincentives for Influencing Conflict Situations, Case Study: Afghanistan*. Paris: OECD.

Van Creveld, M., 1987. *Command in War*. Cambridge: Harvard University Press.

—— 1991. *The Transformation of War*. New York: The Free Press.

Vilsanjuan, R., 2003. "The Increasing Presence of Military Forces and the Independence of NGOs: The NGO Perspective." Summary of Presentation at the ICVA Conference on NGOs in a Changing World Order: Dilemmas and Challenges. Geneva, 14–15 February.

Vogelsang, W., 2002. *The Afghans*. Oxford: Blackwells Publishing.

Waldman, M., 2008. *Aid Effectiveness in Afghanistan*. ACBAR and Oxfam.

Walker, P., and Maxwell, D., 2008. *Shaping the Humanitarian World*. Global Institutions Series. London: Routledge.

Walkup, M., 1997. Policy Dysfunction in Humanitarian Organizations: The Role of Coping Strategies, Institutions, and Organizational Culture. *Journal of Refugee Studies*. 10(1), pp. 37–60.

Walzer, M., 1977. *Just and Unjust Wars: A Moral Argument with Historical Illustrations*. New York: Basic Books.

—— 1980. The Moral Standing of States: A Response to Four Critics. *Philosophy and Public Affairs*. 9(3), pp. 209–29.

—— 2000. *Just and Unjust Wars*. 3rd ed. New York: Basic Books.

Waters, K., 2004. 'Influencing the Message: The Role of Catholic Missionaries in Media Coverage of the Nigerian Civil War'. *Catholic Historical Review*. 90(4), October, pp. 697–718.

Watkins, C., 2003. *Provincial Reconstruction Teams (PRTs): An Analysis of Their Contribution to Security in Afghanistan*. Oxford: Oxford Brookes University.

Watts, C., 2004. "Indicators of NGO Security in Afghanistan." Masters thesis. Monterrey, CA: MIIS.

Weinbaum, M., 1989. The Politics of Afghan Resettlement and Rehabilitation. *Asian Survey*. 29(3), March, pp. 287–307.

Weir, E., 2006. *Conflict and Compromise: UN Integrated Missions and the Humanitarian Imperative*. KAIPTC Monograph, No. 4 June.

Weiss, T., 1997. A Research Note about Military-Civilian Humanitarianism: More Questions than Answers. *Disasters*. 21(2), pp. 95–117.

Weiss, T., and Campbell, K., 1991. Military Humanitarianism. *Survival*. 33(5), pp. 451–65.

Weiss, T., and Collins, C. (eds.), 1996. *Humanitarian Challenges and Intervention: World Politics and the Dilemmas of Help*. New York: Westview Press.

Weissman, F., 2004. Humanitarian Action and Military Intervention: Temptations and Possibilities. *Disasters*. 28(2), pp. 205–15.

Welle, J.W., 1999. Principle, Politics and Humanitarian Action. *Ethics and International Affairs*. 13, pp. 1–21.

—— 2010. Civil–military Integration in Afghanistan: Creating Unity of Command. *Joint Force Quarterly*. 56 (1), pp: 54–9.

West, B., 1972. *The Village*. New York: Harper and Row.

West, K., 2001. *Agents of Altruism*. Aldershot: Ashgate.

Wheeler, V., and Harmer, A. (eds.), 2006. *Resetting the Rules of Engagement: Trends and Issues in Military–Humanitarian Relations*. HPG Report No. 21, March. London: ODI.

Whitehead, A.N., 1938. *Science and the Modern World*. Harmondsworth: Penguin.

WHO, 2014. "Country Cooperation Strategy." Available at: http://www.who.int/country focus/cooperation_strategy/ccsbrief_afg_en.pdf.

Wieloch, R., 2003. The Humanitarian Use of the Military. *Forced Migration Review*. 18 (September), pp. 32–3.

Willets, P., 2001. *What is a Non-Governmental Organization?* London: City University.

Williams, G., 2005. *Engineering Peace: The Military Role in Postconflict Reconstruction*. Washington, DC: US Institute of Peace Press.

Williams, M.J., 2011. Empire Lite Revisited: NATO, the Comprehensive Approach and State-building in Afghanistan. *International Peacekeeping*. 18 (1), pp. 64–78.

Williamson, J.A., 2011. Using Humanitarian Aid To "Win Hearts and Minds": A Costly Failure? *International Review of the Red Cross*. 93 (884), pp. 1035–61.

Woodward, S., 2001. Humanitarian War: A New Consensus? *Disasters*. 25(4), pp. 331–44.

Wrong, M., 2001. "Mixing Arms and Aid Raises Fears: Afghanistan Aid Agencies Deeply Troubled." *Financial Times*. 6 October, p. 3.

Wylly, H.C., 1907. *Special Campaign Series No 4: The Campaign of Magenta and Solferino*. New York: Macmillan Company.

Zeller, S., 2003. "Activist attacks U.S. military relief effort in Afghanistan." *Government Executive*. Available at: http://www.govexec.com/dailyfed/0503/051303sz1.htm.

Ziemke, E., 1990. *The US Army in the Occupation of Germany*. Washington, DC: Center of Military History.

Zyck, S.A., 2012. *Peace and Reintegration: An Introduction, Civil–Military*. Kabul: Fusion Centre.

Index